Tempting the Devil

in the Name of God

The Heavy Hand of Fate

HOWARD BECKMAN

Inspire on Purpose Publishing
Irving, Texas

Tempting the Devil in the Name of God
The Heavy Hand of Fate

Inspire On Purpose Publishing
Irving, Texas
(888) 403-2727
http://inspireonpurpose.com
The Platform Publisher™

Printed in the United States of America

Library of Congress Control Number: 2015951505
ISBN-13: 978-1-941782-24-8

TABLE OF CONTENTS

DEDICATION

To all who feared that the darkness might never end — for all who ever wished they had a second chance — know that a new day shall always dawn, and with it comes another chance to become who you really and truly are.

And to Ricky, I made it, brother! And though I wish you had as well, I dedicate some of what still lives within me to my fondest and dearest memories of you.

ACKNOWLEDGMENTS

While writing about, and therefore reliving the experiences I am sharing within these pages, I remembered so many people that had a positive impact on me during these challenging years. I am forever grateful to all of them, but here I am only mentioning those that stood out during the living of, and now the revealing of, my long-kept secrets.

First, with bowed head I thank my beloved teacher, His Divine Grace A.C. Bhaktivedanta Swami, who truly forced my eyes open with the light of spiritual knowledge. Were it not for what he had inspired within me, I would not have made it through my darkest days, nor would I have eventually concluded what to do with my brightest of times.

Thank you seems almost feeble in expressing gratitude to my family who stood by me during my gloomiest years. Were it not for their love, I wouldn't be here today to tell the tale. My parents, Aileen and Don, and my brother Brad, never gave up hope that I would indeed not only emerge from those days of abject darkness, but that from the ashes of a ruined life I would find myself anew. Their faith in me was strong, even when it was hard to maintain in myself.

A humungous thank you to my friend, diplomat, and attorney, Dick Atkins, for his friendship and all that he did to help my parents eventually secure my release from prison in Thailand. To Dick Hill, the federal parole officer who not only believed in me, but gave me enough rope to either hang myself or use it to swing over the canyon of doubt that lingered in my mind. Thankfully, I managed to land squarely on my feet.

My humble gratitude to my loving wife and partner of over 20 years, Jennifer, who at times stood by helplessly watching my emotional roller coaster while I wrote much of these memoirs, and was forced to relive them along with me. For her, this was a trip through a sordid past in which she played no part.

My thanks to Bill Reid, one of the most realized and spiritually *aware* people I know, who was the first editor to give the book a going over, and to Alice Terry, who also helped me with her keen editing skills and insights. Thank you to Dan Morris, who's brilliant editing skills allowed my story to unfold in print with grace and polish. And last, yet certainly never ever least, my heart-felt thanks to my friend and publisher, Michelle Morse of Inspire on Purpose Publishing. It is her efforts to bring everything together here that have made this production possible.

INTRODUCTION

The Only Way to Go from Here Is Up

Life is what happens when you're busy making other plans.

—John Lennon

This is the story of how life *happened* to me, and how it shaped my destiny. Like most stories, my life boils down to the basic formula of "cause and effect" based on choices made. As a teenager in Philadelphia, I was like countless other kids growing up in the 1960's. Certainly, the pervasive nature of the times had a significant influence on my ability to adapt to the rest of the world. The trends of the era left a profound imprint on the way I perceived my world, and my view did not necessarily see the world objectively and clearly. This resulted in my thinking the world was only about drugs, sex, and Rock 'n' Roll. Life was just one big social experiment. My immediate objective on any given day was to do whatever felt good at that moment. Such an experiential social lifestyle would eventually pave the way for people and events to circumscribe the path my life would take for decades to come. I had no idea that I was defining my destiny in a vacuum.

Struggling with adolescent angst and disillusioned by my perceptions of societal hypocrisy, I began to search for my own answers. Unfortunately, too many of the answers I found were wrong. Every time I tried to do the right thing, something always seemed to derail my goal.

Before I knew it, I had fallen into a pattern of making one bad decision after another. The results were not favorable. I had become a smuggler, an addict, and a veritable Merchant of Death. Looking back now, I realize in those times, I had been clearly delusional, arrogant, and self-involved. Eventually, life *happened* again when I had to face the consequences that had turned my schizophrenic world into a nightmare. Confinement in a Thai prison and ensuing hardships, terror, and the nearly probable and completely palpable possibility of death (excessive risk taking) was not exactly what I had planned for my life.

None of us can escape the hands of fate. Our universal allotments of happiness and suffering are unavoidable and must be either enjoyed or endured as we travel through life. Enduring is always more challenging than enjoying. Many of the things that are thrown at us do not arrive by accident. We often have our hands in the mix somewhere. Once we understand why we are in a challenging situation, we are on the way to learning a lesson.

When we don't know the why of something, we are at a disadvantage when it comes to planning ahead. During our most trying times, we can only accept, adapt, and improve as best we can. However, when we make mistakes, we have to accept responsibility for our actions and learn from them. Whenever we have some salvageable degree of character, guilt will accompany our self-incrimination. Without some degree of guilt, we may not be able to recognize an abject horror in our lives, but it will be there in the afterlife as another scar on our soul. The goal, therefore, is to redeem ourselves in this life, if at all possible.

However, from the depths of despair rebirth can emerge, and with it a new person will replace the old one. The goal of such a transformation is always a better and much improved version of ourselves. Unfortunately, life sometimes responds unfairly as we put forth our best effort. There are tragedies, and no matter how well you try to avoid them, they are often inevitable. There is also the hope that out of the ashes of destruction, a new and favorable day can dawn. We view these days as miracles, and miracles do happen.

This story is neither a Horatio Alger (19th-centry novelist who wrote about impoverished boys who rose to success) primer nor a sugar-coated self-help book. It is not written along the lines of self-help authors like Tony Robbins or Wayne Dyer, or alternative medicine advocate and author Deepak Chopra, nor is it a guide to learn how to weather adversity. It is an authentic account, through my eyes, that includes all the mind-boggling, gritty details and disturbing descriptions of a challenged life that is totally my own. In the following pages, you will see how my life spiraled out of control, and how I battled enormous odds to restore my mind and health, and regain my freedom. Most importantly, how I salvaged my soul.

This memoir not only depicts the story of my transformation as a person, but it also moves on to redefine my inner being as I emerged from darkness into the light. At times, it reads like a psychological thriller. At other times, it reads like a travelogue to exotic lands and cultures. My story is both subjective and as objective as I can describe it in a non-fiction narrative. Every single word, event, and circumstance is recorded as truthfully as my memory allows. Public documents will support the lion's share of my account as verifiable truth.

The ultimate purpose of my story is to hopefully inspire readers to make better decisions and avoid the same pitfalls into which I fell. My goal will be achieved if my story influences one person to make better choices, or if it inspires those who have already headed down the wrong path to change their direction. Yes, I am sharing my experiences to inspire and motivate those who are prone to acting as I once did. The bottom is a dark and ugly place and it is difficult to escape from once you are there. Don't discount an unexpected blow fom the hand of fate because it is not just an annoying interruption; it can be unpredictably destructive and devastating. Returning from the bottom is a long, uphill journey with traps set everywhere along the way.

Truth is, sometimes life seems unfair. Inevitably, it can be extremely painful and even hair-raising for the strongest of us. Unfortunately, these bad experiences are out there waiting on us, especially when we make bad choices.

I am sharing with you my own, once secret and guarded past, one that I even kept from my closest friends. If you have ever had a big pile of *life* land in your lap, then my story may have some answers, encouragement, reassurance, and inspiration for you. There is a full and rewarding life out there waiting on us if we are willing to properly go after it.

CHAPTER 1

Busted in Thailand

The time for change had come. Not incremental change, *profound change.*

A series of unimaginable events brought me to India, and now I sat listening to a complete stranger in a foreign land accurately describe, in detail, an account of what had transpired.

I had flown from Los Angeles, seeking a man named Rabindranath, with only an address and general directions on how to find him. When we finally met face-to-face at his secluded home in rural India, he announced, "Ah, today is the day you were to come."

This man would become my Jyotish (traditional Hindu system of astrology) guru who would educate me in the Science of Light. We spent many days and nights together, and he taught me wondrous things. On one particular day, he said to me, "In three years, your life will again change. At this juncture, you will reach a most important time in your life. But, you still have a great deal to learn. Soon, you'll once again cross the oceans to reside for some time in another foreign land. Don't worry. Your destiny shall find **you.**"

When I retired to my lodgings for the evening to ponder his predictions, my mind drifted back to that dreadful day in Thailand that changed everything.

* * *

Accelerating into the curve toward the house, I zoomed into the driveway and quickly parked the bike. Next, I turned back to close the front gate. All of a sudden, as if transported to another dimension, cops began popping out of the bushes. Then more appeared from somewhere just outside the gate, all pointing rifles at my head. I raised my hands up in the air. My heart was pounding and a wave of fear shot over me, inducing a sense of nausea. A green Jeep-type personnel carrier careened around the corner and stopped short of the entrance to our compound. In less than thirty seconds, there were two more vehicles and a platoon of policemen with weapons locked and loaded.

"What the hell's going on?" I cried out, hands still held high above my head. I was shaking and sweat trickled down my neck and back, soaking my shirt.

The commanding officer, a thin man with slicked-back hair and a thin moustache, walked toward me saying, "We are here to search your house." My heart was beating so hard I thought it would explode. I tried to stay calm as I was allowed to lower my arms.

Shrugging my shoulders, I said, "Go ahead. We have nothing to hide."

I called out to my girlfriend, Jamie. She came to the door and her eyes quickly widened as she took in the virtual army of policemen surrounding the house. Several of them aimed rifles at our heads as we were marched back in through the front door. Ordering us to sit down on the sofa in the front room, the commanding officer walked back out into the hallway, leaving us guarded by three very nervous-looking cops. All kept their guns trained on us, as though they expected us to make a run for the door at any moment.

Getting busted by the police in Thailand is one of the worst fears of any foreigner living or visiting there. You never know when someone might turn you in to the cops, or if they'll just get wind of you for some infraction. Should you not be able to buy your way out, you will likely risk a

50-plus year sentence. Whatever the result, getting busted in Thailand is no laughing matter.

They turned the house upside down for over an hour searching for drugs. We could only see the kitchen and dining room from where we were being held, but it looked like a bomb had hit! The carpets were lifted up and thrown in a heap. Every picture was torn from the walls. All of the kitchen and dining room cabinet drawers were dumped out, contents strewn across the floor. The commander seemed exasperated at not being able to find anything, but he yelled at his men to keep searching. It was like they had been tipped off and expected to quickly uncover a huge cache of drugs, weapons or something equally illegal.

Then, the commander strode over to us, standing so close to me that I could smell the odor of chili and garlic on his breath. "We know you have Number 4 heroin. Why not make it easy on yourself and tell us where it is?"

Right, I thought, but decided to answer by saying, "I don't know what you're talking about. We don't have any heroin."

His response to my denial was, "We know all about you, and we will find it!"

Eyes ablaze with anger, he marched out of the room. He called several of his underlings to his side and whispered something to them that was obviously for their ears only. The two rifle-toting uniformed officers hurriedly walked out of the house. In less than a minute one of them returned, holding a small, clear plastic bottle filled with white powder. The cop said something to him, and handed over the bottle of powder at the same time. "We found this outside," the lieutenant announced to everyone as he held up the bottle.

"That's not mine!" I protested, and I was being truthful. That was not to say that we didn't have any drugs stashed. Yes, we did have drugs stashed, but they hadn't even come close to finding them. The bottom line was they weren't leaving without taking me with them. From the size of this operation, I knew someone had set me up "big time." I had no idea who may have snitched us out, but when drug addicts or runners get busted, they will usually give up someone to stay out of jail. That was simply the reality of the business.

Whoever ordered the search of my house was obviously expecting to make a major bust. I'd never heard of so many cops called out on such a small-time drug bust. I was certainly not a big-time opium warlord like "Khun Sa," who was also known as the Prince of Death and King of the Golden Triangle at one time. Prior to his death, he was one of the world's most powerful drug dealers. With all certainty, I can say that I was in no way in his league and certainly did not require such a show of force to be taken into custody.

The commander again barked orders at one of his officers, who then cuffed my hands behind my back. "Is this really necessary?" I asked, but was ignored.

Poor Jamie was terrified. Tears were streaming down her face. Before the cops could cuff her, I began pleading with them. "Don't take her. She has nothing to do with any of this! It's me you want."

Miraculously, the cop released her when he was told, "Okay, we leave her. Let's go!"

They crammed me into the back of one of the wagons, among the troops. Laughing and joking while casting sidelong glances at me, they were all having a good laugh at my expense. As soon as we arrived at the police station, they piled out, dragging me with them. I tripped on the steps, falling hard onto the ground, which evoked yet another round of snickers and loud laughter.

The police station stood on a cleared lot, but not more than fifty feet from it was the thick, extravagant foliage of the jungle, bordered on one side by a row of coconut trees. Having to traverse the uneven and cracked cement steps into the station, I managed to avoid any additional stumbling.

Inside the large foyer were several large holding cells for prisoners. I was steered to the right of them, past a desk with a short, fat, greasy, little cop with black, beady eyes and a thick moustache. My handler then shoved me through the door of an office. The lieutenant came in and told me to stand against the wall. "Just wait," he said, then screeched some orders at a young uniformed cop. He left and the cop positioned himself just outside the office door. Within a few minutes the captain came in, motioning for me to sit down. His thick lips, puffy eyelids, and chubby face reminded me of a Thai version of Jabba the Hut from *Star Wars*. He immediately started grilling me with questions. "We know who you are," he said. Then he followed up with some ambiguous questions about "the others."

Before answering, I asked him to please close the door. Once we were alone, I began telling him that this was all a big mistake. I didn't know anything about who or what he was talking about. Whatever the policemen had found outside my house had not been mine.

I noticed he was wearing a 5 *baht* (in this instance a baht is not Thai money, but Thai jeweler's weight) gold chain around his neck, a gold watch, and a large gold ring on his finger. Thai cops make a pittance, so without question these items were all gained through highly suspect activity such as graft. Leaning toward him over the desk, I looked him in the eye and asked how much he wanted in order to let me go. Instead of the answer I expected, a monetary figure, he just waved his hand at me while shaking his head from side-to-side. He flatly refused my offer with a sturdy "No."

This was totally out of character for any member of the Thai police force. His refusal to name a price was alarming because Thai cops live to bust foreigners since they usually have money. There's nothing in it for them if you go to court and then on to jail. Locals with the means to do so will often pay their way out of custody. However, foreigners are the ones who can usually pay the higher bribes that can enhance an officer's lifestyle.

"Please Captain Sir. Surely we can keep this just between us?" I asked in a hushed and pleading tone.

"No, not possible!" he kept saying. I figured it was just his game to get more out of me, so I kept at it.

"There must be some arrangement we can come to, Captain Sir?" But he wouldn't budge.

Finally, obviously very agitated, he stood up from behind his desk, opened the door, and called for one of the cops down the hall. "Lock him up," he said. The hairs were standing up on the back of my neck as a strange feeling of déjà vu came over me. This was not my first time in jail.

Marching me down the hall, he led me to one of the large cells. Ordering me to lift up my handcuffed wrists, he used his key to remove them. After opening the heavy iron door, he placed his hand behind my shoulders and shoved me in. The door clanged shut behind me. I looked around and couldn't believe where I had landed! There were at least thirty other people in the cell, so every square inch of space was occupied. This was beyond my wildest imagination. Things like this happen to other people, not me!

My eyes quickly scanned my new surroundings. Everyone in this overcrowded cell was Thai, except for one guy who looked European. People were everywhere, crouching, sitting, or leaning against the filthy, mold-encrusted walls or against the iron bars at the front. The hot, humid air was thick and stifling. The stagnant, stale air nearly choked me as I tried to adapt.

That was not, however, the worst part. There was an overpowering, sickening smell of sweat and body odor mixed with the unmistakable stench of human excrement. It all hit my senses at once, smacking me in the face like a big wave, akin to a scene out of a Hollywood movie. But this was no movie. A feeling of impending doom came over me. I looked around for a place to sit, but there was none. I just stood there, not believing what fate had handed me in just a few short hours. I'd been dragged away from my comfortable home in Pattaya Beach to a nasty place filled with stinking strangers. My new situation was appalling and seemed to exist somewhere beyond the parameters of my worst nightmares.

All of a sudden, a voice called out, "Hey! Over here!" The accent was unmistakably German. Looking around, I saw a hand waving to me. "Here," he said. "Move," he growled at the guy sitting next to him, a skinny youngster dressed only in a pair of shorts and nothing else. The young man moved, albeit grudgingly. After I sat down, Helmut, a tall and friendly Austrian with piercing blue eyes and a generous smile, introduced himself. He was there, he said, because he'd overstayed his visa. With no money or friends to call on for help, he had been forced to contact his embassy. But embassies don't move quickly, at least not on behalf of their citizens arrested in Thailand. I would also soon find this out for myself. For probably no more than a few hundred dollars, Helmut could have bought his way out of this Armageddon in a "New York Minute." Sadly, by being broke, he was at the mercy and timetable of the Austrian Embassy.

Most of the other guys in the cell were staring at us as if we were some kind of oddity in a carnival sideshow. This kind of scrutiny by the natives had unnerved me when I first started going to Asia, especially in India. But I soon found out it was usually quite innocent since most local inhabitants were simply denied opportunities to interact with foreigners. Put on a big smile and most of the time they'd smile back, their eyes lighting up and sparkling with the innocence of young children. Almost nobody had shoes on. Most of the prisoners were wearing shorts or jeans, and some were bare from the waist up. Most of these guys had been arrested for minor drug violations or petty theft. Helmut asked what I was in for. "Drug possession, but it was a plant," I said, recounting the day's events. "After tossing my house and coming up empty, one of the cops goes outside, and a minute later walks back in with a few grams of China White, saying they'd found it just outside my front door!"

For the moment, I was happy to engage in conversation with Helmut. We casually shared our stories. Like a lot of foreigners in Thailand, he had been just hanging out, living the easy life in this Southeast Asian tropical paradise. If you didn't spend your money on drugs, it was really cheap to live in Thailand. You could eat like a king for a few dollars a day. In Pattaya especially, many visitors lolled away their time lounging at the beach, sipping fresh coconut juice through a straw by day, and drinking cheap Thai beer at night. This fit the foreigners' concept of *"My Pen Lai,"* the famous Thai phrase synonymous with the Aussie expression, "No worries, mate."

In Helmut's case, he had run out of money and had resorted to preying on tourists. He became a thief, stealing money and credit cards in order to maintain his decadent lifestyle. Unfortunately for him, he had tried to pay his hotel bill that very morning with a stolen credit card, one that had already been posted to the *hot list*. The hotel manager called the police when the card was rejected and flagged as stolen. Overstaying his visa was surely overtrumped by his criminal activity. To his knowledge though, the Thai police had not yet hit him with anything but overstaying his visa. Maybe he was catching a break.

"After the weekend, they'll take us to court for arraignment, unless you are able to make bail before then. If you have the money, you should try to buy your way out of here now. Things tend to get harder once you're arraigned. Once you cross that arraignment threshold, there will be more outstretched hands looking for a payoff. Before it is too late, you best find out what the captain wants and just pay him off. Otherwise, you'll be off to Chonburi Prison after court." He was speaking literally and without emotion. Evidently, Helmut had a history of run-ins with the Thai legal system. How else could he be such a fountain of knowledge? But knowledge or not, he was flat broke with no resources to call on. Helmut wasn't going anywhere until his embassy managed to help him sort things out.

Just then I heard my name called. Jamie was standing about twenty feet away in front of the duty cop's desk. Thank God! Hopefully, she could arrange some sort of a deal with the captain. I motioned for her to come over so we could talk.

The duty cop said, "*Bai*," meaning, "go," so Jamie approached and reached through the bars to touch my face. I grasped her hand. "I'm so glad you're here," I whispered. She'd brought some food and drinks for me, and after a cursory glance into the bags the cop let her pass it to me through the bars.

"What are we going to do?" she asked in a hushed tone. "Can't we just pay them to let you go?"

I gave her an abbreviated account of my exchange with the captain and his subsequent refusal to discuss a bribe to let me walk.

"See what you can do," I prompted her. "Ask to speak to the captain yourself. Hopefully, you'll have better luck than I did. He must be stalling to pressure me. He's probably holding out for more money. He had to know that I would eventually be willing to pay anything to get out of here. Why else would he not just take some money and let me go?" We both knew that this was how things worked in this country. A few 100-dollar bills in the palm of the officer in charge usually ended any legal hassles right then and there.

Jamie's normally smiling face was now etched into a frown and her dark almond eyes were red from crying. Wiping tears from her pretty Filipino face, she agreed to speak with the captain. "I'll be back soon, hon. Try not to worry." As fretful as I was, I still thought we had a good chance of buying our way out of this mess.

Hunger pangs reminded me that I had not eaten today; I was starting to feel ravenous. Taking the containers of food from the bags Jamie brought, I put them down between Helmut and myself, handing him one. Helmut dug right in and ate as if he hadn't eaten for days! After we had our fill, he said, "Let me introduce you to somebody. He might be able to help you." He introduced me to Wan Chai, a tall, thin Thai man with a thick shock of jet-black hair and a long-nosed aristocratic face. He also spoke fluent English.

After shaking hands, we talked for a few minutes about how we came to be meeting under such unfortunate circumstances. Wan Chai related that he had been arrested for possessing about 15 grams of heroin, enough to be charged with possessing it for sale. The charge could carry a pretty hefty prison sentence, but Wan Chai said that he'd be out by tonight at the latest with all charges dropped. He had already made a deal with the captain. Somebody was coming this afternoon to buy him out.

Once I finished telling Wan Chai about my experience with the captain, he said, "Talk to him again. Just make him an offer. Otherwise, your only chance for bail will be in Chonburi at court. That means not only paying the cops, but the judge, and the prosecutor, too. And they'll cost a lot more. You'll also need a lawyer to make the deals for you. Everybody wants their cut here."

"Thank God for corruption," I facetiously acknowledged under my breath.

Corruption is rampant in Asian countries. India was the worst, not just for getting out of a run-in with the law, but to get even the simplest thing done. And that goes for the locals, as well. A bribe could speed up getting your utilities hooked up in your home or getting you a driver's license. You had to pay the man at the desk or the serviceman doing the work. Even the taxman expected to be paid in order to give you a lower assessment.

Although I wasn't feeling ill yet, I knew it was just a matter of time before I began to get sick. My heroin addiction would have every ounce of me crying out for a fix within a few hours. Sharing this with Wan Chai, he said, "The cops will sell you anything you want. However, it is better to just have someone bring it when they come to visit. Never trust anybody in here." Instinctively, he whispered his advice.

"How?" I asked. "They can't just hand me some dope through the bars." Wan Chai demonstrated his method of getting drugs into the cell by carefully opening the bottom seal of a pack of cigarettes, leaving the top part with the pull strip intact. The dope could then be packed, compressed, and sealed in plastic with cigarettes all around it. Then just re-glue the bottom of the pack. *Voila!* No one could even tell it had been tampered with.

"The cops don't check anything closely, anyway," he said, "They only take a quick look in the bag, if they look at all. They'll let you have all the cigarettes and food you want. Just tell your girlfriend to give the cop at the desk 100 baht each time she comes to see you. They'll just wave her through. No sweat. Hopefully, you won't even be here that long."

Jamie returned in about fifteen minutes. My heart was racing as I pushed my way up to the bars so I could speak with her. "What did he say?" I whispered, but her downcast eyes and trembling lips said it all.

"He won't even talk about it!" Jamie whimpered in a voice choked with emotion. "What are we going to do?" Her lips were quivering and tears were starting to run down her face. "We have to get you out of here! Should I go see Pan? I bet he can talk to them. Pan will know how to get you out."

"Yeah, go see Pan," I agreed. "He knows everybody."

Then I whispered what Wan Chai said about getting some dope in to me. Jamie didn't like the sound of it one bit, but I assured her that there wouldn't be any problems. "Promise, babe. Wan Chai said that after 6 PM the cops on duty are easy, so come back then. When you come back with the food and cigarettes, show the bag to the cop and hand him a folded-up 100 baht note." Before leaving she agreed to return later that evening. Her stride reflected the sadness and helplessness she was feeling. Her tiny 5'3" frame appeared frail as she slowly made her way out the door of the police station and down the stairs.

Soon I started to sweat and my nose wouldn't stop running. I was getting *sick*, the ugly consequences of a heroin habit when your supply runs out. While taking a sip from one of the cans of juice Jamie brought, I offered some of the other snacks to others in the cell. My offer was gratefully accepted. A few of the guys showed their gratitude by making a little more space for me. At least I was then able to lean back against the wall and stretch out my legs.

"How the hell can you sleep in here?" I asked Helmut. "There's hardly room to stretch out your legs, not to mention being able to lie down!"

"We just have to sleep leaning against the wall. We also have to sleep in shifts. Otherwise, our pockets would be empty when we wake up." His advice revealed another reality.

I suddenly realized that I still had money in my pocket, about a few thousand baht or so. Other than taking my passport, they'd let me hang onto my money, as well as a few papers that I had on me. Helmut knew more about being in a Thai jail than a newcomer like me. He hardly even seemed fazed about being here, so I asked him how often he'd been a guest of the Thai police. His response told me that this was the first time he had been here without any money for a bribe.

Adjusting my cramped legs on the filthy cement floor, I leaned back against the unforgiving iron bars of the cell. Dozing on and off, my thoughts were spinning around inside my head like a gyroscope. This could turn out to be very serious if I didn't manage to bribe my way out. I'd read more than a few stories in *The Bangkok Post* about foreigners getting twenty, thirty, or even seventy-five year prison sentences after being busted for heroin. Obviously, not everybody managed to buy his or her way out. Calling for the guard, I asked to see the captain again. A few minutes later he returned. Opening the cell door, he motioned me toward the captain's office, and then he followed close behind me.

The captain's office was bare, except for a few plaques decorating the walls. There was a cabinet, a desk and chair, and two folding metal chairs. Pointing at one of the folding chairs he told me to sit down. "What do you want," he asked with a sneer on his face.

"How much do you want to let me go?" I answered. Surely he would spout off an amount. All cops were crooked in this country.

"Sorry," he said, "I cannot do that."

I looked at him, then whispered, "Come on, Captain Sir, how much?"

Angrily, he retorted, "It's not possible, so if that's all you have to say?" Pleading for my life, I offered him a very hefty sum for such a small bust. "Just take the money and let me out. Nobody will ever know. You are in charge here, Captain," I was pleading with him at this point.

Shaking his head from side-to-side, he stood up and called the other cop back in, yelling something at him that I couldn't catch because my grasp of the Thai language was still pretty rudimentary. The cop led me back to the cell, opened the door, and pushed me in. He slammed the door behind me. The sound of the key turning in the lock was awful. There was something horrifying about my predicament and I read it as a premonition of an unimaginable finality to my life.

Time seemed to crawl as I waited for evening, when Jamie would return. I constantly glanced over at the clock outside the cell as if somehow that would make the time go faster. Finally, the hours passed and the day shift left, including the captain. Only a handful of cops took their places. One was a tall, lanky guy with a boyish lock of hair that kept falling in his face. The other man was short and stocky with a big potbelly hanging over his belt. Together, they were the Thai police version of *The Odd Couple*. The tall guy was pretty friendly and kept coming over to talk to Helmut and me. As do many Thais, he liked practicing his English with foreigners. However, remembering Wan Chai's warning, I said very little about myself or why I was here, just that it was all a mistake, and I hoped to go home soon.

About an hour or so later, Jamie arrived, trying her best to look lighthearted. She made a valiant attempt at a smile, but I saw the apprehension in her eyes. She held two plastic bags in her hands, pointing to the cell and telling the cop they were for me, the *farang* (foreigner). Motioning for her to come over to his desk, he glanced into the bags. Never touching a thing in them, he just looked up at her expectantly. Jamie deftly handed him a folded bill with her hand outstretched, palm down. Smiling, he took the money and waved at her to pass it through to me.

Jamie knelt down next to the bars and handed the bags through to me. Inside were four packs of Krong Thip cigarettes, a few bottles of mineral water, two curries with rice, and some other assorted goodies. She gave me a few large plastic spoons from her pocket while anxiously asking how I was holding up. I told her that I had tried again with the captain, but he was adamant about his resolve not to take a bribe.

"Did you see Pan?" I asked.

"He's in Bangkok until late tonight," Jamie's voice had a disappointing tone. "What are we going to do?" She was extremely frightened and starting to panic. Poor Jamie had never spent a night alone since we arrived in Thailand.

"Try to calm down," I said, holding her hand through the bars. Pan has everybody in his pocket. He'll be able to get me out of here. It's got to happen soon, though. So no matter how late he gets home, you must see him."

I told her how complicated things would get if we couldn't bribe me out of the police station. "I won't be going to court until after the weekend, so we have a few days. If anybody knows who to talk to, Pan will.

"I miss you," Jamie whispered, her voice faltering as her eyes filled with tears.

"I miss you, too," I answered. "Don't worry, everything will be all right." The fat cop called out to her. She had to go now. I squeezed her hand one more time. Now we both had eyes filled with tears, "See you tomorrow."

Pan was a well-known businessman in Pattaya Beach, powerful and well connected politically. He had several businesses, one in textiles and the other selling construction materials. But his real money came from neither. Pan was also in the drug business. A much-feared boss in the heroin "syndicate," he moved hundreds of kilos of pure Number 4 Thai heroin every year. Not only were all the police and government officials paid to leave him alone, but they also looked out for his welfare. Nothing, but nothing, happened in Pattaya that Pan didn't know about. If he couldn't get me out, then I was up the proverbial creek without a paddle.

After Jamie left, I opened one of the packs of cigarettes, keeping it down between Helmut and myself so nobody could see. Wan Chai came over and sat up close facing us, so it was about as private as you could get in this overcrowded jail cell. Inside was a small plastic bag with about 2 grams of heroin surrounded by cigarettes. The others, Jamie had told me were just cigarettes. Even though I didn't smoke, cigarettes were always useful to have in jail. They were used like currency.

Wan Chai told me not to do it here, to go into the bathroom. Helmut had already remarked that the bathroom was something he "guaranteed would blow my mind," but had left it at that. There was a wall in there that I could stand behind, where I couldn't be seen from the doorway. Taking the packet of dope, I walked through the open door into the *hong nam*, (literally meaning "the water room").

Saying what I saw behind that wall "blew me away" would be the understatement of the century. There was a large sink with a water tank next to it, a long metal urinal and another small area with low walls where the toilet was. What I saw there totally grossed me out! Helmut was right. It did blow my mind.

The toilet was western style, not just a hole in the floor, but it was literally full of shit! Not just full of shit, mind you, but a mountain of human feces rising about eight inches above the rim of the toilet seat. To use it you would have to hover over it in a semi-squat, and then proceed to make your contribution to the ever-growing pile of excrement. Never before in my life had I witnessed anything as revolting! The smell was so foul it made my eyes sting.

I had to pee really badly, so my first order of business was to use the urinal. The walls were dirty and discolored with cracks extending from a barred window high above my head down to the floor. Out of the corner of my eye I saw something moving. Turning my head to look, I saw several huge cockroaches running under the sink. I could only imagine that there must have been countless more behind the walls. After emptying my swollen bladder, I took out the packet of white powder and a pack of matches. Scooping up a bit of the white powder with a corner of the flap covering the matches, I brought it up to one of my nostrils and *snorted* it. Immediately, that old familiar cushion of warmth enveloped my body and conscious mind. It washed over me, not only dispelling the sickness in my body, but dulling my mind so that my present situation seemed less precarious. Tucking the packet back into my pocket, I stepped out from behind the wall, strode over to Helmut and sat down.

"How the hell can anyone use that toilet?" My tone revealed my disgust and repulsion.

"You use it carefully, and as little as possible," he replied with a grimace. For the next few hours, Helmut and I sat and talked, with me intermittently closing my eyes and nodding off. My heroin fix could not totally counter my mental and physical exhaustion. This whole experience was the *piece de resistance* of my recent run-ins with the police. In the approximate space of six months, law enforcement agencies in three separate countries had arrested me: the U.S., Mexico, and Thailand. Soon, I dozed off. Vigilant to keep the petty thieves from picking my pockets, Helmut stayed awake.

The Thai inmates hardly seemed bothered by the close quarters. They'd lie down with their arms and legs all over each other. Some even allowed another guy to rest his head on them as a pillow. This was not an intimacy most Westerners would share. Westerners tend to demand that others respect their space and loathe even the thought of close physical contact with a stranger. Here, however, it was merely a way to adapt to one's circumstances and environment.

Most of the other inmates were from very poor families and were incarcerated for petty crimes, usually theft. Not armed robbery, or even burglary, just little things pilfered from food shops for the most part. The majority of those arrested for drugs were busted with only small quantities of either pot or heroin. Usually, someone came to get them out within hours, paying anywhere between 250 and 1,000 baht ($12.50 to $50) for their release.

For me, it was a fitful night. I would doze off for a while, then suddenly wake and bolt upright. Each time I did, the reality of my situation produced a sinking sensation of helplessness. Finally, the morning sunlight ushered in another day; the first rays slipped in through the windows down the hallway.

The first morning that I woke up in this overcrowded pigpen, there was no choice but to use the sewage receptacle from hell. The experience was nauseating, way beyond anything words can adequately describe. I couldn't believe it! Like some sort of sick cartoon, there I was in a half crouch, naked from the waist down, hanging my butt over a cylindrical steaming mass of putrid human feces. The air was so hot and humid that the walls and floors were in a perpetual state of dampness. The last thing I wanted was to slip and fall onto a mountain of raw sewage.

Somehow I managed, using water from the sink, to clean myself afterwards. Returning to the cell, I sat down once again next to Helmut and sighed. "I'll never complain about the toilets in India again."

Helmut just laughed and said, "Yeah, I know what you mean. Even over there, they'd never believe this place."

At about 10 AM Jamie showed up wearing a flowered skirt and a white blouse. Her familiar countenance was comforting, although the feeling was somewhat fleeting. She made her way to the desk and confronted a new cop since the morning shift had already come on duty. Once again, she nimbly passed a folded bank note to a policeman, who quickly took it and waved her over to the holding cell. She carried two bags. One bag was filled with the yogurt drinks that I liked along with my favorite tropical fruit, Mangosteen. The other bag contained various drinks and some sweet rolls. I gulped down several of the small plastic bottles of yogurt drink, handing a few to Helmut along with the yellow plastic bag of purple fruits.

"Did you see Pan?" I quizzed Jamie.

"Yes," she said, "last night, then again this morning. It's not good. There's somebody else keeping you here, and he is much higher up than Pan." She nodded toward the captain's office. "The captain told Pan that he would let you go in a heartbeat if it was up to him. But now, he would be in big trouble if he let you out. We have to wait until you get to court. Pan will try to get a judge to let you out before you're even arraigned. I'm sorry, hon, but there's nothing he can do until after the weekend."

What could I say? I'd have to cool my heels and hope for the best.

I could feel my optimism taking a fall. That sinking feeling once again claimed a spot in the pit of my stomach. Who was it that wanted me in here? And why? I was just a small independent dealer; I had never stepped on anyone's toes here. I knew better than that. Sure, I was wanted in Hawaii for failing to appear in court, but that was a state charge, not federal. So, it shouldn't even be in the U.S. Embassy's computer system yet! The Thais had no reason to even notice me, much less want to make a big case out of arresting me! None of it made any sense, but nothing seemed to make sense in my life anymore. Feeling faint, I sunk to my knees.

"Are you okay?" Jamie asked, crouching down outside the cell to meet my eyes.

"No, I'm not okay," I answered, bowing my head. "It just doesn't add up."

While making an effort to smile Jamie attempted to encourage me. "Don't worry, hon, Pan will come through for us."

"I hope so," I murmured. "Thanks babe, I don't know what I'd do without you." She promised to return in the evening after seeing Pan. She blew me a kiss as she retreated back to the foyer. I watched her turn and fade into the outside world. She was out of sight, but not out of my thoughts.

Most of the policemen in the station left Helmut and me alone, but a few were real assholes. We had seen them smacking a few of the Thai prisoners around outside their cells. They strutted around like peacocks, and barked orders at the prisoners they forced to clean the floors and shine their shoes. Well, you get the idea. I was careful not to take enough dope to totally incapacitate me. I just wanted to maintain my ability to avert a bad withdrawal episode. Several times a day, I had to brave that humiliating sewer for my fix.

My unfathomable situation would appear unimaginable to my friends back in the United States. In the space of a few hours, I had gone from a paradisiacal life of luxury to this filthy, crowded jail cell. Back home, no inmate would be crammed into such a small space with sweaty, smelly bodies and have to suffer the indignity of using a broken toilet overflowing with human feces that emitted such noxious odors. The whole scene now before me would make grown men weep with disgust while holding their noses. This would never occur back in the good old US of A. This place was something out of the Middle Ages.

My emotions shifted frequently and rapidly from anger and frustration to remorse and utter devastation. The Thai prisoners, however, seemed to take everything in stride. Thais, in general, are a very congenial people, taking life as it comes. There was absolutely nothing for me, or Helmut, to fear from them. In an American jail, the strong prey on the weak, dominating other prisoners through fear. Here it was different. They'd pick your pockets if they got the chance, but nobody would try to strong-arm you. Such fear-mongering and bullying tactics were rare, the opposite of what went on in most western countries' prisons. In Thailand it was the police and prison guards that you had to steer clear of. I guess a person would have to experience being locked up in different countries to fully understand the societal contrasts.

Slumping back against the wall, I again surveyed my surroundings. In the large foyer and hallway there was always activity. Women scurried back and forth in sarongs or flowing skirts and young boys hurried about, carrying food or tea. There were even small children playing just outside the entrance to the station. The captain and lieutenant stayed in their offices most of the time, only coming out to give orders or to leave the building. Everyone else sat in the hallway or just inside the entrance in this large open foyer area.

Sighing, I thought to myself that this had to be the lowest I had ever sunk. The possible consequences of my hedonistic and dangerous lifestyle had now finally permeated my thick, stubborn mind. So now what? I couldn't imagine being sentenced to prison in this country. The stories I had heard of what foreigners went through in Thai prisons were beyond frightening. Anxiety gnawed at the pit of my stomach, increasing exponentially by the second.

Trying my best to shelve these thoughts, I went into the restroom to snort some more of the white powder, just enough for my mind to drift away when I closed my eyes. During the day we just sat, sometimes talking, sometimes staring off into space. Whatever Jamie brought in the way of food and drink, I shared with Helmut. Since I had both money and dope in my pockets, Helmut always made sure that nobody picked my pockets while I was asleep. The merry-go-round of confusion and desolation that I felt seemed to gain force as each hour slowly passed. My life was now completely out of my own hands. Fate would have her way with me, and I'd have no say in the matter. No man can change the past.

On the second morning of waking up in this grisly, torturous situation, I saw the captain through the bars of the cell. He had just arrived and was walking toward his office. I stood and repeatedly called for him through the bars. Finally, he acknowledged me. A bit annoyed, he sent someone over to ask what I wanted. "I need to speak with the captain," I said. The young policeman left to relay my words. Soon he returned, unlocked the cell, and motioned for me to go ahead of him down the dimly lit hallway to the captain's office. When I walked in, he was sitting at his desk drinking tea and eating his breakfast. He looked at me as if to say, "Well, what do you want now?"

On the morning I had been arrested and brought to the police station, they had allowed me to use the bathroom located in back of the station. I assumed it was one that the cops themselves used. Recounting my revulsion at the state of the toilet in the cell's *hong nam*, I asked the captain if I might be able to use the one out back instead.

He didn't answer right away, but he smirked at me. Having a 500 baht note neatly folded at the ready, I handed it to him and he quickly slipped it into his shirt pocket. "Okay," he said, "I'll tell them you can use the outside toilet. Two times a day only! Don't you try to run, okay?" He made a motion with his forefinger across his throat, intimating what the consequences would be if I did.

Thank God, I thought. I could handle having to pee in that stinking corroded urinal, but I didn't want to take another crap in there, if I could avoid it. "*Kaup kun mach kap*," I said, meaning, "thank you very much." "I won't do anything stupid." Just being in this sordid environment was demeaning enough, but at least I wouldn't have to stand over that pile anymore. "*Bai*" (go), he said, and I walked out the door. No cop was outside the door waiting for me, so I sauntered over to the desk and tried to engage the cop sitting there in light conversation. The captain came out and spoke to him, saying I could use the outside toilet, and then he returned to his office.

The cop asked, "You need *hong nam* now?"

Not wanting to return to the cell, I answered with, "*Chai kap*" (yes). He told a man in plain clothes, who was sitting on a chair just outside the foyer door, to come in and take his place at the desk. Then he led me out back to the bathroom. Making the most of the situation, I walked slowly, taking in the scenery and the gentle motion of village life. I looked up at the sky and appreciated its warm blue color and the myriad cloud shapes as they drifted by.

There was also a shower in the bathroom so I used it, as well. Never mind asking permission. I figured nobody would care, and I was right. The previous night, Jamie had brought me a change of clothes with a sarong to wrap around my waist when I used the toilet, so I used that to dry myself. I tried talking the cops into letting Helmut use the same bathroom and shower, but no dice. They just said, "Captain gone for weekend" and "Only captain can say."

Jamie came twice a day, making sure I had whatever I needed in the way of nourishment. Monday must have been some sort of holiday since we were told that we weren't going to court until the following day. By evening there was still no word from Pan. Early Tuesday morning, Jamie arrived and said that both she and Pan would meet me at the courthouse in Chonburi. Pan had spoken to a friend of his who said he would arrange bail. I was elated, to put it mildly! I promised Helmut that I would see what I could do for him once I was out.

About a half hour later Helmut and I, and about a half dozen Thai prisoners, were handcuffed, then taken out of the cell. Now we'd take the hour or so journey to the courthouse in Chonburi. One by one, we walked up the steps into the back of a dark green paddy wagon with barred windows. Two policemen climbed in behind us and then I heard the door being locked from the outside. Up until now, I hadn't been handcuffed, not since being arrested at my house four days prior. This didn't bother me because, with any luck, I'd soon be free again.

I watched life whizz by as we raced down the highway toward Chonburi, which was more than halfway to Bangkok from Pattaya Beach. Cars, motorcycles, and trucks piled high with their loads of goods were all around us, jockeying to get ahead. I watched the village scenes fly by, which mostly consisted of people and animals. The details of this subtropical countryside seemed more noteworthy than usual. You only really learn to appreciate the feeling of freedom after losing it. Savoring everything within sight, I prayed that later in the day I would be in a car on my way back to Pattaya with Jamie and Pan.

I'll have to get out of the country, I thought to myself. I have to put this mess behind me and do my best to figure out my life. That was a tall order considering I was a fugitive, having jumped bail after my arrest on drug charges in Hawaii. Somehow I would figure something out. Anything was better than being in jail. I was also making vows to myself, once again, to give up my heroin addiction, this time for good. All these plans and promises that were swirling around in my head were dependent on me first worming myself out of this mess!

In all my adult life, I'd never been stopped for anything more than a traffic ticket, much less being arrested. Recently, all this changed. Since March of this year, I'd been taken into police custody four times. My memory drifted back to my arrest and stay in Hawaii's infamous Halawa Prison. Then came the two close calls in Mexico City after fleeing the US while on bail. A day and a night in a Mexican jail left me in such a frustrated state of mind that I foolishly decided to return to Bangkok. Bad decision! Then it happened again, only days after arriving in Thailand. I was nearly busted by the police in Bangkok. Amazingly, I somehow managed to get out of that mess. I clearly recall the fast one I'd pulled on them, right under their noses.

I was jolted out of my reverie by our arrival at the Chonburi courthouse. The paddy wagon door opened and we filed out, still handcuffed, and were escorted into the courthouse building. Downstairs there were huge cells, large enough to accommodate hundreds of prisoners, yet most were crammed full. Some were literally standing room only.

The cuffs were removed and Helmut and I were locked in the same cell with a few dozen other men. The cell was dimly lit, with the same floor to ceiling iron bars and grimy, filthy floors as in the police station. We saw a fairly large group of women prisoners, including foreigners, in another holding cell that we passed. I assumed that they also had been arrested for heroin possession. I never heard of a foreign woman arrested here for anything else. Sure, it sounds easy enough. Just carry a small false-bottom suitcase on board the plane in Bangkok, and then deliver it once you reach the US or Europe. Everyone who ever agreed to smuggle illegal drugs did so thinking it would be a fast and easy way to make $10,000. The consequences and likelihood of being caught are rarely factored in when making such a decision. Easy money is not often that easy.

Outside our holding cell, people were constantly coming and going. I kept my eyes trained on the hallway, watching intently for Jamie. Expecting to see her at any moment, hopefully with Pan or an attorney, to let me know my bail had been arranged.

Finally, after about an hour, Jamie showed up, but she was alone. She said Pan was upstairs with the lawyer. He would be talking to the prosecutor's assistant, who in turn would get the bail order signed by the judge. "Don't worry, hon," she kept saying, "Pan knows the prosecutor, as well as the judge." But I still had this unsettling feeling that I just couldn't shake. My insides were like butterflies on steroids! Jamie left to go upstairs to wait for Pan.

An hour passed before they came to get us. Helmut tried to make small talk, but I couldn't concentrate on what he was saying. Nervous and scared, I just kept praying for my release. This time we were all handcuffed to each other and led back up the cement stairs, then into the courtroom. This wasn't a good sign at all! I had expected to go before the judge alone. Since we were all cuffed together, we had to stand up as a group as soon as they started calling out our names.

The judge didn't even acknowledge me and I didn't have a clue what he was saying. Actually, I only understood a few words of anything that was said in the courtroom. Ten minutes later, we were unceremoniously led out of the courtroom, and back downstairs to the holding cell. Our handcuffs were removed and we were once again locked inside a cell.

Although I could speak some Thai, the dialect I was familiar with was more of a slang version, spoken by people from the countryside, called *chat*. In court only the "Kings

Thai" (which can be equated with the English spoken by the upper classes in England, often referred to as the "Queen's English") is spoken, called *raja sop*. Although I couldn't understand what was being said, a premonition of doom left me feeling weak and nauseous.

Every minute seemed like an hour until Jamie finally showed up with Pan. Pan was tall and lean, his black hair pushed back on the sides. His appearance was impeccable from the black Italian three-button, collared shirt and cream-colored slacks to the Gucci shoes and designer sunglasses. He strode along confidently, with an air of power and affluence. Seeing the two of them approach the cell gave me hope. Unfortunately, my optimism was short-lived. Neither was smiling.

"I have good news and bad news," Pan said. "The bad news is that you will be transferred to Chonburi Prison today. The good news is we should be able to bail you out tomorrow, if you have the cash."

"How much is it going to cost," I asked him.

"We have to pay the judge, the prosecutor, and the police captain in Pattaya in order to make this charge go away. All together 35 Grand, US."

$35K was a ridiculous amount to have to pay for a charge like this, but I wasn't about to argue. I had it, but all of my money was in American Express traveler's checks in a safe deposit box in Pattaya Beach. "I'll have to write a letter to the bank to give Jamie access to my safe deposit box," I told him.

Turning to Jamie, I asked if she remembered where the key was stashed. She nodded her head yes. I had shown her where I hid it just in case of an emergency like this. "Get me a sheet of paper and a pen."

Pan reassured me I'd be out the next day, while Jamie left to get some paper for me to write the letter. She returned a few minutes later with the paper and took a pen from her bag. I wrote to the bank asking that Jamie be given access to my box, having no choice but to state the truth about my present circumstances — that I was being detained in police custody. "Please do this quickly," I told her. "You'll have to bring me the checks to sign in the morning. Then Pan can get them cashed in time to get the bail order signed by tomorrow afternoon."

Jamie promised to go to the bank as soon as she left the courthouse, in an attempt to get there before they closed for the day. Pan said something to the guards and they treated me somewhat deferentially after that, even asking if I wanted anything to eat or drink.

Another few hours passed in this stiflingly hot house of a jail cell, until finally they opened the door, took us back upstairs, and ordered us onto a bus to Chonburi Prison. Thankfully, Jamie had the foresight to bring me a few changes of clothes, just in case of any delays in getting me out. She'd already brought me a sarong and a few toiletries when I was in the police station, which I had in a small bag with me. Knowing it was likely that I'd be subjected to body searches today, I hadn't brought any dope with me. I was starting to get sick with withdrawal symptoms, but resigned myself to accept the impending suffering. Thinking I'd be getting out the next day, I tried to relax. "All I have to do is just get through another twenty-four hours," I told myself.

CHAPTER 2

Chonburi Prison

A short time later, we arrived at the foreboding stone entrance of a stark medieval-looking prison. Approaching the huge, iron front gates, the driver blew his horn. The gates began to slowly open. We drove through the archway and the gates immediately clanged shut behind us. In seconds the rear door of the bus was flung open, and two uniformed guards quickly ushered us out yelling, "Hurry up! Get out!" They stood on both sides of the door as we drained from the bus. Grabbing and pushing the shoulder of each prisoner to hasten our exit, the guards practically hurled us to the ground in the process. Several prisoners tripped and fell, and were immediately kicked and snarled at to hurry up.

The inner chamber of the prison was huge; it was a large open area with cement block walls and a rough cement floor, but no windows. It looked like a gigantic garage, except the walls were constructed of massive stone blocks and the doors were made of thick, heavy steel. At both ends, left and right, were small steel doors. Ahead was another set of steel doors similar to the ones we entered upon arrival. Those, I assumed, were also for vehicles and led into the inner compound of the prison. Next to it were two smaller steel doors for foot traffic. Far to my right, toward the end of this open chamber, I noticed a large iron-barred area; it looked like a big cage. I wondered what it was for, but didn't dare divert my attention long enough to study it more closely.

We were told to empty our pockets onto the ground and then strip naked. Helmut and I took our cues from what the other prisoners were doing since we couldn't understand much of what they were saying. I had been processed in a somewhat similar manner when I entered Halawa Prison in Honolulu seven months earlier. But the attitudes of those gruff prison guards were nothing compared to the treatment being meted out today. I felt defiled and humiliated as never before in my life. Ordering us to stand in rows, the guards walked along in front of us. One by one they picked up the articles of our clothing, lying in a heap at our feet, searching for contraband.

When they got to Helmut and me, one of them pointed his baton toward my crotch, then at Helmut's, laughing and obviously making some kind of snide comments about our genitals. He barked a question while pointing his baton at me, but I didn't have a clue what he was saying. I simply answered, "*My kowjai*" (I don't understand). He said something else in a loud voice, which the other guard laughed at as they moved on.

If one of the Thai prisoners didn't answer quickly enough or failed to use the requisite honorifics in their speech, they were hit across the back of the knees with the baton, causing their legs to buckle and drop out from beneath them. Berated and kicked until they managed to get to their feet, they would then call out loudly "*Chai kap*" (yes sir).

These guards were nasty pieces of work, taking every opportunity to abuse and ridicule us. In the hour it took to process us into the prison, I witnessed at least a half dozen prisoners kicked or whacked with a baton. I cringed in sympathy as one man was beaten mercilessly across his back. During the search, one of the guards found contraband in the waistband of an inmate's pants. He was dragged away, through one of the doors to our left. We heard his shrieks of pain. I never saw him again, or at least I didn't recognize him if I did.

The realization that I was entering a house of horrors, the likes of which I could never have imagined in my wildest nightmares, was making me feel faint. Steeling myself to stay on my feet, I silently repeated my mantra, "It's only for a day. Tomorrow I'll be walking out through those doors."

Finally, we were told to put our clothes back on. A higher-ranking officer, stripes on the shoulders of his green uniform and several stars on his lapels, walked down the rows. Asking each of our names, he checked them off on his clipboard. One of the new recruits must have been too slow in answering or spoke in a manner they disapproved of because the guard accompanying the officer struck him open-handed on the side of his head. He crumpled to the ground. As he rose shakily to his feet, he loudly exclaimed, "Yes sir, yes sir, I'm sorry sir!"

Our money, and anything else we had in our pockets, except clothing and toiletries, was taken away. The money, we were told, would be deposited into an account at the prison canteen, where cigarettes and other items were available for purchase. I wasn't given a receipt, nor asked to sign one. In fact, my cash simply disappeared. I was told there had been no money deposited to my canteen account when I asked about it the next day.

After the induction experience, we were separated into groups. Helmut and I were the only two in ours. Two guards were assigned to each group; they marched us single file through the doors into the compound where we were stopped and told to squat.

Thais and other Asians have no problem squatting. You often see people in Thailand, India, and other Asian countries squatting while waiting for a bus or while holding conversations. For them it's often as comfortable as sitting. Not so for us, though. My legs began to ache if I remained in that position for more than a minute. Some Westerners couldn't even last that long!

After a minute or two, I couldn't take it any longer. I had to stand up, so I did. Blackbeard, a particularly brutal guard so named due to a dark discoloring of his face that resembled a beard, immediately came over to me, screaming in my face to squat again. Putting both of his hands on my shoulders, he pushed me back down. I tried to keep from falling, but couldn't and fell backwards onto the concrete walkway.

Now a perfect target for his boots, I received a kick in the thigh before I could get back up. Trying to squat again for a minute, I simply fell back and sat on the ground. Helmut couldn't stay squatted either, so he did the same thing. Blackbeard shouted and cursed at us, his spittle spraying into our faces while he held his baton threateningly above his head. But finally he had to just let us sit there. It was either that or beat the crap out of us for not being capable of squatting like the Thais.

When the second name-checking process inside the prison compound finished, the Thais were led in two groups farther into the prison compound. From my vantage point, I could see buildings along the sides, just inside the outer wall, some in the center and obviously more in the back where the two groups of prisoners were heading.

The buildings were made of concrete with open, barred windows. A maze of walkways wound around the prison housing units, forming a kind of concrete spider's web. Looking up to the left, I saw stone guard towers, reminding me of medieval castles, only here and now armed guards with rifles manned them. Above them, along the outside perimeter wall, were even bigger towers. The guards in those were armed with larger caliber automatic weapons.

Helmut and I were taken along a path to the right of the entry that led to a long rectangular building, situated behind a low retaining wall. As we approached, we saw a few white-skinned faces sitting outside on stone benches, and other inmates standing in groups around the area. Most looked up at us, some nodded in acknowledgement, and a few raised a finger or hand in greeting.

We were shown the building where we were to be housed. The guard who led us spoke to one of the foreigners, a heavy-set man with blue-green eyes and brown wavy hair that kept falling in his face. He said, "New *farangs*. You show them where they stay," and then he left after giving us each a stained bamboo mat to sleep on. That was it.

Mike Beetroff, a Cockney from London, introduced himself to us. "Hello mates, welcome to paradise." His smile was warm and disarming, which was somewhat comforting after our initial welcome. He showed us where to put our meager belongings. Helmut had a few pieces of clothing that he had managed to bring to the jail with him when he was first arrested. He also had a toothbrush, toothpaste, and soap that I'd had Jamie bring for him when we were at the police station. In my bag were a few articles of clothing, my sarong, a toothbrush, toothpaste, and a bar of soap.

The building had previously been an infirmary long before there were any foreign prisoners here. It had raised wooden platforms on each side of a center walkway running its full length. Situated at the far end was the one and only toilet, an Asian squat variety, of course. Surrounding it was a low, gray cement wall about eighteen inches high. Next to the wall, there was an open trough filled with water and a dirty, green plastic pitcher.

Having spent considerable time in India, I had learned what that was for many years ago. You fill the pitcher with water from the trough before you starting doing your business. Once you're finished, you pour it over your rear end, holding the pitcher with your right hand, using the left to clean yourself. There was no toilet paper at this "hotel," so no matter what you were accustomed to before your unfortunate arrival, you had to learn to take a dump Asian style.

In this situation, even foreigners who had a hard time squatting had no choice but to learn to use it long enough to defecate. More than a few fell over in the beginning; or worse, they simply plopped down on their butts into the filthy, stinking hole. Eventually, of necessity, everyone develops enough leg strength to use it. I remember once seeing a fat American guy taking his first dump, trying desperately to hold himself up over the hole to keep from falling in. He held his body weight up with his hands at hip level just behind him on the filthy rim of the toilet. Suddenly, the poor guy's arms gave way and he fell backwards into the hole. The entire room burst into laughter as they watched the guy struggle to get out.

It was a whole new experience using the toilet with twenty to thirty people watching. There was never any privacy. Around the clock you ate, crapped, washed, and slept in the company of dozens of other inmates. We all slept in a row on one of the platforms, shoulder to shoulder, our feet pointed toward the aisle, our heads toward the barred windows on the sides of the building. Whatever personal belongings we had were placed underneath the platform.

Later in the evening, the building was locked down for the night. For a while, Helmut and I shared our stories with a few of the other foreigners. Practically every single white foreigner in there was in for possession of heroin. But white-skinned prisoners were also the minority among the foreign population. There were only eight of us the day Helmut and I arrived. Helmut was the only one charged with something other than a drug offense.

There were a few Pakistanis in for visa violations, some Chinese who didn't talk much (especially when it came to why they were there), and a few others from other countries. There was even one guy named Mohammed who claimed to be the finance minister of Oman. He was in for heroin possession after being turned in by a prostitute he'd slept with at Pattaya Beach. Later, we heard he was indeed an Omani minister. He was out within a few days.

Most of the inmates had straw mats as well as blankets to sleep on, all of which had been sent in for them from the outside. "You can have pretty much anything you want in here," a Canadian guy named Paul told us. "Just make sure whoever sends it in for you also gives money to the guards at the office. Then it will get to you." Paul never smiled while speaking to us. His blue eyes were always expressionless and his mouth was set in a permanent frown. After giving us these words of wisdom, he rolled over and closed his eyes, retreating into his own world as if he'd simply had his fill of us.

Helmut and I spent more time talking with Mike, the English Cockney who had introduced himself upon our arrival. Through him we learned that you could keep cash in here, besides having it deposited to your canteen account. He explained that some of the guards could be induced to allow contraband. Salaries were miniscule, and taking bribes for favors earned them many times over their salaries.

Soon, withdrawal symptoms began to hit me with a vengeance, and I had to lie back, retreating from the conversation. My head throbbed and my nose ran. All night long, I repeatedly ran to the toilet with diarrhea. My stomach was cramped and tied up in knots. Lying there, using my sarong to wipe the mucous flowing endlessly from my nose, I bemoaned my predicament, but repeated my mantra "It's just until tomorrow, only until tomorrow." All I could do was patiently await the arrival of morning.

Just when I thought the night would never end, the first light of dawn began to glow, casting shadows outside our windows. Soon after the first rays of the sunrise became apparent, a short, stocky uniformed guard sporting a grin came to unlock the door. "Be careful of that one," Michael warned. "I've seen him beat the crap out of some of the Thais. The smile's a front. He's a mean SOB, not one that you want to ask any favors of, believe me."

There was no regimented program for foreign prisoners. We could stay inside the building or go out into the prison compound. Although the majority of Thai inmates had to work, the foreigners didn't. As soon as the door was opened, everyone got up to exit the building. Except for me. I was too nauseous to move right then, so I stayed put.

Eventually, I got up and went outside to bathe. Each building had a large open concrete water tank behind it that measured about ten feet across and twice that in length. Using a plastic bowl filled with water, you douse yourself, soap up, and repeat the process to rinse off. After washing my sarong, I wrung it out and used it to dry myself off. I was too sick to have any interest in exploring my new abode, which, as expected, was a wretched place. So I walked back inside to lie down.

The prison served two meals a day, but very few foreigners ate the prison food. Helmut, however, had no choice. He got in line for food the first morning, but I was still too sick to even think about eating. He returned with an aluminum bowl filled with a foul-smelling soup. Floating in it were fish heads and other unidentifiable chunks. It also contained a scoop of *kow dang* (red rice); the result was a nauseating concoction.

Red rice looks somewhat similar to brown rice, but it's a lower grade and completely unwashed. There were always small rocks and other bits of foreign matter in it. You had to chew very carefully, lest you break a tooth. Many a prisoner suffered broken molars from eating prison red rice. That often meant having to get someone to pull the damaged tooth with a pair of pliers. Agonizing though that may sound, you'll do anything to get rid of an abscessed tooth. Anyone who has ever had one knows how excruciatingly painful it is. There are no dentists in a Thai prison. In other words, unless you had outside support, you carefully ate the swill or starved. Most foreigners from western countries had access to money, so they were not forced to eat it.

The day wore on with no sign of Jamie. Finally, about four in the afternoon, she showed up. A guard came to get me, taking me back to where we had entered the prison. He pointed to a set of cement stairs not far from the entrance. I went through a doorway and entered the area I'd seen and noted as an iron-barred cage upon my arrival at the prison. It was the visiting room; this caged enclosure was divided into two sections by rusty iron bars running from floor to ceiling. I sat on the bench on my side facing Jamie on the other side of the bars.

"Did you manage to get the TCs?" I asked her, my anxiety obvious by the strain in my voice. Jamie looked totally stressed-out and had large bags under her bloodshot eyes.

"No, babe, they wouldn't let me in with that note you wrote." The bank had given her a form for me to fill out and sign before they would allow her access to my safe deposit box.

Jamie called over a guard on her side of the barred enclosure and showed it to him, telling him I needed to sign it and give it back to her. He passed it to another guard who handed it through to me, along with a pen. Hurriedly signing it, I asked if she had told Pan why she wasn't bringing the money today.

"Yes, I called him but he wasn't home so I talked to his sister. Don't worry. I'll get them first thing tomorrow morning and bring them here for you to sign. I promise." She was doing her best to smile and reassure me.

She brought some food for me, so I asked her to give it to the guard before leaving, along with 50 baht. We both sat there looking at each other, tears welling up in our eyes.

"This is the most diabolical place that I have ever been in," I said dishearteningly. Suddenly, Jamie began sobbing uncontrollably.

Forgetting about myself for a second, I realized that my complaining was only adding to her feelings of desperation. I quickly added, "But I'll be out tomorrow night, and it'll all just be a bad memory. Hang in there and we'll be okay." She nodded, wiping her face with a tissue she'd fished out of her bag. The guard motioned that our time was up. I blew her a kiss and sat watching as she walked out the door.

In a moment, another guard handed me the bag of food and told me to hurry back to my building. Carrying it, I dejectedly shuffled off, the feeling of impending doom numbing my mind again. Lost in thought, I was soon at the door to our building where a guard was waiting for me. It was time to lock us up for the night.

I opened the bag of food and tried to eat a little, even though I wasn't really hungry. Jamie had brought two of everything, knowing that my new friend Helmut had no one else to help him. Opening the rice containers, I scooped a little out to put into the curry. Then I noticed a plastic bag slipped down the side. Inside it, I found 1000 baht in cash. Slipping it into my pants' pocket I continued my meal. We weren't allowed drinks from outside, so there was no choice but to drink the tap water. All I could do was hope I wouldn't get parasites from drinking it. In India, if you drink tap water, you're guaranteed to get sick. Until now, I had always enjoyed bottled water in Thailand.

The next day was Thursday; again I waited for Jamie, but this time she didn't show up. I was beginning to panic. My withdrawal symptoms were also at their peak. Weak, despondent, and utterly miserable, I was plagued with constant diarrhea. Still too sick to eat more than a few bites, I gave most of my food to Helmut, who voraciously consumed every morsel. For someone so thin, he was like a bottomless pit.

Late Friday afternoon Jamie arrived, saying she'd just managed to get them to let her into my box. Thursday had been a holiday. Now we would have to wait until Monday to do anything, because the courts and government offices were closed on the weekend. Jamie brought more food, blankets, and towels for us. She also gave me a new pair of sandals, since mine had fallen apart.

A guard brought me the American Express travelers' checks, along with a pen, and I set to signing my name on each one. After handing them back, Jamie put them in her bag. "I'll be here Monday," she said. The guard was already pointing to the clock, indicating that her time was up. Once again, we made the motions of giving each other a kiss, fingers to lips, then touching the metal fence covering the bars separating us.

"Monday," I murmured.

"Monday you'll be out," she answered; then she mouthed the words, "I love you."

"I love you, too" I mouthed back and waved, my eyes following her until she disappeared. I sighed, resigning myself to another three days. Slowly walking back down the stairs, I followed the path back to our building. My body was now starting to tingle, especially when lying down at night. The worst of the withdrawal symptoms had passed during the five days since I'd last had a fix, but every nerve ending prickled with that pins and needles feeling. Heroin depresses your nervous system. You cease to feel anything much at all. No pain, no worries, and no desire for anything else, except your next hit.

Now all of my senses were coming alive. As if asleep for years, even the "bald headed butler" between my legs woke up. Sunday night, I actually had a wet dream, the first since I was a teenager. There was so much semen that my pants were literally soaked. After that, I started sleeping in a sarong, which was more comfortable to wear in this hot, humid atmosphere anyway.

By Monday, I was starting to feel much better, at least physically. For the first time in a week, my stomach growled with hunger pangs. Up until now, I'd had to force myself to eat and drink just so I wouldn't completely deteriorate or dehydrate. I gave one of the guards some money to buy us rice, cream of wheat, and vegetables from the outside. Like me, Helmut was a vegetarian. Unlike me, though, he was a fantastic cook. Using an open flame pit, he cooked up some cream of wheat with vegetables for lunch — an Indian dish called *upma*. Although we'd only known each other for ten days, we had formed a brotherly bond.

Time seemed to crawl while I sat and waited for Jamie, so I decided to take a walk around the compound after eating. Asking Helmut if he wanted to explore a bit, we set off down the path toward the center of the prison complex. As we passed a building with a few groups of Thais sitting in front, I nodded and smiled. Several returned my smile. One said, "Hello, how are you?"

"Just great" I answered sarcastically, though the wit was lost on him. We stopped for a moment to shake hands and exchange names and pleasantries. Looking down at the ground, I noticed that many of them had on thick chains attached to iron rings around their ankles. "Holy shit" I said, to nobody in particular. Pointing at one of them, I said to the guy "Those look heavy!"

"Heavy, yes, but, *farangs* no have to wear," he replied.

"Man," I said, "Thank God for that! Why do you have to wear them?" The answer was that for many crimes, the prison time included having to be kept bound in chains, and not lightweight leg cuffs. My estimate was that they weighed at least six to ten pounds. Later, I found out that there were larger sizes, too. The heaviest links weighed in the vicinity of twenty pounds or more. Shaking my head, I called out "See you later" to Arthit, the guy I'd been talking to, as Helmut and I resumed our tour of the compound.

The sun was blazing hot and the air oppressively thick with humidity. The entire compound was wall-to-wall concrete, making it feel like a cross between an oven and a steam bath. Gazing up at the mold and mildew-stained prison walls, iron stakes and barbed wire at the top, my heart felt heavy. What if Pan couldn't get me out? How the hell was I supposed to live in this place? Jumbled thoughts crisscrossed through my mind. I felt so low, lower than at any time in my life.

The day passed slowly. Alone, I watched the sun inch closer to the western horizon. Still, there was no sign of Jamie. Where the hell was she? I wanted to scream. Finally, I had to accept the fact that, for whatever reason, she wasn't coming. Dazed, confused, emotionally crushed, and despondent, I wanted to break down and weep. Sitting there in my own lost world, I passed the remaining hours of the day until one of the guards shook me out of my reverie. It was evening, and time for lock-down.

A few new foreigners had come in that day, so I took some time to talk to an American who had just arrived. He was from Hawaii, interestingly enough, so we had a lot in common. Sonny was part Hawaiian, part Samoan, part Chinese, and part Japanese, a real *local da kine*, as they say in the islands. As one might expect, he had been arrested for heroin possession. With over a kilogram in his hotel room when he was busted, he would need some serious cash if he expected to get out of here any time soon.

Memories came flooding back after our talk about Hawaii. I even got teary-eyed thinking about them. I did my best to block out reality, even if only for a little while. Finally, for the first time since my arrest, I fell into a sound sleep. The next thing I knew, I was awake; it was that darkest time just before the break of dawn. I quickly jumped down, and went to the toilet to relieve myself.

One bonus of waking up before everyone else was being able to use the toilet first. It was in constant use from just before the crack of dawn until the door was unlocked at seven. Once everyone was awake, you had to keep eyeing the bog like a vulture. When the guy using it reached for the water pitcher, you had to jump up and claim the next place in line before someone else beat you to it. Not an easy feat. Being the first to rise in the morning gave me a definite advantage. I could relax while everyone else waited to compete for his turn.

Nobody wanted to be one of the last to go because the tank of water was usually empty by then. Since these were not flush toilets, you had to pour enough water down them after you were finished to wash it down the hole. As there was only the one tank of water for everyone to use, you couldn't just keep pouring water every time you cut the proverbial cable.

You had to wait until you were completely finished, your excrement lying below you, stinking in the sweltering heat. Meanwhile, the others had no choice but to inhale the foul odor. Only when you were completely finished, could you then use water to clean yourself and flush. There was never enough water for everyone. Just imagine running to the toilet to finally get to empty your bowels, only to find that there was no water to clean yourself with afterwards. Honestly, there is nothing quite like smelling that kind of aroma for two hours every morning in a hot, stuffy room shared by dozens of guys with bad body odor who are burping and farting while waiting for their turn to add their bit to the sickening stench. Then, when you finally got your turn to contribute to the revolting brown pile, everyone else was glancing sideways at you. In some mentally deranged way, they just stared at you, as you performed your ass-cleaning ceremony. Whoever was fastest would then push over to the toilet, hovering over you to claim the next turn.

On Tuesday, at about four in the afternoon, Jamie finally showed up. "Where have you been?" I asked. She wasn't smiling, so I knew something was wrong.

"I cashed the TCs and went to see Pan to give him the cash. But now he says that his guy at the court insists it can't be done without a lawyer's involvement." She sounded exhausted, and she had dark circles under her eyes from all the stress and fatigue.

"So where's the money?" I asked.

"Right here," she answered while putting her hand on the bag she was carrying over her shoulder, "I came directly here from the court to tell you. Had I gone back to put it away first, I'd have been too late to see you."

"Where do we get a lawyer?" I asked, the feeling of impending doom wafting over me yet again.

"Pan said he'll introduce me to a good lawyer and we'll take it from there," Jamie replied. About ready to cry, she whispered, "I miss you."

"I miss you too," I softly responded. "When do you meet with him?"

"Tomorrow morning. Pan will drive me," Jamie murmured. "Try to relax."

"I'll do my best," I managed a half-hearted smile. The guard was motioning that our time was up. Jamie turned for one last look before slowly walking out the door. It was painful to see her depart with tears in her eyes. Departing with tears was the new norm for her. I had to remember that this nightmare was just as frightening for her as it was for me. When you're fighting for survival, it is good to have someone in your corner, and she was the one in my corner. She was my rock.

I slowly returned to my building to lie down. All I could do was stare at the ceiling. Before long Helmut came in to see what was up. After relating the story to him, I added, "I have a bad feeling about all this, but it's out of my hands. Fate always has her way with us, whether we like it or not."

Late the next morning, Jamie showed up with a lawyer. He was dressed in a light blue suit with a pair of oval shaped glasses resting on his nose. He introduced himself as Somwan. I was not allowed out of the inmate side of the visiting room, not even to speak with an attorney, so we had to talk through the bars. Somwan got right down to business by saying, "I have obtained your case files and I am sure we can get you out on bail. But it may take some time."

"Why?" I asked, obviously upset, "Why can't you get me bail right away? Isn't it just about the money? I mean, they only got me with a gram or so, and it wasn't even mine, not that that matters any."

"No," he said, "The Americans are blocking your bail."

My heart sank to a new depth and my heavy head felt like it was going to fall off my shoulders. I was stunned, and for a moment I couldn't even summon any words in response. Now, I knew for sure that the Feds were involved. Still, the case at home was a state charge, not federal, so why were they interested?

"Isn't there somebody higher up that we can pay to sign a bail petition?" I pleaded, my voice strained and close to cracking.

In Thailand, you can accomplish almost anything, if you have money. All officials are corrupt, from the bottom to the top. At this point, I didn't care if it took every single penny I had. Staying in here was not an option!

Mr. Somwan went on to explain that his firm had the connections to accomplish it, but time was of the essence. I knew that. If it got past the next hearing, the price would skyrocket or it might simply become impossible. Wishing the earth would simply swallow me up, I sat there, dejectedly, waiting for what was to come next.

"It will be more expensive to arrange than Mr. Pan previously told Miss Jamie. This is not an easy task, I assure you. Our fee will be $25,000 US and I will tell you how much additional money is required once it has been arranged. Expect it to be in the vicinity of $30,000, in addition to our fee."

Slack-jawed, I just sat there on the hard bench, staring at him in disbelief. This amount was astronomical, but what choice did I have? "Do it," I said definitively, looking at Jamie. "I want out of here." Somwan informed me that he would need the entire $55,000 up front because once he managed to secure my release, he'd have to be ready to make the payments immediately.

Jamie looked at me and said, "I'll have to go to the bank and get the rest of the traveler's checks." She then turned to Somwan, and asked, "Can I just have Howard sign them and give them to you or do I need to cash them first?"

"We can cash them, that's not a problem, as long as both signatures match, which I assume they will," he answered. Turning to me, he said, "Okay then, Mr. Beckman, we will now set about arranging your freedom."

Jamie touched her palm to the bars, with a sorrowful look in her eyes. Speaking so softly that I could barely hear her, she said, "I'll be here tomorrow with the TCs for you to sign. Try to be strong."

After watching them leave, I reluctantly turned to walk back into the compound. My mind was spinning. Depression was beginning to set in despite how much I tried to shrug it off. I have to be positive, I told myself. But I felt completely drained. On one hand, I was wary of this lawyer's ability to even be able to do what he promised. He might just rip me off and never come back. There'd be nothing I could do about it. But on the other hand, I had to chance it. After all, Pan got him for us. I have to get out of this place before I crack, I thought to myself. In a thick mental fog, I slowly ambled back to my building.

Helmut and Mike were waiting for me. They could tell from the look on my face that things hadn't gone well. Sitting down, I sighed heavily, "This doesn't look good. The price has already almost tripled. And there's a big complication. The DEA (Drug Enforcement Agency) is blocking my bail. Unless this lawyer can get somebody with enough clout to arrange my release so I can get out of the country, then I'm screwed." I slumped back on the bench and wearily extended my legs.

Helmut said, "Let's hope the gods smile on you. How about something to eat? I can cook us up some tofu and veggies in the wok, Chinese style. There's some jasmine rice that Michael's little lady friend brought to him." He meant the bar girl Michael had been hanging-out with before he got busted. At least she was coming to see him.

"Sure, why not." I said. "Starving myself won't help matters any, that's for sure."

Jamie showed up the next day and I nervously signed the checks, all $75,000 worth. "There's not much left," she said.

"Put back what you don't need, but keep some money for yourself."

Jamie needed money to live on, besides what I would need while I was incarcerated. She deposited some cash to my canteen account, and gave the guard some dough to give to me, including something for him, of course. I had no idea when Somwan would come through, so I wanted to have some cash in my pocket.

CHAPTER 3

A Junkie Never Learns

Drugs were readily available in the prison. Just about all the white foreigners, except Helmut, did heroin when they had money to buy it. The purity was the same as on the outside, it just cost more in prison. Still, compared to the price in the U.S., it was dirt-cheap. My fragile and vacillating mind convinced me that I really needed a hit. The immense pressure in my head now seemed too much for me to fight any longer. For almost two years now, heroin had been my crutch, the panacea to all the sorrows in my life.

The sorry thing about the mentality of a drug addict is that your decision-making skills are terrible. Here I was, almost completely over the physical withdrawal symptoms, but my mind was still that of a heroin addict. Rather than dealing with the emotional upset, pain, and frustration, an addict retreats into the fog of the all-encompassing heroin high.

I told myself that I couldn't deal with the pressure of being incarcerated any longer. I needed a mental lift, but the truth of the matter was that I had been depending on the heroin high for my so-called mental equilibrium for a long time; thus the psychological addiction. Had I followed through with my intentions to give up heroin after leaving Hawaii, I would have learned how to cope with the everyday struggles of life. In all likelihood, my life may have been in turmoil, but it would have been manageable. However, I didn't take that route because I was an addict, and addicts don't always act rationally. So I ended up locked away in a Thai prison. Yes, the proverbial best laid plans of mice and men. My mind was screaming in frustration because I still had the mindset of an addict.

Within an hour, I had scored a gram of pure Number 4 heroin, as well as a syringe and needle. Now, crouching down behind the bathing tank, with Helmut nervously keeping a lookout for me, I hurriedly shot it into my vein. In a flash, I was calm and collected, worries cast to the wind. It's all in the hands of fate, I told myself in denial. But, just a moment ago, I certainly wasn't so cool and collected about that very same indisputable fact of life. Once I finished, I bathed, so the guards wouldn't be suspicious of me. Feeling better now, I decided to take a walk around the prison compound. First, to the canteen to get a carton of orange juice and some bread, then to just wander around a bit.

All of the buildings around the compound were the same rectangular shape, constructed of gray cement and steel bars. Looking inside the open doors of the other housing units that I passed, I noticed that they only had a bare floor for sleeping. There were no platforms raised above the ground like in the one the foreigners stayed in. Inmates were segregated depending on the severity of their offenses. Most were allowed out during the day for their work details.

There was one building, though, which was kept locked twenty-four hours a day. Inmates in this unit were only allowed out once daily, and then only to bathe. Even while they were bathing, guards watched their every move. This building was called *hong suua*, *The Tiger Room*. These guys were in for the most serious offences, ranging from murder and racketeering to drug trafficking.

You'd think that these inmates would be the most tightly controlled in every aspect of prison life, yet most of the heroin in the prison actually originated from this high-security unit. The largest of these individual units had its entire front constructed of heavy steel from chest height to almost the ceiling.

The rest was made of thick solid concrete block. In the back were small windows cut out of the concrete block with bars on them, but at a height of about eight feet, just below the ceiling. It really was like a tiger cage. Every single inmate inside had chains manacled to his ankles.

Taking a counter clockwise tour of the prison, I ended up across from my building again. For the first time, I noticed that just inside the front of the prison, below the entrance and visiting room, there were three individual cells. They were like underground dungeons. The cells had steel doors about three feet wide with a tiny barred window in the center. An inmate would have to crouch and then step down to enter it. The dimensions inside were a little less than six by four feet and they were less than four feet from floor to ceiling. From the inside, a prisoner could look out through the mesh-covered window in the steel door, but would only be able to see up to about a foot above the ground. I don't remember what they called them in Thai, but everyone referred to them as *The Hole*. They were used to break a prisoner for whatever reason, or for punishment. If confined to The Hole, an inmate would only be allowed out once a day, if lucky, to bathe. You'd have to use a small water tank in the front courtyard about thirty feet from the cell. After bathing, you'd be immediately locked up again.

I developed a daily routine consisting of going to the canteen, taking a walk around the compound, and taking a shot of heroin in the early morning. Later in the afternoon, I'd do another hit behind the bathing tank. Heroin was a way of life for the majority of the Westerners who were incarcerated here. Regardless of the fact that we were in prison, charged with possession of heroin, or even worse trafficking in it, nobody ever considered the risk of another bust inside. The drug is so enticing, the euphoria so powerful, that a junkie will ignore any and all such risks.

If there were too many guys shooting-up behind the bathing tank, you could do your fix in a shower stall situated near the bathing tank, but it was a lot riskier. Guards were always walking around, and from inside the stall you couldn't see them coming. At least the bathing tank was far enough away from the front of the building that the lookout had time to give ample warning should a guard approach. If caught, the best you could hope for was a severe beating and being thrown into The Hole. Added to your misery, if caught, was the possibility of having to contend with an additional criminal case in the courts. A second case from inside the prison would get you a much longer prison sentence than the one that landed you there in the first place. But drug addicts never think about consequences, just getting high.

Jamie showed up every other day, bringing food, supplies, and money, when I needed it. She also brought some cooking utensils for the chef at Chez Helmut. Up until then, Helmut had been using some old aluminum pans and a really funky iron wok. Tofu was easy to get, so we ate a lot of it, fried and then put into Thai curries, Chinese stir fries, and even Indian dishes in place of *paneer* (fresh curd made from whole milk). You couldn't do anything about the ambiance, though. You had to eat your meal while zillions of Thais stood nearby staring at you. It was unnerving. Not only that, but the decor included the open sewers nearby.

All day, every day, we'd sit and watch while Thai prisoners, bent over and shuffling along holding their thick heavy leg chains, passed by in a stream. Psycho guards walked among them, looking for any excuse to use their batons across the back of an inmate. Above it all, surveying the scene, were the guards in the gun towers, their eyes constantly roving back and forth. Each day merged into the next, and was indistinguishable from the preceding one; the monotony induced apathy towards everything.

Somwan, along with Jamie, came back the following week, but they didn't have anything reassuring to tell me. Somwan said that it was proving very difficult to get me bail. He went on about his many hours of work on my behalf, the opposition from the Americans being extremely difficult to circumvent. Blah, blah, blah. Then he said he had finally managed to convince a highly placed government official to pull the necessary strings to allow me bail.

The bottom line was he needed another $25,000. I was desperate. Jamie would now have to use almost every cent we had left to do it. I didn't care. I was frantic. I just had to get out of this place. "Can you get the money for him?" I asked Jamie.

"I think so." I knew she wanted to say something more, but it was time for them to leave. Jamie waved goodbye with tears in her eyes. Too numb to cry anymore, I just held up my hand and watched as they disappeared. I waited for the guard to hand me the plastic bags that Jamie had brought for me.

Walking back to the building, I tripped over a large crack in the concrete pavement and pitched headlong onto the hard ground, skinning both arms and one of my hands.

"God, please get me out of here," I cried to myself. Tears welled up in my eyes. Never before had I felt so utterly helpless and alone. But I knew that whatever fate held in store for me would soon unfold. No amount of crying or self-pity was going to change the outcome. There was nothing I could do to influence the outcome of my situation. Crossing the doorway to my building I sat on the platform and collapsed.

Somehow, I shook myself out of it after a while, but a dark despondency continued to plague me. I wanted to believe it would all soon be over. But the longer I was in here, the realization that freedom might be a long time coming became more apparent.

A few days later, Jamie returned to visit. She was my lifeline, the only thing I had to look forward to in a daily routine of abject boredom and misery. She tried to make small talk, attempting to sound hopeful of my imminent release. Yet, even she was forced to accept the fact that this might take a lot longer than we'd thought. As usual, our time together was up too quickly. She handed the plastic bags to the guard to pass through to me after she'd gone. Putting fingers to her lips to throw me a kiss, she turned to leave. All of a sudden she stopped and glanced back at me again for a few seconds, eyes brimming with tears.

I couldn't control myself. I broke down right there in the visiting room. Sobbing uncontrollably, my body heaving, I couldn't catch my breath. I sounded like a wounded animal in agony. How much longer could I go on like this? My life had become a living hell, and I was beginning to lose my will to fight.

Finally, I stopped and collected myself. Pulling up my T-shirt, I used it to wipe my eyes and nose. The guard hadn't said a word. Then, he said "*Bai.*" I had to go. He handed the bags to me and I walked through the door, returning to my building with my arms hanging listlessly by my sides.

CHAPTER 4

A Day Destined for Infamy

We gave all the guards nicknames, based either on their appearance or their personalities. One of the guards that worked the visiting room when Jamie came, who usually handed in the supplies she brought for me, was nicknamed Idi Amin. He was not quite as gargantuan as the original, but he had the same rotund build. It was his face that earned him his nickname, though. He looked exactly like the real Idi Amin.

The guard that locked us down most nights, we named Hitler, a name earned entirely due to his demeanor, as he bore no resemblance to Adolf. He was a real son-of-a-bitch, and took every opportunity to throw his weight around. Often, when we were walking out to bathe in the morning, when our backs were turned to him, he'd shove someone from behind. That inmate would inevitably fall down, crashing into others and causing a few more to do the same, like a line of dominoes. "*Layo, layo*," (quickly, quickly) he would scream at us, laughing evilly. We all despised Hitler. Idi Amin was a super schmuck to the Thai inmates, violent as hell, but he was easy on the foreigners. After all, he probably quadrupled or more his salary from the bribes he collected from us.

By now, I'd been inside Chonburi Prison for six weeks, yet it seemed like six months since that fateful day at Pattaya Beach. I'd even established relationships with some of the Thai inmates, as well as some of the foreigners that were here. One guy, Louie, had a lot of influence in the prison. The guards treated him with deference, nothing like the manner in which they treated most of the other Thai prisoners.

Louie was a gangster. He was in for drug trafficking as well as dealing in firearms. He was a major source for handguns, which were illegal for anyone outside of law enforcement to possess. Louie spoke fluent English, so once we became acquainted I spent some time sitting and talking with him every day. We'd engage in long conversations on many different subjects. Louie was surprisingly well educated and knowledgeable about world affairs. The time we spent chatting together was the highlight of my more dreary days.

Running the canteen was Louie's *job* in the prison. Eventually, he revealed to me that he was distributing most of the heroin in there. The source was one of the big syndicate bosses, presently incarcerated here in Chonburi Prison. Facing several life sentences, he was being kept in the Tiger Room under total lockdown.

The next few weeks went by at a snail's pace. Each day seemed like a week, every week a month. Jamie still came to see me every other day, bringing the usual stuff. She spoke to the lawyer regularly, but he still hadn't given a definitive answer as to when I'd be getting bail.

At long last, Somwan came early one morning and said that it was all finally arranged. We'd be going to court within a week. I was going to get out, end of story! I questioned him as to how it was happening. Would it be a bond? If so, could I leave the country while I was supposedly waiting for my trial? "Just leave all that to me, Mr. Beckman," Somwan replied, adding, "Does it really matter? We're going to get you released."

No, it didn't matter a fig. I was getting out! Practically skipping back to our building, I was in a good mood for the first time since the cops showed up at my house in Pattaya. As soon as I walked through the door, I relayed the news to Helmut and Mike. They seemed sincerely happy for me, and there were high fives all around. Deciding to go out back to use the shower enclosure to do a fix, I grabbed my towel and soap dish.

After showering I prepared a shot. Just as I was putting it into my vein, I heard a noise above my head. Looking up I saw a Thai kid peering in at me over the top. He quickly disappeared. Shit, I muttered under my breath. I needed to get out of there immediately and get rid of my stash before the guards came. The Thai kid was a well-known snitch. As I opened the door and emerged, two guards came running toward me. In half a second, they were on top of me. One pushed me up against the wall, holding me there, while the other searched me. In an instant they had the dope and the syringe, as well as the money I had in my pockets.

Marching me up to the main office building, they knocked at the prison warden's door. After being told to enter, they pushed me ahead of them and told the warden what I had been doing, placing the syringe and packet of heroin on his desk. With eyes full of contempt, the warden began screaming at me, berating me as a worthless scumbag junkie. He was barking in Thai so quickly that I couldn't understand anything else that he said.

Finishing his tirade, he stormed out of the office, calling for some of the other guards. Two came running, stopping only long enough to salute and say, "Yes Sir!" One of them was Blackbeard, notorious for his cruel and demented penchant for severely beating prisoners. Swinging his right hand in a half-fist with incredible force, he smashed it against the side of my head. Flung against the wall by the sheer power of his blow, I crumpled to the ground. Blackbeard kicked me relentlessly while screaming epithets at me. The other guard, one I'd never had any interaction with, made Blackbeard stop. Grabbing me under one arm, he hauled me to my feet.

"Are you okay?" he asked. I nodded yes. Turning away from me, he spun around, executing a roundhouse kick to my chest with such power that I thought my heart would stop. Falling again to the ground in a heap, I feared they would beat me to death. Blackbeard started kicking me again, first in my side, then in the small of my back, while the other guard struck me repeatedly on the legs with his baton.

Within a matter of seconds I'd been beaten to a pulp. Never before in my life had I experienced such staggering physical pain. Curling up into a ball on the ground, I tried my best to protect my face, chest, and stomach, but then both of them grabbed me, one under each arm, and dragged me outside and across the tarmac from the office toward the front of the prison. Barefoot and bleeding, the heels of my feet were now being scraped raw from being dragged across the hot, rough cement of the courtyard floor. I was going to die.

They dropped me to the ground at one end of the courtyard next to the office. I fell heavily onto my back, smashing the back of my head at the same time. Several Thai inmates were summoned to the scene. One lifted my legs, one by one. After slipping a heavy iron ring over each of my feet, connected by thick iron chain links, they placed my legs on top of an anvil. One of the inmates held my leg in place while the other, wielding a sledgehammer, pounded on the iron ring until it closed around my ankle. I was being put into leg irons, bigger and rustier than any of those that I had ever seen the Thai prisoners wearing. Later, I found out that the chains and rings weighed a total of approximately nine kilograms, just about twenty pounds.

I was stunned. It all happened so quickly that I had no time to assimilate what was happening. By now, several other guards had gathered round. Many inmates were watching, from the foreigners' building as well as from another building near the front of the prison. Blackbeard sneered at me, "Get up!" Kicking me several times before I could react, he held his baton menacingly above his head.

Another guard had opened the door to one of the underground dungeons. I lifted myself to my knees, then to my feet. Blackbeard hit me with his baton at the back of my thighs, and then screamed in Thai "Move!" Reaching down to hold up the chains, as I had seen the Thais do, I was barely able to shuffle the few yards to the entrance of The Hole. "Get in!" Blackbeard screamed. I crouched down, leaning forward slightly to put one leg down. But, before I could crawl in, he kicked me violently, pitching me forward onto the hard dirt floor from a height of about three feet. My forehead and knees hit the ground first, but the force caused me to smash the top of my head into the wall at the back of the cell. The door was slammed shut, bolted, and secured with a large padlock.

I lay there on the floor in shock, bleeding, bruised, and in excruciating pain. I was dazed and confused, and I couldn't move my limbs. I have no idea how long I lay there, but when I regained consciousness, it was dark outside. Slowly, I tried to sit up and determine if anything was broken. I lifted each arm, then attempted to move my legs, but I couldn't lift them with the chains on. My knees were injured and bleeding through my jeans, and my shoulders were badly bruised. My head throbbed and my vision was blurred. Putting a hand to my forehead to wipe away the dirt and sweat, I felt the caked-on blood mixed with dirt.

There were two buckets in the corner just inside the door. I had seen a Thai filling one of them just before they threw me in. One was for drinking water, and whatever else I needed water for. The other bucket was my toilet. Taking off my now torn and filthy shirt, I turned it inside out and tore a piece from it with my teeth. Then I did my best to begin cleaning my wounds. The pain was so bad that when I wiped my forehead I almost screamed.

It took a long time for me to gingerly clean the wounds on my head, but when I did, the newly formed scab came away in the process. Fresh blood dripped from my head. I tore off one of the sleeves from my shirt. Tying it around my head, I used it to stem the flow of blood. Moving to where I could lean back against the dank rough wall of my subterranean cell, with great effort, I managed to stretch out my legs. Tearing off the other sleeve, I ripped a smaller piece from it, dipped it into the water bucket and began cleaning the dried blood from my chin. My shoulders and forearms were next, and finally my feet. The pain was unbearable.

My jeans covered the more severe wounds on my legs, hips and butt. There was no more blood coming through, so I didn't even bother trying to pull them down. With the chains secured around my ankles, I wouldn't be able to take them off anyway. I must have had a concussion, for I lapsed continually in and out of consciousness. Finally, I found myself awake, though still very much in shock.

Countless thoughts swirled around in my mental devastation: What have I done? Why couldn't I have just stayed clean while the lawyer was sorting out my release? Not wanting to think about it anymore, I closed my eyes. But sleep wouldn't come, nor could I stop the voice inside my head: Now you've totally blown it! You're a complete idiot! If they decide to bring another charge against you, it's all over. Somehow, I knew that there were going to be serious repercussions. My chance at freedom was gone, owing to nothing but my own stupidity and my self-destructive behavior.

Glancing around and taking stock of my surroundings, I saw that what I had been told about The Hole was accurate. It was just a windowless, underground box cut into the foundation of the building beneath the entrance to the prison and the visiting room. The small steel door had a tiny four by twelve inch barred window that allowed some outside light to enter. When looking through it, my eyes were at ground level. If anything, all a man could see from this vantage point were feet passing by. Prisoners were not allowed to go near The Hole, except for those whose job it was to service them, so the feet I saw were mostly those of guards.

The length of the cell was less than six feet. That was obvious, as I was just over six feet tall and I couldn't lay down flat without bending my knees. The cell was about four feet wide and only about four feet high, so it was like being in a grave before the dirt was shoveled back in. The walls were ancient stone blocks, thick with mold and mildew. The floor was just dirt. Hanging precariously on a frayed wire from the ceiling was a single light bulb casting eerie shadows on the wall.

I had no idea what time it was, but what did it matter? I lay down on the filthy dirt floor, bruised and battered, my head and entire body aching, not knowing how serious my internal injuries were or if I'd live to see another day. Falling in and out of consciousness again for who knows how many hours, I finally awoke and sat up. The realization of my hopeless situation flooded over me like a river breaking its banks in the rainy season. What had I done?

My body was wracked with pain from the multitude of injuries inflicted upon it just hours before. I lay still, softly crying out to God in my mind, "My dear Lord Krishna! Is this where it all ends?"

CHAPTER 5

Seeds of Destiny

My love affair with drugs began when I was thirteen. As with many of my generation, it began with smoking pot. It was the mid 1960s and thanks to Tim Leary, psychedelic drugs were becoming the generational rage. I was living in Philadelphia, far from San Francisco's Haight Ashbury and the hippie movement that began in California. But, the refrain: *Tune in, turn on, and drop out* had by now spread to the East Coast, as well. At fourteen, my friends and I started taking LSD. By the time I was sixteen, we were smoking pot constantly and dropping acid more days than not.

The *pièce de résistance* came just before my seventeenth birthday when I met Leah. She was two years my senior and the most beautiful, alluring girl I'd ever seen. Of course, I'd only really been with a very few girls until then, so I lost myself in the ecstasy of newly found carnal pleasures. To me, she was a goddess with her waist-length, jet-black hair, milky-white breasts, and tiny waist. I'd have done anything she asked.

They say that at this age young men are at their sexual peak. I can only speak for myself, but I literally seemed to have a perpetual hard-on. Leah took full advantage of my devoted infatuation, stoking the fire of my never-ending teenage passion. She drew me to her, coaching me in the art of satisfying a woman, and then rewarded me when I pleased her. She was a sexual dynamo.

Unfortunately for me, Leah was also a heroin addict. She loved having sex, but even more so, she loved the gratification and bliss of the heroin high. I paid dearly for my lessons in the art of lovemaking. In due course, she moved on to greener pastures, but her parting gift was to leave me with a taste for heroin.

Trying to figure out how to help me was a hopeless effort for my parents who were navigating uncharted waters. They watched helplessly as I slid downhill. However, Dad was an attorney with great integrity. He believed in truth, justice, and the American way. Yet with a misguided faith in "The System," he called the police one evening to pick me up at home. He had signed an incorrigibility petition against me thinking it was the only way for me to get the help I needed. I was taken into police custody. The following morning, they transferred me to the juvenile lockup at Montgomery Hall.

My father probably should have known better than to think the state would facilitate my rehabilitation. But he was extremely idealistic back then. Soon enough, though, he realized that no *help* would be forthcoming. If a final decree of incorrigibility were decided upon in court, I'd be sent straight to Camp Hill Juvenile Prison until I turned eighteen. Camp Hill would have made mincemeat out of me. It was basically a stopping place for underage criminals. Most of the kids there continued on a life of crime after their release, having learned more tricks of the trade while incarcerated. Dad testified at my hearing that he felt I had changed, that the six weeks I'd spent in juvenile hall had done the trick. The judge sent me back home on probation until my eighteenth birthday. He gave a stern warning that any infractions would result in my being sent straight to Camp Hill. I promised him and my parents that I'd stay the straight and narrow course. And I did, for about three weeks, then I went right back to doing drugs, especially heroin.

One night I almost overdosed in the bathroom. My father found me barely conscious on the toilet, with a bloody needle in the sink. My parents reached out for help, making another call to the local police. This time they not only found drugs on me, but in nice neat little packets all ready for sale. Yet, my parents still really didn't want me going to Camp Hill, so they helped me dodge the parole violation by packing me off to Eagleville, a drug rehab center. But even then, I couldn't follow the program without screwing up. A few months into the program, I was tossed out on my ear for having brought some Psilocybin (psychedelic mushrooms) back in with me from a weekend pass.

My parents' last ditch attempt to help keep me out of juvenile prison was having me voluntarily check into the Philadelphia Psychiatric Center to live with a bunch of psychos: from guys who thought they were Jesus or Napoleon to others who just sat and stared at the walls all day. There were also a few druggies like myself in there; it was a real mixed bag of psychotics, lunatics, and self-destructive misfits.

For a few months I managed to stay put, biding time until my eighteenth birthday. Without going into all the ins and outs of life in the nuthouse, suffice it to say that I just couldn't take being there any longer. So, I escaped only ten days before my eighteenth birthday. Quite a stunt, actually. First, I removed the inside panel from an air-conditioner in one of the ward's windows. I managed to pull it in and set it on the bed, then, climbing out of the window, I hung down from the frame and dropped to the ground. It was only the second floor, not exactly a death-defying feat.

The rest of the nut jobs had been called upstairs for lunch, leaving the yard and recreation area empty. As fast as my legs could take me, I ran around the building to where the wall enclosing the hospital grounds met a slatted fence. I climbed the fence easily, stood on top of it, grasped the top of the wall and vaulted over.

There was some construction work going on just outside, but only one worker saw me come flying over the wall. I can just imagine what was going through his mind when I landed on my feet right in front of him. I said "hi" and started walking quickly away from the building, then broke into a run, determined to get as far away as possible before anyone knew I was missing. I ran across a busy intersection like a bat out of hell.

On the other side of the road was a golf driving range. Beyond that, was a long, open field that extended several blocks to City Line Avenue. I knew the area well because my grandparents used to live nearby. Hauling ass across the driving range like a madman, I headed for the freeway entrance in front of an apartment complex at the far end.

People were yelling "FORE" while driving golf balls down range. A few balls whizzed by just inches past my head. Guys were screaming, "Hey you, are you crazy?" Running as fast as my legs would take me, I made it across the driving range without being hit and reached City Line Avenue. I then continued sprinting the last block to the freeway entrance. There was a big construction sign just inside the entrance, which provided the perfect place to hide. When I heard cars coming, I'd pop out just before they got there, extending my thumb in an attempt to hitch a ride.

Amazingly enough, the third car that came along was someone that I'd met a year before at a friend's house, Randy Smith. He almost went by before he recognized me, but managed to pull over a little ways ahead. Dashing to his car, I jumped in. But before he could say a word I cried, "Get going quick!"

Randy took me to a train station some miles away. He even lent me some money, which I promised to repay as soon as I could. Once the train arrived, I headed over to the Greyhound Bus Station. I had decided to go to Atlantic City where I would hide out among the summer tourists for the next ten days. My thinking was that once I turned eighteen, my probation was finished. If I could make it until then, the "Long Arm of the Law" couldn't touch me. No new charges had ever been filed, nor had any parole violations been reported.

After successfully making myself scarce for ten days, I turned eighteen and went home to throw myself on the mercy of my parents, promising to make something of my life and stay away from drugs. Where else was I going to go?

CHAPTER 6

Searching for a Deeper Meaning to Life

Shortly after returning to my parents' home, I came upon a book written by Alan Watts. The spiritual questions he raised stirred something inside of me. I needed spiritual answers to the angst that plagued my restless mind. It seemed that nothing in this world that I'd known, thus far, brought me any kind of satisfaction. Is this it? Is life all about joining the ranks of society, working for a living, and aspiring to live the American Dream? Somehow, I just didn't see myself fitting in with established society. My folks thought the panacea was to return to school, get a university degree, and then get a law degree. However, my parents' approach to life simply didn't resonate with me. My spiritual questions demanded answers.

I decided to seek out a spiritual teacher. Over the next year, I sought out every spiritual teacher that came to the Philly or New York area. From Muktananda and Maharishi Mahesh Yogi to Guru Maharaji and Baba Ram Dass, I went to them, listened, and tried to assimilate what they were saying. However, it was Ram Dass's book *Be Here Now* that made the greatest impression on me. It spoke in a language I could relate to. The book became my bible.

At the same time, I began a relationship with Rhonda, a girl a few years younger than me. We'd hang out at her place mostly, since she had a private room on the lower level of her parents' house. Utilizing all of the bedroom talents I'd learned from Leah, we spent an inordinate number of hours conversing, listening to music, and having sex. Rhonda also came from a dysfunctional background. Her father had little to no time for her when she was growing up because he was always working, and her mother spent most of her days anesthetized on tranquilizers.

Since I'd been avidly reading everything I could find on Eastern spirituality, I shared philosophical concepts with Rhonda who listened and seemed to truly appreciate what I was saying. She joined me in my new spiritual quest. After sex, reading *Be Here Now* was our next favorite activity. Now, I finally knew what life was about! The practicalities of making a living and building a career were relegated to a position of little to no importance. Why worry about such things? Just *be here now*, which was fine when we were talking to each other, but I made a big mistake by not keeping it that way.

When Rhonda's parents invited me to dinner one night, her father inquired about my plans for the future. He was a management consultant so money meant everything to him. My answer definitely was not what he wanted to hear. I replied that I wasn't worried about the future, that all we have to do is to be here now.

Moments later, Rhonda's parents summarily threw me out, along with her. Her father literally threw her down the stairs to the back door, telling her never to come back and that she could go live with me, and 'be here now' *somewhere else*! There wasn't much else I could do, so I brought her home to my parents' house. Amazingly, my parents let her stay. However, now I would have to join the real world, get a job, and support Rhonda and myself. We could stay at my parents' house until we were able to stand on our own two feet.

After a week or so, I managed to get a job at a department store. Another few weeks, and we moved into our own apartment. I guess Rhonda's father had expected her to quickly come crawling back home because when she didn't, and he found out we'd moved into our own apartment, he gave me an ultimatum. Since Rhonda was only sixteen, I could either marry her or he'd bring statutory rape charges against me. I made the only decision that made sense. One month later we were married amidst cries of Mazel Tov as I crushed the obligatory glass beneath my foot and the rabbi pronounced us man and wife.

We moved to Germantown in Philadelphia, where we attended the local Hare Krishna Temple. Some of the Krishna devotees seemed very balanced, but others were a bit wacko, yet we made some new friends there. It was their guru, His Divine Grace A.C. Bhaktivedanta Swami Prabhupada, who was the deciding factor in my joining the Krishna movement. The books he wrote, English translations of the Eastern spiritual classics, *Bhagavad-Gita* and *Srimad Bhagavatam*, spoke to me. His words entered my heart. Inspiration found a home there. His teachings were light-years beyond anything I'd managed to glean from any of the other gurus I'd already sought out. His most famous devotee was George Harrison, and it was his song "My Sweet Lord" that melted my heart. I still wanted to "get high," but this time, on God.

When George brought out his album *Living in the Material World* in 1973, I decided to devote my life to the spiritual path of Bhakti Yoga, which Prabhupada called Krishna Consciousness. Nothing else mattered anymore. Rhonda, my wife of six months, my close friend CB, his wife and son, and I all drove out to LA in my 1954 Ford sedan and joined the Hare Krishna community.

Prabhupada had captured my heart. The powerful yoga philosophy he espoused in his books inspired me, and that prompted me to spread this timeless philosophy to others. That was his only mission in life. No other guru had come to the west with such goals. Others seemed to want something in return from Western students, but Prabhupada seemed to only want to *give* something to Western society. No matter how much money came his way, he continued to live the same Spartan lifestyle, and his personal motto of "simple living and higher thinking" was one he lived by.

My only regret was that I was unable to spend much personal time with him. Some disciples had more access to him than others. Since he was always traveling, nobody could be with him all the time, except for one or two devotees who personally served him.

Becoming a Bhakti Yogi wasn't easy. My heart's selfish desires needed to be gradually purified before I could serve unconditionally. I think that everyone I knew in the Krishna movement was sincerely trying to do just that, at least back in those early days. Sadly, most of us had too many impressions from our pasts lingering and haunting us.

During those years, I followed a very strict lifestyle. I had already become a vegetarian when I joined the Hare Krishna faith so that was no problem. Giving up all intoxication, even tea and coffee, was also not that difficult. But not having sex, except once a month and only to have children, was a different story. Rhonda, however, found it very easy. She liked the regimented institutional lifestyle of the community.

Everyone had to attend the temple programs beginning at four-thirty every morning, so you really had to get up early to get there on time. There was actually a guy with a clipboard at the temple door when you entered, checking names off a list. When we lived in LA, I went along with it, but when an opportunity came to move to Hawaii to help run the Honolulu Temple's program, I jumped at it. I even shipped my old '54 Ford over to the islands.

Soon we were living in Honolulu's Nuuanu valley at the Krishna Temple. The environment was divine. Filled with the scents of beautiful tropical flowers, the atmosphere was almost intoxicating. Even in the city, trees were hanging heavy with fruit, especially mangoes. Although our accommodation was just a converted greenhouse on the temple's property, I didn't miss our apartment in LA one bit. Sometimes, I even found time to slip away to a nearby waterfall. Below it there was a pool of crystal clear water where we could swim. For me this was surely heaven on earth.

A few months went by uneventfully. Then one day in early February of 1975, on the way back to the temple after shopping at a local supermarket, I had a major car accident. Sruta, a close friend of mine who had arranged with Srila Prabhupada for me to come to Hawaii from LA with him, was in the front passenger seat. Rhonda was in the back seat with another woman and her baby. A car sped down the cross street toward the light we were approaching, apparently attempting to make it through the yellow light before it turned red. But it had already turned red before he got there, and, not noticing him, we had already moved out into the middle of the intersection. Both Sruta and I were tossed out of the car and into the street by the severity of the crash. The front of my car was crushed, but the other driver's fate was worse. He and his passengers were riding in a '65 Ford Mustang. The Mustang was no match for my '54 Ford so no one in his car survived. In comparison, it was like a Sherman Tank taking on a Jeep.

In our car, we all made it through with only minor injuries, except for the more serious lower back problems that stayed with both Sruta and me from then on. Since my back was badly injured, Rhonda and I jumped at an opportunity to go to the Big Island for a year while I recuperated.

On the Big Island, I met Bill, a Krishna devotee who had left the temple years before. Bill had a business selling honey to food stores. He was also a great storyteller who'd grown up on the Big Island, and I loved listening to his stories about Hawaii.

One day he asked if I wanted to smoke some *da kine*, referring to Hawaiian pot. I experienced a momentary flash of confusion, remembering the No Intoxication rule of the Hare Krishna lifestyle. Then I said, "Ah, what the hell! Sure." Back when I was smoking it in the 60s, nobody had pot like this. It was the most powerful herb I'd ever sampled, so it didn't take me long to get used to it. Soon I developed a penchant for smoking *da kine* on a daily basis.

[This is a good place for a reflective note. Recently, while relating this story to my present wife, she asked me "Weren't you beyond wanting to smoke marijuana because you were on your spiritual path of Bhakti Yoga?" My answer was that just because you find a spiritual path that opens a window on truth, doesn't mean your sensual desires for enjoyment will suddenly evaporate. In the past, yogis used to meditate for years, even decades, before attaining a worthy elevated state of consciousness. Many people, like myself, have grown up in environments that were the antithesis of healthy desires. A state of mind is not easy to alter. Years of *Sex, Drugs and Rock 'n' Roll* created a library of memories and imprints in my mind that could not be easily dismissed with a passive wave of the hand. Thus, a strict lifestyle of abstaining from all intoxication and sex was not an easy one to follow; at least it wasn't for me.

Although I had found important spiritual answers, I wasn't cut out to be a monk. As Arjuna replied to Krishna in the *Bhagavad Gita*, after Krishna recommended he follow the path of sense and mind control, "Controlling the mind seems to be as impossible as controlling the wind." Once I started smoking pot again, it was easy for me to rationalize my reacquired poor behavior. Why should I pretend to be something I wasn't? After all, who am I going to fool?]

After a year on the Big Island, Rhonda and I ended up moving back to Oahu. We lived in Honolulu for a while and then moved to the north shore. Learning to surf from one of my die-hard surf buddies, I swiftly caught the surfing bug. Making money wasn't hard, either. I'd buy Puka shells in bulk, string them into necklaces and find tourists on the beach to sell them to. We weren't getting rich, but it paid the bills. This new vocation gave me ample time for surfing and hanging out on the beach. For a guy in his early twenties, I was living the life.

Within a year, my wife became pregnant, and naturally I soon realized that the meager income I made selling shell necklaces just wasn't going to cut it. By the time our daughter

Debbie was born, I'd begun a side business of selling pot. Not a lot, but along with the jewelry sales (I was now selling silver and semi-precious stone necklaces, rings, and more as well as the shell), I could better support us.

Lately, I'd been hearing how wonderful the island of Maui was. It used to win Island of the Year every year, or so said the travel magazines. Itching for adventure, I decided to see what the island of Maui might have to offer. We'd never had the opportunity to spend any time there, so I decided to go on a reconnaissance mission, thinking maybe we'd move there. We had a friend, Cindi, who lived on the island and she had offered us a place to stay should we ever want to visit, so I decided to take her up on her offer.

In the town of Wailuku, Cindi had a guesthouse on a beautiful piece of property. The place was private with lush vegetation. Veronica, who lived in the main house and held the lease, had a little shop fronting the road. She sold crafts and objects d'art from Nepal and India. She was very much an old-school hippie chick, draped in beads and always scented with essential oils. She also possessed a deep love for India's mysterious spirituality, especially its iconography. She graciously offered to let me stay in the loft above the store while I checked out the island.

I looked around for a few days, and then realized it was going to take more time to find a place that I would really like. There were other areas on the island that I wanted to check out before making a decision. Since Veronica was getting ready to go to India on a buying trip for her store, she offered to let us stay in her house during her absence. The timing was perfect. She wasn't leaving for four weeks, which would give me time to go back to Oahu, pack everything up, and give notice to my landlord. I now had enough time to look around for the right place.

CHAPTER 7

Life on Maui, the Valley Isle

After tying up all our loose ends in Honolulu, I packed almost everything we owned into my Nissan pickup. A few days after putting it all on an inter-island cargo ship, we flew into Kahului, Maui. We took a cab from the airport to the docks. Toting our suitcases, Rhonda, Debbie, and I picked up the truck and drove to Veronica's house. She had departed for India on the previous day, leaving the keys to the house with Cindi. Coconut palms, fruit trees, and flowers were growing everywhere, and the atmosphere was indescribably delightful.

A few weeks after arriving, I was not only able to find a great rental house on five acres in Haiku, but a new financial opportunity presented itself. I ran into Sarva, someone I knew from Honolulu who had lived on Maui for years before joining the Krishna Temple. He was visiting the island and offered to introduce me to a few of his old friends. Sarva was the perfect person to show me around Maui. As we passed the famous windsurfing beach "Ho'okipa" near Paia, I marveled at the ocean, which was stunning. The mountain scenery along the two-lane road to Hana was breathtaking. Hana was nicknamed Heavenly Hana, and for me, that said it all.

Cordova was one of the old friends that Sarva introduced me to. Originally from Cuba, he had taken up residence on Maui many years ago, and had married an American. He was now one of the old granddaddy pot growers on the island.

He sported long black hair and a thick black beard. Cordova's dark eyes seemed to flash whenever he spoke.

Growing marijuana was big business on Maui back then. It flourished, creating its own economy. These were the days before "Green Harvest," a federal government operation that used helicopters to search out and destroy marijuana crops. The first time I was shown a patch, I was amazed at the powerful fragrance generated by the plants and their size was astonishing. The most powerful variety, however, smelled like skunk, thus, it was known as skunkweed, not to be confused with another skunkweed that is not cannabis.

The circumference of these plants was so great that two men facing each other couldn't join their hands together around one. They could grow easily up to twenty feet high, but were kept pruned down to about eight feet to encourage them to bush out. This way, they'd get maximum growth of the flowers (buds) and plants could be more easily cared for.

Most of the growers had small operations. Rather than live on welfare and food stamps, they grew pot. Lots of Maui growers bought and paid for their land with profits derived from their pot sales. Putting their plants and investments before their own comfort, they often lived in tents. After harvesting a crop, they'd start buying building materials for their houses. I knew people who had lived in partially finished houses for years until they managed to get enough cash to complete them.

You couldn't grow too much at one time without drawing unwanted attention. Not only would law enforcement target your crops, but thieves would also. In those days, there was an abundance of jungle foliage on public land where growers could cut out a patch without inviting too much attention. Naturally, many growers preferred to use government land instead of growing on their own property. An additional benefit to using state owned land was that if it was discovered, the pot would be lost, but a grower probably wouldn't be caught and prosecuted. Reducing one's risk was always a good goal.

Initially, I didn't envision any involvement in the pot-growing business. That was until fate threw a curve ball at me. An old friend from Philadelphia, a drug dealer I'd known in my teens, suddenly appeared on Maui. There he was, having dinner in the booth next to mine in a local restaurant. He didn't even look up when I passed by, but after sitting down I turned around and said, "Hey Andy!" He was surprised to hear his name called out and when he recognized me he broke into a huge smile.

"Howard, what are you doing here? It's been years!"

"I might ask you the same question," I replied.

"Come sit with us," Andy said, and I moved over to his booth. I was also there with a friend, so after introductions all around, I related an abbreviated story of my years with the Hare Krishna movement, moving to Hawaii, and only recently to Maui.

Andy was still following his old ways because he was in Hawaii to buy up as much of Maui's finest pot as he possibly could. Living in a rented house up in Kula during the harvest season, he'd buy anything from a single pound to dozens of pounds at a time. If the quality were Top Shelf, he'd buy it all. The idea was to obtain a variety for his sophisticated clientele. There are subtle differences in the best cannabis, and Maui growers were the world's experts.

[Another noteworthy reflection is in order at this point. During more recent times, when growing pot became more challenging and risky in Hawaii and California (before decriminalization and legal medical marijuana) due to both the population explosion and constant police surveillance, many growers moved to Amsterdam. There, they grew the world's strongest marijuana indoors from seeds they'd originally brought from Maui. Their customers were the *coffee shops* that legally sold marijuana to the public for personal consumption.]

Thinking of Cordova, I told Andy that I had some great sources for what he wanted. From that day forward, we became partners in crime. It was a piece of cake: Cordova would give me ten pounds at a time, and I'd carry it to Andy's house in a big, black trash bag. After sampling some, he'd get out his scale to weigh it. Soon I'd have a paper bag full of cash for Cordova, along with a nice profit for myself.

For the next six months, the rest of my time was spent pretty much lolling around, much of it with my baby daughter. She was seven months old by this time and still the light of my life. Every morning I'd carry her down to a small waterfall behind our house. We'd go under a fence at the backside of the property, down a gently sloping hill and Voila! The most beautiful hidden waterfall and crystal clear pool of water came into view. The sheer beauty of it was mesmerizing. The sight and sound of the falling water completely captivated Debbie. Those days were wonderful, and life felt like an unending vacation. Until one day I received a wake-up call.

CHAPTER 8

The Passing of My Spiritual Father

I'll never forget the day a friend knocked at my door bearing the news of Prabhupada's passing. His health had been failing for some time, especially during the past few months, but his loss still shocked and saddened me. Memories of our meetings flashed through my mind like a touching movie. My tears poured out uncontrollably. The last time I was this upset over anyone's passing was when I had visited my grandmother's bedside just before she died. I recall how lost I had felt. Now, once again, I was experiencing that same feeling of loss. My guru's passing left me with an insecure feeling.

Prabhupada had always said that there were two facets of the guru, one being his physical form, and the other his instructions. The latter, he had stressed, was by far the more important, as the guru's body was always destined to leave the material world. He left a legacy of such magnitude it was inconceivable to everyone who had known him, or even those who had only known of him. Prabhupada authored more than eighty books on Vedic spiritual philosophy and culture.

In only twelve years, he opened over 100 temples, several of them were extremely large and famous in India. The magnificence of these temples will live on as part of his legacy. They continue to attract pilgrims from not only India but around the world. To say that I will miss him would be a vast understatement. Through his passing, my world appeared to be caving in.

Right up until his last breath, Prabhupada was teaching, as he had always done. His teachings were recorded and often filmed. When he was about to pass from his body, some of his senior disciples told the cameraman to stop filming. But Prabhupada said, "No, this is the final lesson."

He began his great journey to the west from India at the age of seventy. Following the orders of his own guru, he brought the ancient philosophy of Bhakti Yoga to the English-speaking world. His accomplishments, in just over a decade, were monumental.

In his absence, the beautiful island of Maui was losing its mystical appeal for me. I could hear India calling me to her shores. My intuition was telling me that a new chapter in my life would soon dawn. But first, we'd return to Honolulu; my wife wanted to be near the temple.

Soon, my truck was on a barge and we were boarding a flight. Within a day, we found a house to rent in Nuuanu, just a few blocks from the Krishna Temple. Rhonda and Debbie could now walk about in a safe environment. After making all the arrangements, just a few days hence, I was on a flight to New Delhi.

CHAPTER 9

India, Thailand, and Back Again

India is a place of sights, sounds, and smells that are utterly and completely unlike anything most Westerners have ever experienced. The streets were bustling with throngs of people, all seeming to have someplace to go, but rarely in a hurry to get there. Beggars were commonplace, and no visitor could go anywhere without being approached by one, regardless of the time of day. This is still true in most of the big cities in India, especially in Delhi and Bombay, now called "Mumbai," as a result of the shedding of the British colonial names.

After collecting my bag, I caught a taxi into the city and took a room at the Imperial Hotel. This was the old Imperial Hotel, which was very inexpensive back then.

[Note: Today the New Imperial stands in its place, a five-star luxury hotel that rivals the finest hotels in New York, London, or Paris, with prices to match. Today the cheapest room at the New Imperial is well over $300 a night.]

The next morning I checked-out and continued my journey. Having cash to spend, I decided to take a taxi for the four-hour ride to Vrindavan, rather than take the train. I hated taking trains in India. People stare at you the entire time you're on board, which gets unnerving after a while. You also have to keep a constant eye on your luggage. Using a bathroom on a train meant having to lug your baggage with you or expect it to be gone when you returned to your seat.

In India, nobody bothered to stop at traffic lights. Hardly any Westerners dared drive on the roads of India, which was something like playing a fast-moving video game. The consequences of driving yourself could be catastrophic.

Moreover, inhabitants of India haven't lost their compulsion to constantly lean on their horns. At least most of them do make an effort to stop at red lights now.

Arriving finally in Vrindavan, the Krishna Balarama Mandir Temple, built by Srila Prabhupada, loomed into view. It was still not completely finished, but it was functioning and the guesthouse was open. I rented a room there, bathed, and went outside to Prabhupada's *Samadhi* tomb to pay my respects. Kneeling in front of it, I felt a wave of sadness wash over me. Until now, there had been a lot of drastic changes to my life and I knew another one was about to take place. Yes, I was now at a new crossroads and I was clueless about which road to take.

I spent my time visiting Vrindavan's temples, where I chanted, prayed, and meditated in their holy sanctums. Deciding to put the future out of my mind for the time being, I concentrated on mantra meditation for the next few weeks. My thinking was that an opportunity to do so might not come again for many years, and I was right.

At the time, if you didn't get an Indian visa before your trip, you would simply get a landing pass upon arrival, which was good for a stay of three to four weeks. I hadn't had time to get a visa before leaving Hawaii, so three to four weeks it was. On the day before my visa expired, I made my way back to New Delhi. The next morning I would begin my journey back home.

I planned to visit some friends who, like myself, had formerly lived within the Krishna movement and were now living in a beach town south of Bangkok, Thailand. I wanted to share my thoughts and feelings with others who I could relate to. Surely, they would be going through similar emotional feelings regarding the loss of our guru.

CHAPTER 10
Pattaya Beach, Thailand

It was late when I arrived in Bangkok. I took a taxi to a nearby hotel, figuring to head down south in the morning. At this late hour, Bangkok's traffic was noisy, but it was much more orderly than New Delhi's. The hot, steamy atmosphere was similar though. My friends' house was in Pattaya Beach, about a two-hour drive from Bangkok. The next morning after breakfast, I grabbed a rickshaw to the bus station and boarded a tourist bus bound for Pattaya. The highways were more modern and better maintained than those in India. Even in the mid to late 70s the buses were new, making the ride quite comfortable. I sat looking out the window, watching the beautiful tropical scenery pass by. Time passed quickly, and before I knew it, I had arrived.

The atmosphere in Pattaya Beach was laid back and that was refreshing. Pattaya was an old fishing village that had become a tourist destination. The majority of visitors were European, American, and Australian men. The beer bars, filled with beautiful young women, were famous all over the world. It should be noted, too, that in the 1970s, US soldiers were returning home from Vietnam telling their stories of rest and relaxation (R & R) in Pattaya Beach.

[Note: Today Pattaya Beach is teeming with bars and nightclubs, but back then there were only a handful. The most famous was the "Marine Bar," but it was tiny compared to the large sprawling complex it has now become. It was also the only bar that had a separate nightclub inside. A couple of shops and restaurants rounded out the center of town, but for the most part it was still pretty mellow.]

Upon arriving at my friend's house on Soi 5, I took my bag and knocked on the door. Both Kerry and Bob seemed genuinely glad to see me. After some light conversation and laughter, we began speaking about Prabhupada, and the tone quickly became somber. It was the end of an era that would mark us forever. Prabhupada had given us a spiritual direction that most of us could never have imagined before he came into our lives. After a while, Kerry showed me to my room.

He and a few other Americans I knew were now living in Thailand. They loved the tropical weather and the laid-back lifestyle. The cost of living was also next to nothing. But, to be perfectly honest, it was either the easy availability of drugs or women that made so many guys want to stay there.

After unpacking, I went out for a walk, crossing the street to the beach. The turquoise water was calm and clear. You could see to the bottom when you waded in. The beach was absolutely pristine with fine white sand that stretched as far as the eye could see. The scene was captivating and soothing to my emotionally bruised mind, although my thoughts were still racing around in circles. At a crisis point in my life, I simply didn't know where to go from this point.

Eventually, I got up and walked slowly back toward the house, stopping at a gaily painted wooden stand on the corner. Behind it was a large mound of fresh coconuts. After living in Hawaii, I had acquired a taste for fresh coconut water. A young boy deftly sliced the top off and made a small hole in the now flat surface with the tip of his machete. After dropping a drinking straw through the hole, he handed it to me. I stood there sipping the sweet fresh coconut water until I had drained it. Still wanting to be alone with my thoughts, I decided to walk into town and see what the place was like. Although I've never been much of a drinker, I stopped at one of the outdoor bars, figuring it was a good place to kill some time. Sitting on one of the barstools outside of B.J.'s Bar, I nursed a bottle of Singha beer. Languidly, I watched the steady stream of tourists pass by. Most were men, alone or with a friend or two, although I saw the occasional couple from abroad. Some guys had young Thai women hanging on their arms, no doubt *rented* for the night from one of the bars. Many girls walked by alone, purposefully heading somewhere, quite a few likely heading to work at one of the bars. Nighttime was when Pattaya Beach came alive.

Suddenly, I saw someone I knew walking across the road. Calling out his name, I stood up and waved to him. Ron smiled warmly when he recognized me and came over. We embraced, not having seen each other since we were both living in the Hare Krishna community in Los Angeles. Offering him a seat on the barstool next to me, I inquired about his reason for being here.

Like me, Ron was at a crossroads in his life, but being single and without any family responsibilities, he'd decided to live in Thailand for the time being. After my offer to buy him a beer, he answered, lowering his voice, "I still haven't developed a taste for it. I do like my weed though."

Grinning, I said "And so do I."

"Come on, let's go over to my place," Ron invited. "It's not far. We'll go on my bike." Draining the last of the Singha, I paid the bartender and off we went. Minutes later, I was on the back of his motorcycle for the short ride to his house. He lived in a nice four-bedroom house, a stone's throw from the beach, but well away from the center of town. Two of the bedrooms he used for his garment business. He bought women's clothing in Thailand and sold them in the US.

He brought out a tray with some buds and rolling papers. Moments later, we were kicking back and sharing a joint. Plenty of cheap pot was available here. The Thais grew a powerful variety of Cannabis Indica, and then painstakingly tied the buds onto sticks, thus the name Thai Sticks.

We sat together inhaling the heavy, thick smoke, holding it in for a moment and then slowly exhaling. Ron told me what he'd been doing, and I brought him up to speed on my own life, sharing how I'd just come from India having felt the need to go there as soon as I'd heard the news of Prabhupada's passing. I had thought that going to the land of his birth would somehow lessen the grief.

Just thinking about it made my eyes well up with tears. Looking at Ron, I could see that he too was tearful. For a moment, we sat in silence before resuming our conversation. Ron had left the temple community quite some time ago. The only plans he had were to build up his business and eventually buy homes in both Thailand and India. India was also a source of textiles for his company. Our sentiments regarding the current state of the Krishna movement were the same. Neither of us wanted anything to do with the newly self-proclaimed successor gurus. We talked for hours; sharing our thoughts was good therapy for both of us. As it was getting late, I asked Ron if he'd give me a ride to where I was staying. After arriving back at my place, we exchanged hugs, once again promising to stay in touch.

After spending a week at Kerry's house, I decided it was time to leave. He'd now become a heroin addict, a road I didn't want to chance going down again. Somehow, I had to make the transition from a life centered on a cult community to one centered on the real world.

CHAPTER 11
Making Difficult Decisions

A few days later I found myself back at home in Honolulu. Rhonda was fully involved with the temple again, and I was holding back on voicing my opinion. I needed to decide on a Life Plan before confronting her. I sat with my infant daughter for hours at a time, making faces and playing little games with her just as if I hadn't been away. One evening after Debbie fell asleep, Rhonda and I talked about what she'd been up to in my absence. As for me, I was forthcoming on sharing my experiences in India.

A few days later I found a new job, selling jewelry, but not on the beach. Some of the hotels were renting spaces large enough to have a jewelry stand right on the streets of Waikiki. It was less hassle and far more lucrative selling jewelry this way instead of peddling my merchandise on the beach. Making a "hard sell" to tourists at the water's edge was exhausting.

On the streets, they came to us. We carried all kinds of shell necklaces and bracelets, as well as silver and semi-precious stone jewelry. Working a stand meant working from 5 PM until midnight, since the tourists were mostly on the beach all day. But it was well worth the change. On a good night, you could take in as much as a thousand dollars. Half of that was gross profit. Even after rent and expenses, it was still a good living.

My new work schedule left my days totally free, which meant plenty of time to be with my daughter as well as go surfing. Meanwhile, my wife had become fully immersed in the temple. I was fine with the arrangement as long as she wasn't hassling me to spend much time there. For me, my temple affiliations were mostly a thing of the past.

But, before long, the local government started to impose new restrictions on street vendors. The hotels also started charging higher rents. Reading the handwriting on the wall, I knew this way of doing business wouldn't last much longer, so I decided to get a degree as a Graduate Gemologist. Then, I could parlay my knowledge of gems and jewelry into a real career. With my father's blessings and his willingness to pay my tuition, my little family and I left Honolulu and returned to LA.

At Rhonda's behest, we rented a cheap apartment in the midst of the Hare Krishna community. I'd be attending classes at the Gemological Institute of America in Santa Monica. We had agreed to stay there while I attended school, as she had friends in the community. Our plan was to return to Hawaii when I finished school. My hope was to be able to get a job with a jewelry store. With a Gemologist degree, I could get a sales position at one of the big stores. From that point, it was a wait and see game. At least I now had a definite goal, one with potential and greater opportunities.

For eight months, I worked hard, never missing a day of classes, and I diligently studied nights and on the weekends. In February 1979, I graduated, diploma in hand. I was ready to return to Hawaii and eager to embark on a worthy career.

However, there was a big problem. My wife had been completely brainwashed by one of the new Hare Krishna gurus. She had become a religious fanatic — a zealot who believed that this guru was akin to what the next coming of Christ meant to Christians. Flat-out refusing to return to Hawaii with me, she voiced her dedication to her guru's worship and service. He and ten others were now the so-called spiritual heads of the Krishna movement.

All but two of these new autocrats were swamis who would have everyone believe they were beyond the realm of worldly sensual pleasures. In time, most of them would become exposed as imposters. They would fall to unimaginable depths of depravity. In the world of religion, more than a few modern-day swamis, priests, or ministers have been exposed as sexual deviants or predators, some as pedophiles. The Hare Krishna movement was no different.

Over time, some of the swamis fell from grace, and gave up the saffron cloth to get married. A few homosexual pedophiles at the very top weren't discovered until long after they'd committed unspeakable heinous crimes of sexual degeneracy. Using the movement's schools as their own *garden of tender young boys*, they plucked them at will in order to fulfill their perverted sexual desires. Many young boys were sexually abused on a daily basis for years, until they grew old enough or brave enough to expose their abuse. Unfortunately, as is common in such cases, many of those abused boys went on to become abusers themselves.

After becoming leaders and role models, some turned to a sex, drugs, and rock and roll lifestyle. One even became a gun-packing gangster. Even my wife's new guru would eventually be caught dating the fifteen-year-old daughter of one of his female disciples. Subsequently, he was forced to leave in disgrace. Others simply left with the millions of dollars they had swindled from the movement.

Over a ten-year period following Prabhupada's death, it all came to light. There was even a famous murder-for-hire case in the 1980s among the Hare Krishnas. The victim, a young man, was killed because he was about to expose a swami's life of depravity in a book he had authored. Although his book was never published, another was: *Monkey on a Stick*.

However, these revelations had not yet come to fruition and would not for another six to ten years. It was still the late 1970s and Prabhupada had only recently passed on. I don't even know if he had any knowledge about the ugliness that was fermenting in the movement. However, I intuitively felt that evil was developing a stronghold among some of the members. Without Prabhupada leading the Krishna movement, I no longer wished to be a part of it. Not much different, I suppose, than a Christian becoming disillusioned with his or her church, yet remaining faithful because of a strong faith in Jesus Christ and His teachings.

I tried repeatedly to reason with my wife, but to no avail. She was convinced of her duty to follow some self-appointed *savior of the fallen masses.* Prabhupada had always taught that a guru is never appointed, nor is he elected to his position. 'Within his heart, he was beholden to nobody but God.' These new supreme leaders had managed to set up an ecclesiastic system similar to the Catholic Church, the exception being there were eleven "Popes," instead of one.

Although my own path wasn't at all clear yet, I wasn't going to stick around all of these pseudo-spiritual absurdities. When Prabhupada was alive, the Hare Krishna movement that I had once joined had been promulgating an ancient spiritual culture, which was grounded in ancient India. Due to Prabhupada's phenomenal knowledge and obvious spiritual clarity, he had gained the respect and admiration of the academic and religious communities worldwide. However, the influx of new leaders was destroying all the respect that the group had garnered, and the movement was being transformed into a cult run by a group of power-hungry despots.

The thought of leaving my daughter was devastating. She was the greatest joy I had ever experienced. Around the time Debbie was born, Stevie Wonder had come out with the song, "Isn't She Lovely," written for and dedicated to his own newborn daughter. Hearing it always brought tears to my eyes. I was crushed at the thought of not seeing my daughter's smiling face every day. She always seemed excited to see me when I came home. She'd run to me, jumping into my arms and hugging me tightly. "I love you Pita," she'd say, using the Hindi word for father. Although I didn't know what the future held, I hoped that my wife might eventually come to her senses. If not, I'd have to cross that bridge at some point. For now I was returning to Hawaii, alone.

CHAPTER 12

Opportunity Knocks

On the flight back to Hawaii, I ran into Lani, a female acquaintance, standing in the aisle next to my seat. She was on her way home after a trip to San Francisco and LA. I let her know that I had earned a degree at the Gemological Institute of America in Santa Monica, and that I was returning home to find a job. Lani was a local surfer and remembered me from when I sold Puka shell necklaces on the beach.

After she returned to her seat, a voice from behind me said in an unmistakable Texas drawl, "Did I hear you say you're a gemologist?"

"Yes, I am," I answered, turning to look at him.

"I sell emeralds," he said smiling.

"That's a coincidence," I replied. Then he asked me, "Would you be interested in seeing some?"

"Sure, why not." I handed him one of my cards. I told him I'd be staying in a hotel for a few days while I looked for a rental house.

We shook hands and he introduced himself as John Baines. I told him to call me at my hotel to arrange a time to meet. This was John's first trip to Hawaii, so he didn't know anyone there. I took his claim of having a good stock of top-quality emeralds with a grain of salt. I had nothing to lose and everything to gain, if he was for real. I already knew just about everyone in the business on the island, so wholesale customers wouldn't be hard to find.

Internally, I was still in turmoil. Although my relationship with my wife had been dysfunctional for years, I'd stuck with it. However, I was missing my daughter and feeling very disjointed, even a bit depressed. This latest turn of events with my wife had really thrown me. Somehow overnight, she'd become this crazy religious fanatic. Maybe she had been that way for some time and I just didn't notice. We didn't do much talking these days, other than about Debbie.

As soon as the plane began its approach, the sweeping views of the ocean and the majestic mountain ranges towering above her shores made my heart surge. I loved this tropical paradise. Beholding the natural beauty that is Hawaii through the plane's window raised my spirits and renewed my hopes for the future.

It was mid-afternoon when we arrived. The sultry tropical atmosphere was intoxicating, with its fragrant scents of plumeria, gardenia, and pikaki flowers. After collecting my luggage and renting a car, I drove the familiar route along the Nimitz Highway from the airport. Shortly, the road's name changed to Ala Moana Boulevard, then I made a right turn onto Kalakaua Avenue, and drove on into Waikiki. The twin towers of the Hyatt Regency were across the street from the beach, but the hotel offered a greatly discounted rate for *kama'aina* (residents of the islands).

After checking into an ocean view room at the hotel, I sat for a while on the balcony, watching the small winter waves roll in. I felt happy to be back, regardless of my anguish. There was no place on earth that felt more like home to me. The Hawaiians call it the *Aina*, the magic of their land. Temporarily, I was at peace.

After a long night of fretting over my life, I was startled out of a deep sleep by the phone blasting away at 8 AM. Almost knocking the thing onto the floor, I put the receiver to my ear and managed a raspy greeting, "Hello."

"Good morning Howard," a cheery Texan voice said. "Ready to see some emeralds?"

"Sure," I said, "but can you call me back in an hour? I

need to get up and shower." My expectations were low, but he was keen to show me his goods. Looking wasn't going to cost me anything.

John called back an hour later, on the dot. "Where should we meet?" He asked eagerly. I figured he didn't want to show me gems in the hotel restaurant over breakfast, so we arranged to meet in my hotel room. A few hours later he arrived, and after some brief pleasantries he unzipped his shoulder bag. When I saw the contents, my jaw dropped. He spread packet after packet of emeralds across the coffee table.

The man was carrying around a veritable showroom of gemstones! He had everything from single stone papers holding three to twenty carat plus stones, to parcels of stones from one to two carats. All of the larger stones, three carats or more, had certificates from a gemological laboratory in California. The paperwork included value appraisals, and the numbers were high. When I asked what my price would be, he replied, "Twenty to thirty percent of the lab appraisals." He gave me prices on other stones that didn't have certificates, mostly parcels of one and two carat sizes and smaller stones under a carat. The prices were all extremely reasonable.

"Think you can sell some?" he asked with a smile.

"Do bears shit in the woods?" I answered, returning his smile. "Let me make some calls. I'll try to set up some prospective buyers for later today." Once John had gone, I started calling everyone I knew in the business to arrange appointments for that afternoon and the following day.

An hour later, having garnered some very serious interest in seeing the emeralds, I called John.

"How are we going to work this?" I asked, knowing he wasn't going to let a guy he just met on an airplane walk off with his stones. We agreed that we'd go together. I'd tell my customers that John was my partner. "Just let me do all the talking," I insisted. He agreed to let me handle all the business, and twenty minutes later he was at my door, bag in hand.

For the next week or so, we sold so many stones it made my head spin. Never before in my life had I done so much cash business, not to mention in such a short period of time. As a result, I'd also managed to deliver John quite a tidy sum of cash. He was extremely pleased, as was I, at the good fortune of our chance meeting on a plane.

Every night at dinner, John would grin ear-to-ear while repeating the same line in his heavy southern drawl. "Howard, you sure can sell!" We both agreed that this was only the beginning of a mutually beneficial business relationship. He and I were both in our mid-twenties and looking forward to many years of working together.

When it came time for him to return home to Texas, John felt confident enough in my integrity to leave a significant number of his emeralds with me. We had enjoyed each other's company while sharing a lot of laughs over drinks and dinner. The whirlwind of daily business had taken my mind off my personal life.

I had not only found a new job opportunity, I had literally fallen into my own business. I was selling emeralds that knocked people's socks off, and all without a penny of investment, other than my time and effort. Our benefits were mutual, John had the goods, and I had the contacts.

Day in and day out, I worked tirelessly at finding new customers. It was a win-win situation for us. John had somebody he could trust in Hawaii to sell his goods, which was what he had been looking for when he arrived, and I was making far better money than would have been possible working in a retail jewelry store. My customers also prospered since most of the emeralds came complete with certificates of appraisal from laboratories. They sold them at a discount from their appraised value, so their customers were just as thrilled.

Before John left for home, I'd found myself an apartment. I spoke to Rhonda regularly, but there was no change in her attitude. She was still steadfastly determined to follow her new guru. Concerning Debbie, we were relegated to telephone conversations that were often heart wrenching. She constantly asked, "When are you coming home, Pita? I miss you." My wife and I were still legally married, but I knew that would soon change. For now, it was all too overwhelming for me to deal with so I focused on selling emeralds and saving money.

Without question, I was sick and tired of the pretenses within the Krishna community. Rhonda fit right in where she could practice her own pseudo-austerity. Her parents had pounded feelings of guilt into her throughout her childhood. However, once you got to know what was really going on in the LA Krishna community, you realized that there were many sexual affairs going on between married devotees. There, the divorce rate in the early 1970s was already far higher than the national average. I wondered what kind of precedent this was setting.

Sex is a natural desire for all people. But when it came to Hare Krishna followers, it was reduced to a mentality of "Do as I Say, Not as I Do." So it should come as no surprise that there were a lot of unhappy and strained relationships within their ranks. The society repressed and even abused its female members. A significant number of married men actually beat their wives. The mindset of many men in the movement was that women enticed them to think about sex. Sexual encounters were troublesome since the men often professed a desire for celibacy. Of course, most couples had sexual relationships, but there was an unspoken public pretense that they did not. Ensuing feelings of guilt often manifested as anger, which sometimes led to domestic violence.

This general view of women was even encouraged by some of the leading swamis. The result was young married men and women walking around with feelings of shame simply because they were unable to keep vows of celibacy. Likewise, unwed celibate monks were having the same experience. In a nutshell, sinful behavior won't get a person a nice place (paradise) in the afterlife. All religions tend to have similar beliefs for their followers. Fear of going to Hell is a big motivation and the anticipation of going to Heaven is equally as strong for those who followed the right path. In any case, I'd had enough. I didn't know where life was taking me, but my days of living an institutionalized lifestyle were over.

One evening, I met a very attractive Filipino woman through a mutual friend in Waikiki. By now I'd had business cards made with a new mailing address and telephone number, and I gave her one. There was an obvious attraction between us, but being in such a quandary about my family situation, I decided not to pressure Rhonda with a divorce.

A few weeks later, while shopping at the Ala Moana mall, someone tapped me on the shoulder from behind. It was Jamie, the Filipino woman I'd recently met in Waikiki. "Fancy running into you here," she said with a warm smile. We stood and talked for a while until she asked, "Want to get some lunch? I haven't eaten all day and I'm starving!"

"Sure, where do you suggest?" I prompted.

Not keen on any of the restaurants at the mall, we agreed to meet at a Japanese restaurant in Waikiki, which was not far away. Over *inori*, a type of tofu appetizer that I love, miso soup, and some veggie tempura, we talked about our lives. I even ended up confiding in her about my screwed-up marriage and personal life.

Jamie had been born and raised in Hawaii. She'd gone to school here and started working pretty much right after high school. She was so relaxed and easy to be with, very simple, yet straightforward in demeanor. After a two-hour plus lunch, I walked her to her car, and we agreed to meet again.

A few days later I called her, extending an invitation for dinner that night, which she immediately accepted. After enjoying each other's company at dinner, we went for a walk on the beach. Still not wanting the night to end, I asked, "Would you like to come over to my place?"

Jamie nodded and said, "I'd love to." Once alone at my

place, it didn't take long before we were locked in an embrace that moved into my bedroom. It had been a long time since I'd been to bed with a woman, and she undeniably made the moment worthwhile.

Jamie and I started seeing each other regularly after that. Before long, she was spending several nights a week at my place. We really liked each other's company, just spending time together and talking, and the sex was great. Neither of us seemed to be able to get enough of the latter. It was actually the first *normal* sexual relationship I had ever had.

In contrast, Rhonda had subscribed to the philosophy that married devotees in the Krishna movement should be celibate, and that didn't wash with me. For a young couple in their twenties to renounce sex completely simply wasn't normal, at least for me. On occasion, even when she relented to do the *act*, there was no reciprocation on her part, no warmth or affection. Eventually, I simply stopped approaching her.

I realized that I had to do something about a divorce, which couldn't remain on the back burner much longer. Although I spoke to Debbie on the phone regularly, when I called to talk to Rhonda, she'd change the subject whenever I brought it up. Poor Debbie was always asking when I was coming home. I decided that I had to fly to LA to visit her, and while there I'd force my wife to talk about getting divorced. Hopefully, we could do it amicably and sort out shared custody, visitation rights, child support payments, and whatever else we needed to agree on.

The day after I decided to make reservations for LA, Rhonda called to inform me that she had made reservations to come to Hawaii. She gave me until that evening to call the airlines and pay for the tickets. She and Debbie would stay with me, but this was not to be a rekindling of our childhood love affair. Rhonda would be spending her days at the Krishna Temple. Her new guru wanted her to work at the temple because he was now the movement's presiding guru for the Hawaiian Islands.

Additionally, in the evenings, they would only come to

my place for sleep, which would provide an opportunity for me to spend a few hours with my daughter before bedtime. This "New Plan" floored me, but I acquiesced. It was hard enough to hold a conversation with her face-to-face, let alone speak on the phone. I chose to wait until after she arrived before discussing a divorce.

Immediately, I called Jamie to break the news to her. She was crushed, but I promised we'd still be seeing each other just as often. Only it would have to be at her place, until I managed to work things out with my soon-to-be ex-wife. Having already told her the whole story, Jamie knew there wasn't any relationship left between Rhonda and me, except that of parenting our daughter.

The day of their arrival, I picked them up at the airport. Debbie was exuberant during the drive home, chattering away, telling me all about her daily life in LA. I was so happy to have her here, but being with Rhonda was just plain painful. Debbie jumped into my arms, but her mother was like ice. Trying to shrug it off, I carried Debbie, telling her how much I had missed her. Hugging me, and clinging tightly to my neck, she whispered softly into my ear, "I missed you so much, Pita."

CHAPTER 13

Living a Lie

For the next few weeks, I took full advantage of my time with Debbie. The only time we had together was when she wasn't at the temple with her mother, but I savored every minute we had. Each time I approached Rhonda about a divorce, she ignored me. Every time I tried to pin her down, she was either on her way out or would say, "Not now."

But the worst was the way she acted toward me. We had shared the past eight years of our lives with each other. Six and a half of them were as husband and wife, but you certainly couldn't tell by looking at us now. It was sad and frustrating. Each night Debbie and her mother headed to the bedroom to sleep and I'd go over to Jamie's. Rhonda never even asked where I went, but it was no secret. She'd told a mutual friend that she didn't care. She'd already told me I could do as I liked. Her spiritual service to her guru was all that mattered to her, and I would never be a part of it.

My feelings were hurt, but worse, she was just so damned mean to me. Jamie acted as my sounding board as I went through so many scenarios in my head: I had to end this marriage. I decided to force the issue of divorce with Rhonda the next day.

My standing with Rhonda and our marriage fell short when compared to that of her devotion to the new guru. Ending our relationship would be painful, but it had to be done.

Jamie proved to be a good confidant. She was extremely sympathetic and understanding of my emotional turmoil and she certainly was there for me.

As fate would have it, I didn't get the chance to execute my plan. Every morning after Rhonda and Debbie left for the temple, I'd go back home to make phone calls and plan my workday. On this particular morning, however, Jamie followed me over to my apartment in her car. She was going to take some of my shirts to the dry cleaners along with some of her things. We were sitting in the living room when I heard a key in the front door. The door swung open and in walked Rhonda with Debbie.

Great, I thought, this is not exactly how I planned it, so I started to make the introductions, "Jamie, this is Rhonda," but I never got to finish. The minute Rhonda laid eyes on Jamie, her face contorted into a snarl and her eyes flared up like burning coals in a high wind.

"Just look at your father's whore," she screamed, ostensibly to Debbie. "Look at his f***ing whore bitch!" Honestly, I'd never heard Rhonda curse like that. It was like a scene from a lowbrow soap opera.

Jamie started to cry. Complete opposites in personality, Jamie was soft-spoken and somewhat timid. I'd never seen her anything close to what I would call angry. No match for the sheer depravity of Rhonda's temper, Jamie was rendered speechless by the volley of malicious words used against her and literally in shock due to the relentless and vilifying verbal abuse hurled at her.

Rhonda, however, was just the opposite. Born when four planets were in Scorpio, she had an outrageous temper and a terrible proclivity for vengeance. She charged into the center of the room screaming, ranting, and raving. Jamie got up and pushed by her to get out the door. With tears streaming down her face, she ran out heading for the elevator. I went after her, caught her, and told her to go home, I'd come once I'd dealt with things.

Meanwhile, Rhonda was inside overturning tables,

throwing anything she could lay her hands on, all while trying to shove clothes into bags. I tried to talk to her, but there was no way to get a word in. Finally, she gathered her bags and looked at me with the most wrathful expression I had ever seen, "You bastard. You and your whore can go to hell!"

Debbie had been wailing ever since her mother's outburst began. She had her arms outstretched toward me crying, "PEEEETA, PEEETA!" But Rhonda wouldn't let her go. She held her under her arm like a sack of potatoes, behaving like a madwoman. I kept saying, "It's not like you didn't know. I've been trying to talk with you about our lives for some time now. I have to move on with my life."

But all I got in return was, "F*** off you, you bastard" and other choice epithets.

Finally, Rhonda headed downstairs, followed by me carrying some of their belongings. I asked her, "Where are you going to go?"

"Anywhere away from you, you bastard!" was her reply. Worried for her and Debbie's safety if she drove her car in this frame of mind, I said, "I'll drive you." But, she just jumped into the car and careened wildly out of the parking garage. I let her go. What else could I do?

I felt terrible. Regardless of Rhonda's personality shift and her complete rejection of me, I still held some affection for her. You can't completely stop caring for someone you once loved, but our split was long overdue so we both had to pick up the pieces and move on. It seemed to me that we owed it to our daughter to sort things out and come to some understanding. Debbie still needed both parents in her life. But, how do you have a serious conversation with someone who won't talk to you?

Later, after finding out where Rhonda was, I called several times that evening to try to talk to her, but she refused to come to the phone. The next day I called again and after a short pause she finally got on the phone. She had somewhat calmed down by this time. At least she wasn't screaming and swearing.

Her demeanor, though, was like ice. This new person, the one she'd become, was a complete stranger to me. Shivers traveled up and down my spine. But, we had to sort this out, at least for our daughter's sake. She agreed that she and Debbie needed a place to live, and I said I'd see what I could find, and then come to see them that evening.

I bought the paper and found a small rental house about a three-minute drive from the Krishna temple. I called Rhonda and asked if she'd like to see it, then picked her and Debbie up on the way to meet the owner. Rhonda didn't say a word to me other than to say that the house was acceptable to her. I paid the security deposit and the first and last month's rent, and they moved in that afternoon.

After a few weeks, I managed to get Rhonda to talk to me about us. She agreed to an uncontested divorce as well as to sharing legal custody of our daughter. Rhonda would have physical custody. There were to be no court-imposed restrictions on how often I could see Debbie. We also agreed on child support payments. Within a matter of weeks, we were divorced.

Following the divorce, we began getting along better than we had in years. I set aside several hours daily to be with Debbie, either staying with her at her mother's place or bringing her over to mine. Jamie and I could now be together without a dark cloud hanging over our heads, and for the first time in years, I dared to be optimistic about the future.

CHAPTER 14

Just When You Think Life Is Good

*I can only say that Fate is more powerful than all the valor of man.
We may try our level best to do something, but if Fate has decided
to do the opposite, there is no use blaming it on one or another.
Fate watches our actions, but in the end it all turns out as Fate
wants it to. The results are always in the hands of Fate.
We can only try our best.*

Radheya, *Mahabharata*, Ch. 24

Fate is unpredictable. You never know what she has in store for us. Fate can scare the crap out of you, shake you to the depths of your soul, and even chew you up and spit you out.

One day I got a phone call from an old friend, AJ, another Hare Krishna devotee who was ejected from the movement when the new gurus took over. Like me, a few years back, AJ used to sell jewelry on the streets of Waikiki. AJ said he needed help moving some goods. But, when I asked him what they were, he grew cagey, saying he'd rather not discuss it on the phone. Alarm bells should have been going off immediately. Since I rarely listen to bells sounding inside my head, I invited him over.

An hour later, he showed up at my apartment carrying a briefcase. After a few minutes of idle chitchat, I asked him what the goods were that he referred to on the phone. He countered by asking me if I still had any of my old drug connections. It was no secret. Many of my old friends had known about the pot dealing I was involved in when I lived on Maui. When I asked why, he simply snapped open the locks of his case, lifted the lid, and turned it toward me so I could see its contents: two large bags of white powder. AJ said it was China White, 99% pure heroin. At first I was speechless, looking at the dope in the briefcase. I couldn't believe he'd brought it into my apartment.

Truth was, I really didn't have a clue where to sell that kind of stuff and its presence in my apartment was making me extremely nervous. The penalties for possession of heroin made those for pot pale in comparison. I told him that I didn't think much of his plan to move the stuff. But he pressed me. "Just think about it. Maybe you might think of someone. I really need help getting rid of it."

AJ had gotten involved with some dealers in Thailand and had managed to successfully smuggle his cache into the US. However, the thing that was missing in his plan was a buyer. Try too hard to sell that kind of stuff without knowing where to go and you're sure to end up being caught in a police sting operation.

"All right, I'll think about it," I said. That night I remembered a guy I'd met on Maui who was part of *the syndicate* on the Big Island. He and his associates were authentic gangsters, definitely not the kinds of people I was used to working with. The people I had dealt with on Maui were all old hippies, none of whom were into cocaine or heroin, only pot. The guy I'd met was part of the Hawaiian *mafia*, most of whom were of Samoan, Hawaiian, or Portuguese ancestry. They all wore Aloha shirts and dark sunglasses, and were very bad news. They carried guns and were very scary! These guys sold pot, growing it themselves on the Big Island, and peddled coke and heroin that had been smuggled into the islands from abroad.

The syndicates were so serious about their pot-growing operations that their patches were booby-trapped. Wires were strung at strategic places around their plants; when tripped, a gun would fire at the spot. Hippie growers never did things like that. These weren't people I generally crossed paths with, but I did know one particular guy who might be able to help AJ.

The Big Island syndicate was into everything from drugs and gambling to prostitution; they needed people on the other islands to sell their weed for them. The *possible connection* had given me his number and asked me to call, but I never did. Why? Because these were very scary dudes, and the last thing I ever wanted was to get involved with them.

After searching through an old phone book, I finally found his number and called him. All I got was an answering machine, so I left a message asking him to return my call. Within a few minutes he called back. I told him I needed to talk to him about something important and I needed to be discreet. Why? Because I was already paranoid about getting involved. He said his line was secure; however, I chose to call him back using a payphone.

The phone was picked up after two rings, but I heard only silence. "Kimo?" I asked.

"Hang on," came the answer. "Yeah, Howard? How's it going?"

"Do you remember me from Dave's, on Maui? Remember, I told you I used to live in Waipunalei." I was trying to break the ice.

"Oh yeah, sure, chipped front teeth and a green Nissan pickup, right?" he answered. "What's up? Did Dave tell you to call me for something?"

"No," I said, "I still had your number. You gave it to me. I've got something I thought you might be interested in. Pure China White, a couple of kilos."

After a short pause, Kimo responded, "If it's really pure China, I'll take it all, if the price is right."

"It will be," I answered. "I'm right next to the owner, no middlemen."

"I need to inspect it before we talk," Kimo answered. He gave me a mail drop to send a sample to and hung up the phone.

By now, I was so nervous that my shirt was soaked with sweat. After folding the slip of paper with the address, I put it in my pocket, got into my car, and drove home. Next morning, I picked up a gram from AJ, then mailed it off. By the following afternoon, Kimo was on the phone.

"Good shit. What's the price?"

I gave him the price, then paused for his answer.

"I'll take it, all you got, but it better check out. I expect it to be exactly the same shit as what you sent me. Same purity. We clear, *brah*?" (Hawaiian pigeon-slang for "brother.")

"Yes," I answered, slowly letting my breath out. "Guaranteed."

I was shaking when I hung up the phone. I was dealing with ruthless gangsters. Never before had I dealt with people of this caliber. These were real syndicate guys. Concerns aside, my commission was substantial and that made the situation more bearable.

I called AJ and told him it was a done deal. "Drop it off to me" I said.

Less than an hour later, we were weighing the packages on my triple beam scale, 2020 grams, or 2 kilos and 20 grams. He left it all with me, and I promised to call him as soon as I had the money. Right after he left, I went out to the payphone to call Kimo to let him know I was ready. He said he'd catch a late afternoon flight and arrive in the evening. At seven that evening, he called with the address and room number of a small backstreet hotel.

"Come on over," he said and hung up the phone.

My nerves were on edge. What if this was a setup? What if he was going to kill me and just take the stuff? Such things were not unheard of in the drug world. All kinds of dark scenarios ran through my head. I was way out of my league and didn't like the feeling that was growing in the pit of my stomach. Dealing with pot growers or the buyers never scared me. My only concern back then was getting busted, but the penalties for weed were fairly minimal. Getting slammed for selling China White, however, would be no laughing matter.

I couldn't shake the anxiety and fear of the risk I was taking and considered backing out. No, I was already in too deep to back out now. Kimo's people were not the kind to piss off. I managed to get in my car and drive to the hotel.

Within twenty-five minutes I arrived, parked a block away, and walked to the hotel. I took the stairs to the third floor and went directly to his room. As expected, a big gnarly-looking goon answered the door. Waving me in, he looked both ways down the hallway before shutting the door. Kimo was sitting on a bed. There was a scale on the table and a briefcase on the floor.

"Let's see it," Kimo said, skipping the pleasantries.

I opened my case and handed him two bags, a kilo each. Kimo took a little out of one bag with a knife, put it on a piece of aluminum foil, and held a lighter under it.

"As long as this is the same stuff you sent me, your money's there," he nodded at the briefcase by the table.

"Burns clean," he said, smiling. Next, he did the same with some product from the other bag. Afterward, he sat back, smiled and said, "Excellent shit, kid."

Kimo bent over and started taking stacks of 100-dollar bills out of the briefcase. I'd never seen that much money at one time in my life! As one of Kimo's guys counted the money out in front of me, Kimo looked me in the eye and asked me if I wanted to count it again.

"No, that's all right. I saw him count it," I answered.

Wanting to remove myself posthaste now that the deal was done, I put the money in the same case I'd brought the heroin in. Standing up to leave, I stretched, trying not to show my acute case of nerves, and said as casually as I could, "Nice doing business with you."

"Ditto, let me know when you have more," Kimo replied.

Never, I thought while hearing myself say, "Sure, will do. Take it easy." I then walked on out the door.

A few minutes later, back in my car and on my way home, I kept looking in my rear view mirror, making sure nobody was following me. The coast was clear, and finally I relaxed. As soon as I got home I called AJ.

"Come on over. Mission accomplished," I said.

I couldn't wait to get rid of all the cash so I could start breathing normally again. My nerves had been totally frazzled ever since I agreed to do the deal. When AJ arrived, I handed him the money, having already taken out my cut.

"Thanks, I knew you'd come through," he said.

When he'd finished counting it, I still had that nervous feeling. Wanting our business over and done with, I said it was late and I needed to get some sleep. I stretched to get my point across.

"Thanks a lot, man," AJ said.

We shook hands and I let him out the door. My take was a small fortune, at least by my standards and compared to any deals I'd ever done before. That was it, I told myself, adding that my heart can't take it. Fate, however, is a funny thing: something made me keep the extra 20 grams, only selling Kimo the two kilos. Had I not kept it, things might have turned out very differently. But, I did.

CHAPTER 15

Road to Ruin

The next day, I decided to smoke a little bit of the stuff. I put a tiny pinch on top of some weed in a bong. All it took was two hits. The intense euphoria spread through my body and immediately calmed my restless mind. I remembered the high when using cut stuff in my teens, but that was nothing compared to this. The warmth that I now felt profoundly made me feel like *all things were right in the world.*

It's hard to explain, really. Whatever may be ailing you is gone once you get that intense and orgasmic *rush.* No pain, no worries. A surge of pleasure begins in your stomach and spreads throughout your entire body, "via the functioning of the soma sensory cortex in the brain," which is how a medical journal described it. This is by far the most dangerous drug in the world. Not just because you might overdose, but also because just trying it once can be enough to make you want to experience the high again. No other drug compares to the high of heroin. A heroin high is the ultimate painkiller, the ultimate antidepressant, and the ultimate thief of any life worth living.

At first, I only smoked a little every few days. Then, it became an every night event. Somehow, I didn't think I'd become addicted because the idea of smoking it didn't seem as severe as snorting or using a needle. What gave me that idea? I don't know. No matter how you take it, within a week, *you are hooked.*

In five or six weeks I'd finished the lot. Twenty-four hours after smoking the last of it, I felt a bit feverish, like a cold was coming on. The next morning, I woke up feeling really weak. I had a bad case of diarrhea and felt nauseous. By that evening, I realized that my anti-addiction thesis on smoking heroin was dead wrong. Withdrawal symptoms had slammed into me like a ton of bricks. It was like having dysentery, the flu, and a stomach virus all at once. You just have to get through this I told myself, but by that night it was so bad all I wanted was to end the pain. Calling AJ at his home, I asked him if he had any more.

"Funny you should call," AJ said. "I was going to call you in the morning. Any chance your guy might want to buy some more of the same stuff?"

That's how it all began. It was the most hair-raising and self-destructive time of my adult life, a complete and total breakdown, a virtual demolition of normal life. My business, my relationships with friends, and the one relationship I held most sacred, my relationship with my daughter, would all soon be torn away from me. My hopes and dreams would be shredded and disintegrate into nothingness. And, before it all ended, I would go to hell and back.

But at that moment, all I could think of was getting some of that dope into my system in order to make the sickness go away. I asked AJ if I could come over that evening.

"Sure," he said, "anytime."

Twenty minutes later, I was at his door attempting to compose myself. I didn't want him knowing that I'd become addicted. Putting on a smile and stretching out my hand to shake his, I walked through his door.

Since the most noticeable symptoms of withdrawal are a runny nose and other flu-like symptoms, I tried to joke, "Don't kiss me. I think I'm coming down with something."

AJ didn't notice anything though. His first sojourn into the world of drugs was with the two kilos he'd smuggled in from Thailand that I'd sold for him. As of yet, he hadn't tried the stuff himself, but eventually he, too, would fall victim to its enticing and deadly charms.

The Chinese have given the demon heroin a name, *Ta Yen*. They say *Ta Yen* is an unforgiving taskmaster that demands the rent on time. To get money to support the habit, an addict's need for heroin has been responsible for many crimes: burglary, robbery, murder, as well as kidnapping. Junkies only think of getting more. Guys like me, well, we just sell the stuff to finance our habit. We consider ourselves above *street junkies*. Yeah, sure. As above, so below. Looking back at it now, the karma for selling it had to outweigh anything street junkies generally did to get money for dope.

There was a bag of it on the table. Obviously, AJ was only unpacking it from whatever container it had been transported in. A larger duct-taped bag was sitting next to the table.

"Can I taste it?" I asked upon seeing it. I had to have some, in spite of not wanting him to know I was doing it myself.

"Go right ahead," he answered.

I took a tiny scoop out of the bag with the sharp end of a pocketknife and put it to my left nostril. Closing the right with a finger, I sniffed it up my nose.

"I didn't know you indulged," AJ said.

"Once in a blue moon," I answered, "just to taste it. I have to know what the product is like, don't I?" Then I asked for some aluminum foil. While AJ looked on with interest, I performed the same procedure I'd seen Kimo do. Holding a lighter underneath, I rolled a small amount around on top of the foil until it was completely burned up. If there is no carbon or dark black residue left on the surface of the foil, then it's as close to pure as it comes. There should only be a very slight oily residue left afterwards. It burned clean.

"Where'd you learn that trick?" AJ asked.

"My guy. He told me to taste it and then to do this to check the purity before I called him."

This time, AJ only gave me one kilo, saying he had someone else he'd promised some to. So, he now had a second outlet for selling the dastardly stuff! I didn't care. I just wanted to do the deal and keep some for myself. Leaving with it in a gym bag, I drove home.

During the initial month, while I was smoking up the 20 grams left over from the first deal, I'd shared some with a couple of guys I knew who smoked it occasionally. Calling them both as soon as I got home, I said that a friend of mine had some top shelf China White and he'd given me a few ounces to move for him. Both of them wanted to try it, so I invited them over.

After a few hits I asked, "Well, what do you think?"

"It's the real deal, definitely pure," they answered as they leaned back in their chairs. You could see that they were feeling the *all is well with the world* rush.

"Know anybody who might want to buy some?" I asked, looking at one, then the other.

"Maybe not a whole ounce," Sal said, "but definitely a few quarters. Most of the people I know want grams. They're just weekend warriors like me. I'll ask around."

There was no way I wanted to meet his friends, so I gave Sal a quarter ounce up front. "Bring me the money and I'll give you more," I told him. The other guy, Danny, said he'd get back to me. He didn't want to take it unless he knew for sure that he could quickly turn it around. Two days later, he was the one who called. Someone had given him enough money to buy an ounce.

As it turned out the guy came with him. He was waiting in the car while Danny scored at my place. A few days later, the guy told Danny that he wanted to meet me. I didn't like the idea, but Danny said that he'd known him since he was a kid. He was definitely cool, he said. Now the guy wanted to buy several ounces, but didn't want to go through Danny. I finally agreed, hoping the guy was okay.

Thus continued my sojourn further into the murky and dangerous world of the heroin business. I wasn't dealing with street junkies that were robbing houses, stealing stereos out of cars, or committing other crimes for money to buy their dope. Some of my customers were guys much like myself, independent dealers doing it to support their habits and earn a few dollars to boot. Other buyers were syndicate, like Kimo and his gang on the Big Island. On Oahu, there was a syndicate for almost every ethnic group. There were the Hawaiians, the Samoans, the Tongans, the Japanese Yakuza, and the Chinese Triads. Not just one group of Triads, either. They were always vying with each other for control of their businesses. The Italians or others of European descent like you have on the mainland were conspicuously absent.

Dealing with those kinds of guys made this a far more dangerous game than I'd bargained for. Most of them carried guns, and they weren't afraid to use them. Only the big bosses didn't pack heat, because the guys watching their backs did. Most of the syndicate guys wouldn't rip you off unless you crossed them, and then you were history.

I had no idea there were so many drug-dealing operations in Hawaii before I found myself in the thick of it. Within a month, I had four people who either bought from me outright or I fronted dope to. By that time, I'd moved everything AJ had given me, paid him, and gotten more. At the same time my own habit was growing, since I was smoking a gram a day. To give you an idea of the cost on the street, a 50% pure gram sold for $500. What I was using was 100% pure.

This went on for months. I was moving quite a bit of stash for AJ, so not only did I have all I needed, I had stacks of Ben Franklins in my safe deposit box. One day I decided that I needed a new car. Without even thinking about it, I walked into the dealership with cash in a bag. An hour later, I drove out in a brand new BMW 530i, one of the first ever made for the US market.

When I first started using, I kept it away from Jamie. She wanted to try it, but I said, "No!" Then one day when I was nodding out on the couch, she took advantage of my comatose state and put some in the pipe and smoked it. After that, she started doing it regularly, albeit without my knowledge which wasn't especially difficult because I nodded out every night.

Then one day she asked to smoke some with me, adding, "I've been doing it for weeks. When you were asleep on the couch, it was just sitting there on the table."

I just shrugged, watching as she took the pipe, and put a tiny bit of pot in it with a sprinkle of heroin on top. She put the lighter to it, and inhaled through the bong. Monkey see, monkey do.

Jamie smoked with me every day after that. What was I going to do about it? Tell her to do as I say, not as I do? In sober moments, I felt like a real jerk. Following my lead, Jamie now had a heroin habit, too. But somehow the high makes you think everything is cool. I was always telling myself that I'd quit soon and she'd get clean with me. Always tomorrow. Tomorrow never comes. Whenever I'd get down to my last few grams of stash, I'd tell myself, this is it. Once this is gone, I'm through. Then I'd tell Jamie, "We're going to get clean once this is finished."

But after abstaining for a morning, or, on a couple of occasions, for an entire day, one of us would eventually cave. Usually it was Jamie, but what does it matter? It didn't take much to convince me. Even if AJ wasn't around, scoring in Honolulu was easy. After all, I knew all the dealers in town.

I was getting sick and tired of the hamster wheel, but I didn't have the guts to quit. I would have had to move away from the islands, at least for a while, because you can't quit and stay in the same environment. It's too easy to run out and score some dope in a moment of weakness.

I was also getting sick of AJ having me by the balls. He knew it, too. He no longer expressed his appreciation for my selling it for him. I also wanted to cut loose a few of the people I was dealing with, especially a couple of Hawaiian dudes who were always late paying. One of them, a guy named Mel, was into me so deep that I decided to cut my losses and not give him any more until he paid up. I was also leery of his partner Stan, who was one huge dude. He looked to be about 6′4″ and weighed about 350 pounds. What do you do if a guy like that tries to pull something? Not a lot. Not unless you want to shoot him. No way would I shoot someone. Better to write it off. I called Mel, telling him that I needed my money before I'd give them any more.

"Don't worry," he said, "I'll have it for you in two days."

By this time, I'd changed apartments to one farther away from Waikiki in the Nuuanu Valley. It was also closer to my ex, so I could visit with my daughter more easily. After spending time with her, a self-loathing feeling often came over me. I hated what I'd become. Inside, I desperately wanted to give up this destructive lifestyle. What kind of father was I? She was too young to know anything was amiss now, but she wouldn't be a little girl forever. Yet, every time I tried to quit, after a half-day of withdrawals, the sickness made me cave. An hour later, I'd be nodding out on the couch again. I felt helpless. Really, *Ta Yen* had me by the balls, not AJ. It was *Ta Yen* who controlled my life.

The day after Mel said he'd have the money, Stan called and said he was coming over with it. "I'll be there in half an hour, and I have cash to buy an ounce, too." Thirty minutes later, he rang the bell. I buzzed him in while waiting in the doorway, keeping one eye trained down the hall. When I saw him get out of the elevator alone, I relaxed.

Bringing him in, I sat down in my favorite easy chair, and pulled an ounce out of the drawer in the table next to me, throwing it on the coffee table between us.

"Here's the OZ," I said, waiting for him to give me the cash. Opening a paper bag, he reached in, pulled out a banded packet of bills wrapped in newspaper and handed it to me.

"Thanks" I said, getting a pair of scissors to cut the bands and count the cash while he was still there. As I started to unwrap it, I immediately saw that it was filled with nothing but paper cut to look like stacks of cash.

"What the *hell*?" I shouted, looking up.

Stan had risen from his chair and held a pistol pointed at my head.

"Sorry, *brah*. I didn't want to do this, but you made me. You'd never have given me the OZ without the cash, and I don't have it."

"Just take it," I said. "Take it and go."

Pointing the muzzle of his gun toward the drawer in the table, then back to me, He said, "I know you've got a piece in there. Open the drawer slowly and hand it to me."

I did what he wanted. "Take it easy, Stan. Don't do anything stupid."

He popped out the clip, checked to make sure there wasn't a round in the chamber, and then tossed the pistol onto a chair on the other side of the room. Opening the door with his left hand, he backed out of the apartment and into the hallway, his .45 still pointed at my head. "The clip will be in the ashtray next to the elevator. Don't leave the apartment for ten minutes. If I see you, I'll empty this into your head."

I just looked at him, waving my hand dismissively as he closed the door.

That night all I could think about was getting out of this treacherous business. There are only three roads a junkie can take. Road one goes directly to prison. Road two sends you to an early grave. Road three leads to getting clean and going straight. I knew my current behavior was unconscionable for someone who had once given up everything to follow a spiritual path. My heroin addiction had taken away all of my sensibilities as well as all of my spiritual merits and locked them away somewhere beyond my reach.

For the time being, at least, I had to be more careful about the people I dealt with. This was the drug business, not the jewelry trade. The people in it were not nice. They were ruthless. Selling hard drugs meant you always ran the risk of being killed, for either money or dope. I needed to find just one person I could trust to sell it for me so I could reduce my exposure. Since AJ was away getting another load, I decided to cool it for a while. I'd just tell everybody I'd run out and lay low.

About a week later, I was in Waikiki having lunch at the California Pizza Kitchen. I'd just finished a gorgonzola-walnut mixed greens salad and was waiting for the goat cheese pizza when I saw an old friend from when I had lived in Southern California. He was being shown to a table on the other side of the restaurant. I jumped up and walked over to where he was being seated.

"Hey Mickey! Haven't seen you for ages! Come on over and share a table."

Smiling, he accepted my invitation. "Howard, great to see you man. Sure."

The hostess handed him a menu and we walked back to my table. Mickey was visiting from the mainland, taking a little vacation, or so he said. We talked about old friends and what was going on with them now. It seemed there was a whole contingent of former Hare Krishna devotees who had descended into the murky, dark world of drug smuggling. It was mind-boggling. What caused a person to take up an occupation doing something that they knew was so inherently wrong, not to mention dangerous? Naturally, money played a big part in the decision. Who wants to get a job and work for a living?

Almost all of us had been hippies before we joined the movement. Few hippies had the prerequisite qualifications and experience for the job market. Without business know-how and capital to invest, you couldn't start a legitimate business. There were a few devotees that used to be in the drug business who returned to it. When they offered to bring in other Krishna devotees, now lost and disillusioned since Prabhupada's death, many jumped at the opportunity. Where else could you make that kind of money without a degree or experience?

A significant number of former devotees were now smuggling drugs, mostly the ones from California. They tended to be centered in the south, in and around Laguna Beach.

When we were finished eating I asked Mickey, "You smoke bud?"

"Bears still shit in the woods?" he answered with a big grin.

"Come on, let's go over to my place. It's not far."

Mickey followed me over in his rental car and a few minutes later we were smoking some of Maui's finest. After kicking back, toking and reminiscing for a while, he asked me if I did Blow.

"No," I told him, "I don't like it. Coke makes me paranoid and I feel like I want to jump out of my skin and that's not my idea of a good time." I asked him if he ever did China White.

"Definitely, there's nothing better to use for coming down off a coke binge."

Taking out a small vial of it, I brought out a pipe. Putting a little weed in it with a tiny bit of the white powder on top, I handed it to him.

"I wish I knew someone with stuff like this in Laguna," Mickey said, after the rush of the first hit washed over him. "All the coke heads buy it for the *come-down*, and the dealers buy ounces for their own stashes. Never seen anything this pure, though. Shit, I'd buy a stash of this to keep for myself if I knew where to get it."

Immediately the wheels started spinning. "I know where I can get some, but he's out of town right now," I said. "If I can get him to front me enough to make it worth our while, you want me to come over with it?"

"Hell yeah," Mickey answered without hesitation. "Think you can get at least a quarter pound?"

"I'll let you know as soon as I talk to the guy. Give me a few days," I added, knowing damned well I could get a lot more than that.

AJ returned the next week, and I managed to get twelve ounces out of him. "I'll give you more when the rest gets here" he said, "I only have one 'key' right now." I assumed he had several people selling for him, since he only gave me a third of it. The next day Jamie and I were on the plane to LA, each carrying six ounces.

Airline security back then wasn't like it is today, especially since 9/11. In those days, you could pretty much carry anything on your body that wasn't metal and never worry about getting caught. Carry-ons still went through an x-ray, but otherwise things were pretty lax. I knew guys who brought large suitcases full of weed on the small interisland airlines between Maui and Oahu, as well as between the Big Island and Oahu. All passenger luggage was stowed in the wing compartments on the prop airplanes, and you only had to wait on the tarmac while they off loaded it after arrival. One time, I remember when they opened the wings and whew, it reeked of "Skunk" (potent cannabis). I figured somebody was definitely going to get busted. I mean, everyone knows what Skunk smells like! But nothing happened. Everybody collected their luggage and went on their merry way. Today the DEA, FBI, or whoever else had jurisdiction would be waiting upon arrival for bags like that.

Once we arrived at LAX, I rented a car. We drove to Laguna Beach, where we checked into a beachfront hotel. Over the next three days, Mickey sold everything we'd brought. He would pick up a few ounces at a time, returning within hours, cash in hand, all in 100-dollar bills. Our return flight wasn't for another week because I had no idea that he would sell it so quickly. After collecting the last of the cash, I changed our reservations so we could leave the next day. Preparing for the trip home, we bundled all of the money in tight packets to make it easier to carry in a body wrap.

The morning of the fourth day, we checked out of our hotel, drove back up to LAX and caught a plane for Honolulu. Selling dope through Mickey in California wasn't only fast, but I didn't have to deal with anybody else. No dealing with the mobsters or junkies like Stan and Mel. Nobody knew I was there, except for Mickey: *Fly in and Get out, ASAP* became my new business model. I started making the trip every few weeks, only selling to a few guys at home that I really trusted, *haoles* (a person who is not a native Hawaiian, but used mostly for anyone with white skin), and guys from the same background as myself. No more dealing with the local mafias or even other small dealers like Danny or his friends. Mickey was moving so much of the stuff, I decided to rent an apartment in Dana Point, just south of Laguna.

There weren't many hotels in Laguna at the time and employees there could get really nosy. When you're selling something that could get you sent up the river for years, you don't feel like answering unnecessary questions. Dana Point was super quiet in those days, and it was only a few minutes' drive to Laguna. Renting a garden apartment in a small complex gave us privacy and anonymity.

It seemed the yogi in me had become bound, gagged, and held captive somewhere deep in my subconscious. I'd become something unimaginable to myself only months before. I had become a veritable merchant of death. After all, that's what a heroin dealer is! If it doesn't kill you, it certainly causes the death of any kind of worthwhile life you may have had. More than that, I was providing the means for countless faceless souls to ruin their own lives and those of their families. How many people overdosed on the heroin I was selling? The karma racking up for that had to be monumental.

CHAPTER 16

The Hare Krishna Drug Smuggling Syndicate

At this same time, there was an extensive drug smuggling underground of ex-members of the Hare Krishna movement, most of them centered in Laguna Beach. It began as a small syndicate, devotees in the Laguna Beach Krishna temple, smuggling in hash oil from Pakistan. They smuggled it into the US in IBM typewriter cases. In those days there were no laptop computers, so reporters and others who needed to type on a daily basis during their travels had to carry a typewriter. Pretending to be a freelance reporter was an easy cover.

The IBM typewriter case that smugglers used was composed of a double layer of hard plastic. It wasn't custom built for secret stashes; that's just how the cases were made to withstand rough handling. Runners would fly to Karachi, then on to Peshawar where the hash oil connection was. There, the typewriter cases would be pumped full of hash oil. It was injected between the two layers of the typewriter case, then plugged, and fixed cosmetically to hide any trace.

The then temple president had begun running the entire smuggling operation. He actually used temple devotees as his mules. Once this came to the attention of the higher-ups, he was removed from his position. But not before he'd single-handedly caused one of the worst public relations nightmares the Hare Krishna movement ever had.

Consider this: a so-called spiritual leader used devotees who had joined the Hare Krishna movement to follow a spiritual path. They were first told to renounce drugs and intoxication of any kind, and then they were used as part of a smuggling operation. It eventually became a huge operation, involving a large number of the devotees from the Laguna Beach Temple.

Everyone on the west coast knew that the Hare Krishna movement was behind the smuggling operation. Before long, this golden colored hash oil was commonly referred to as Hare Krishna Honey Oil. Back then, more than anywhere else in the country, Laguna Beach seemed to have an inordinate number of young independent drug dealers. Everywhere you looked, you'd see young guys in their twenties and thirties with expensive cars, big houses, and lavish lifestyles, yet they had no visible means of income.

Two very wealthy local drug dealers that had joined the Krishna movement were the originators, except now they had a team of devotees willing to become drug runners for them. Back and forth they'd go, smuggling vast quantities of the stuff to California. It didn't take long before the mules wanted a piece of the action. Now corrupted, they moved out of the temple and started demanding more money for their services. Many started up their own independent operations, since they knew the dealers in Pakistan.

The Krishna temple opened a restaurant in Laguna Beach, admittedly a fantastic vegetarian restaurant, but it was funded with money from selling hash oil. It became a hang out, not only for the Hare Krishna drug smugglers and dealers, but for others as well. The parking lot would be filled with expensive cars like BMWs, Mercedes, and Italian sports cars. The Krishna devotees themselves owned a good many of them. They'd gone from living as renounced monks who slept on the floor of an ashram (monastery), to driving expensive cars and living in high-end beachfront houses and apartments.

Eventually, the entire operation became too well known. Some of the devotees had graduated into coke smuggling from South America, others to smuggling heroin from Thailand. I knew a handful of them, but never had anything to do with their smuggling enterprises. Once the honey oil operation went underground, due to the higher-ups in the Krishna movement finding out about it, the now ex-temple devotees had their own independent ventures.

No other genuine Krishna temples were ever involved in smuggling drugs. Only the one in Laguna Beach. The only reason I even knew about it was because one of the members of the operation was a friend of mine, Bo. He had asked me if I could sell some of the oil for him, and I did. It was to Andy, the old friend from Philly whom I'd sold pot to when I lived on Maui. The money came in very handy since I had nothing coming in while going to the GIA. There were at least twenty-five, maybe more, ex Krishna temple devotees now engaged in the drug business.

Some of them had connections for buying oil overseas, but they had no connections for selling it once it arrived in the US. After a while, the idea of heroin smuggling began to spread to a few disaffected ex-members of the movement. They had left after the hijacking of the Hare Krishna movement by the eleven new "gurus."

Many of them started out as mules, making ten to fifteen thousand dollars to pick up a loaded case in Thailand, then bring it home with them. However, just as happened with the honey oil operation, mules could quite easily go back to the Thai connection themselves. They could make more money working for themselves than working for someone else. A fifteen thousand dollar investment could return as much as three hundred fifty thousand dollars, and that was selling it pure, by the ounce. The profits were unparalleled, but the risks to life and limb, not to speak of your liberty, were perilous.

Once you start making that kind of money though, it's hard to stop. Most of these guys started out doing the business, but they were not using. After a while though, many succumbed. All it takes is one try. Then, when you're an addict, giving up becomes nearly impossible. Heroin addiction is so powerful that statistics say that only ten to twenty percent of addicts ever quit completely. Of those who do stop using, most remain on methadone or other legal drugs for the rest of their lives. Some end up serving long prison sentences or dying. Of those who die young, some overdose, while others are gunned down in incidents of drug-related violence.

Eventually, most of the drug smuggling Hare Krishna's were arrested. Many did prison time, either in the US or abroad. The guy that started it all was actually one of the founders of the famous Brotherhood of Eternal Love, known for its association with Timothy Leary. Some thugs hired by another dealer later kidnapped him. They held him for a ransom of a hundred thousand dollars. Once released, he hired some hit men to go after the guy who ordered his kidnapping. They turned out to be ex-Mafia snitches in the Federal Witness Protection Program.

The evening of the day they made the hit, he was so whacked out on heroin that he nodded out in his Stutz Bearcat in a parking lot. An old lady next door saw someone in the car slumped over the wheel and called 911, thinking he must have had a heart attack. When the police came and knocked on his car window, he awoke from his stupor. Unfortunately for him, they found a few pounds of heroin on the seat next to him. This case made the Orange County Register's 50 Most Notorious Crimes in Orange County History." If you find this hard to believe, just look it up: http://www.ocregister. com/articles/kulik-577220-murder-style.html

He and another early engineer of the Laguna Beach Hare Krishna drug smuggling operation died of drug overdoses after serving prison terms. Another ex-Hare Krishna heroin smuggler was thrown off the balcony of a hotel in Laguna Beach, probably over a drug deal gone awry. Paralyzed from the neck down, he lived as a quadriplegic for some years before he died. Both he and his brother were heavy heroin users and, of course, they were smugglers. Most of the rest of the Hare Krishna drug smugglers and dealers eventually cleaned up after being released from prison. Some actually went to school and earned academic degrees. Others went into legitimate businesses or learned a trade. Only a few got away clean.

One of the few who didn't do prison time was the ex-president of the Laguna Beach Krishna Temple, the one responsible for using the devotees under his charge as drug couriers. He was finally arrested in a big police/DEA roundup of drug dealers and smugglers. By then, he was involved in the more financially lucrative heroin business and no longer doing hash oil from Pakistan. To avoid going to prison, he turned state's evidence.

Most of the rest of the Hare Krishna drug smugglers accepted the results of their actions and did their time. More than just the two guys who started the whole debacle died from drug overdoses. Another was dying of AIDS, last I heard. He'd contracted it in prison. A few others were killed in drug-related acts of violence. These were dark days, and the antithesis of everything that our spiritual mentor had taught us.

CHAPTER 17

Thailand Neighbors Burma

At this point, I was still dealing in gems and jewelry as well as doing my drug business. Gemstones are an excellent way to *shrink* down cash and are easily transported. Being in that business, I was able to get top dollar for the best goods. At that time, the Japanese came to Hawaii in droves, some spending fortunes on gems and jewelry. The Japanese-owned jewelry stores were naturally ones with the wealthiest customers. Many thought nothing of spending tens of thousands of dollars on gems. Rubies were my favorite gems to buy overseas. When it comes to what are called *serious* or *important* rubies, prices always carry a premium. They are so rare, creating such a strong demand for them, that I never felt pressed to sell them. I'd just let my customers know what I had in stock. They'd call me when they had buyers.

This is how many storeowners were able to sell expensive gems, as well as big pieces of jewelry. They didn't have to actually invest their own money in it to do so. Those with good credit ratings, who had big customers coming from Japan, would take pieces on short-term consignment. If they sold, they'd make good profits. If not, it didn't cost them anything to show them to their customers. Deals were made with a handshake back then, in both the diamond and colored stone trades. If you were trusted, dealers would happily *memo* (consign) gems or jewelry to you to sell on a limited timeframe, usually between three to ten days.

Chai was my best source for rubies in Thailand. Whenever I was in Bangkok, I'd visit him to see what he had. He travelled to Burma and managed to avoid border checkpoints. He bought rubies from small dealers with limited inventories. Their prices were extremely low compared to the big *government licensed* dealers. In Burma it was illegal and therefore very risky for anyone to sell gems without government approval. The government tightly controlled everything. Getting caught selling outside their control meant either a long prison sentence or even being executed. Chai told me he'd found another dealer there that had some top shelf rubies, but he needed someone to go in on a larger buy with him.

Sneaking into Burma sounded like an adventure, so I agreed to accompany him. Our plan was to cross the Mekong River from a small town on the Thai side. Chai said that he never stayed overnight. We'd leave at dawn and return just after sunset. I was, by now, used to flirting with danger and getting away with it, so I really didn't entertain the possibility of anything going wrong. I trusted Chai's judgment. After all, he'd been doing this for years. We made the arrangements together. I would travel up to Bangkok from Pattaya in two days' time with my part of the cash. US dollars were always the best currency for buying gems or anything around the world.

We crossed in the early light of dawn, silently slipping into the jungle on the Burmese side. Chai led the way through the dense foliage for about forty-five minutes, until we reached a small village. Staying on its outskirts, we took a side path leading to a clearing with three or four houses where women were outside cooking on open fires. Several carried children in their arms. A few older children were playing a short distance away.

Chai motioned for me to follow him up to the door of one of the houses. He knocked, and instantly the door opened.

Two men were inside. One looked to be in his forties and the other much younger, probably about eighteen or twenty years old. Chai and the older man spoke together in Burmese, and soon he took several packets from his pocket. Chai then called me closer, and we all sat down at a table together to examine the stones.

The rubies, all between one and three carats, were eye-popping gorgeous. Most were a deep pigeon-blood red and completely flawless to the eye. A few had slightly visible imperfections, but they were all excellent quality. The second packet had a few larger stones in it, which looked to me to be around three carats or so each. The older man took out a balance scale and indeed they were. Chai did all the talking and finally told me to fork over my share of the funds. We didn't talk about who got what, or how much was being paid per carat until we'd made our way back to the boat, and crossed the river safely back into Thailand. Suffice it to say, I was more than pleased with my share.

A few months later, Chai asked me if I wanted to go again. The first time was not only an adventure, but profitable. Chai wanted to do as much business as possible with this particular Burmese dealer to entice him to provide the best stones for future deals. But, Chai only wanted the smaller stones, up to two carats each. That was what his clientele purchased. He knew I liked the larger stones; therefore, it was a win-win situation for us both.

On the second trip to Burma, I took more cash with me than I'd ever before carried on my person. Tightly bound in stacks, I slid it into my boots, strapping some more to my waist. Usually, when I traveled to Thailand, I'd make a bank transfer to pay for any gems that I purchased, or I'd have traveler's checks with me. After all, it was totally legit. Why risk carrying undeclared cash out of the States? But buying gems from Chai's Burmese contacts had to be done in hard cash. So, I cashed my checks on Bangkok's black market to get US dollars instead of Thai *baht*.

We began our trip as we did the first time, leaving from a small town in Thailand situated on a tributary of the Mekong River. From there, we took a boat across to Burma. The atmosphere was thick and mosquitoes attacked us mercilessly; we had to wear long sleeves regardless of the stifling heat. It was beautiful though. Early in the morning our surroundings were quiet and still. Only the sounds of insects or frogs and toads could be heard, except for our boat's oars slicing through the water. So surreal was the scene, it reminded me of old Vietnam War movies. I could almost see the soldiers stealthily crossing the river. Once on the other side, we trekked through the jungle for about an hour until we reached the same village as before, then on we went to the same house. Chai's contact was waiting for us.

This time, I got three flawless, pigeon-blood red gems that were between 5 and 8 carats each, plus a packet of 2 to 3 carat stones. The quality was no less than magnificent! Rubies of this quality were the rarest of all. After examining everything closely, we paid for them and shared some tea before leaving.

After saying our goodbyes, we headed back into the jungle where our boatman would be waiting patiently for us. This same old man had been taking Chai across the river for years. But it was Chai who knew this area like the back of his hand. He'd grown up trekking these jungles, and said he could find his way with his eyes closed. Without Chai, I would have been totally lost. Even though there was a trail, the foliage was so incredibly thick that most of the time you couldn't even see it.

A few times Chai stopped us, holding up his hand while motioning *be quiet* as he strained to listen for human sounds (the military was the big worry). Luckily, the only people we'd seen were locals going about their own business. They always looked at me with surprise, as white foreigners were a rarity in this part of the country, especially hiking through the jungle.

On our first trip, the only potential danger we encountered was a King Cobra crossing our path a few yards ahead. Chai had stopped me and pointed it out. To witness this massive and majestic snake so close was awesome, truly a sight to behold. The King Cobra was magnificent with its thick, long body. We stood very still, holding our collective breath, while it silently moved across the path and disappeared into the jungle.

On this trip, so far so good. We were about halfway back to the river now. Chai quickened the pace, and I closely followed him. All of a sudden, we heard some rustling in the bushes behind us as we circled around a small clearing. We always wanted to avoid walking out into the open where we could be easily seen. About eight to ten men with machine guns leapt out of the thick foliage surrounding us. Chai immediately started speaking to them in Burmese, I'd assumed at the time, but later he told me that he was actually speaking in Mandarin. Thank God Chai was multilingual! He motioned for me to keep my hands where they could see them, while he kept jabbering on, pointing toward me every so often with one of his hands.

I was scared to death. I had absolutely no idea what was going on, and didn't know who these men were or what they wanted from us. My first thought was they wanted to rob us. I expected to have to hand over our stones or be shot dead where we stood. Still, I just kept praying that we'd be able to walk away with our lives!

The discussion between Chai and the officer-in-charge became more heated. Suddenly, one of his men pushed me down on my knees. I felt the cold hard steel of the barrel of his rifle against the back of my neck. Chai signaled for me to stay down. I was so petrified, I could hardly breathe; I didn't move a muscle.

All of them had their guns trained on us now and the officer in charge was saying something very quickly, which of course I couldn't understand. But what I heard next I did understand. **C-I-A!** Again and again he ended with C-I-A.

"My God, they think I'm a CIA agent!" I screamed inside my head. "Me, a CIA agent!" I couldn't believe what I was hearing. I was afraid I was either going to pass out or shit myself because if they believed that I was CIA, I was a goner.

Slowly Chai dropped to his knees. With palms clasped together at his chest, he pleaded for our lives, denying again and again that I was a CIA agent. The words were pouring out of his mouth like a river, resounding and insistent. When I saw Chai get down onto his knees, I figured it was all over. They were going to kill us right then and there. Trying to rise above my terror-flooded mind, I accepted inevitable death at their hands. Trying desperately to focus on my sacred mantra, I endeavored to block out everything else from my conscious mind.

Chai kept pleading with the officer. After what seemed like an eternity, the officer barked a command. The others lowered their guns. He shouted something angrily at Chai without giving me a second glance. Waving his hand in a backward arc in front of his face, he indicated we were free to go. I couldn't believe it; a moment ago I was preparing for death. Now, I was walking away, not only with my life, but with the rubies still in my pocket! Still in shock from what had just happened, I struggled to keep up with Chai. We hurriedly made our way back to the boat and immediately set off across the river back to Thailand.

Later, Chai explained to me that the men who had ambushed us were involved in all facets of opium production. That was how they funded their cause (whatever their cause was). Formerly, they were related to the Kuo Min Tang (KMT), who were originally under Chiang Kai Shek in Taiwan decades before. I knew who the KMT were, as I'd read about them years before. They hadn't been interested in robbing us, but had Chai not convinced them that I wasn't a CIA agent, they would certainly have executed us. In fact, the officer had been totally convinced that I was a CIA operative. No one ever saw foreigners in the bush there, certainly not American foreigners. But, the CIA were still operating in the Golden

Triangle, including Burma, Thailand, Laos, and Cambodia. Chai confessed to me that up until that last second when they lowered their weapons, he thought we were dead men. The experience marked my last sojourn into Burma through the *back door* or any other kind of door, for that matter.

When I returned to Bangkok, I boarded a bus back to Pattaya Beach, my Thai home. I stayed in a simple, but very clean and spacious guesthouse there, about a ten-minute walk from the center of town. The tropical air suited me, laden as it was with the sweet scent of jasmine, gardenia, and other beautiful and fragrant tropical flowers. I arrived home thinking about our hair-raising incident in the jungles of Burma and, in hindsight, I still wonder why I failed to take the ominous experience to heart rather than simply shrug it off and walk into town to fill my belly.

After an Indian dinner at a restaurant just off the main drag, I sauntered slowly back toward my guesthouse. The moon was full, and twinkling stars reflected on the ocean's surface. In no rush to get back, I sat down on a bench along the promenade. Facing the shoreline, I embraced the scene's calmness.

It occurred to me that my life just couldn't keep going on like this. A feeling of helplessness and frustration overwhelmed me. How was I to *stop*? By now I'd become completely entangled in a world of drugs and easy money. AJ was bringing in more and more of the stuff, so much so that there was hardly a lull between shipments. Every time I brought him his money, he gave me more to sell. Heaving a heavy sigh, I pushed away those thoughts, rose from the bench with a stretch, and continued my walk back to the guesthouse.

Passing by a street where some friends lived, I decided to drop in, unannounced. Just as I sauntered up their walkway, I ran into another old acquaintance, Steve. "Howard, how's it going?" he asked, adding, "They're not home. Terry's girlfriend said they both went to India."

Steve had just arrived in Pattaya that day. He was headed back to his hotel, which was on my way, so we stopped off for drinks and conversation. We sat in the open-air bar off the hotel lobby making small talk and enjoying the aura of the night's full moon. Exhausted from the past few days' events, I decided to call it a night, but not before arranging to meet for lunch the following afternoon.

Over the next few days, Steve and I shared many meals together; we even enjoyed some water biking one afternoon. Coincidently, we were booked to return to the US via Hawaii on the same day. He had already planned to spend three days in Hawaii before returning to LA, so we arranged to have dinner together on the island before we left.

CHAPTER 18

Taking Risks Up a Notch

Steve was another ex-Hare Krishna involved in heroin smuggling from Thailand. He hoped I wouldn't take it personally, but he didn't want to sit with me on the flight, nor acknowledge that he knew me during the trip. "Nothing against you. It's just my policy to keep to myself on business trips," he explained. I fully understood. You don't want to take chances on associating with someone else who could possibly bring heat on you.

After an exhausting flight, the captain announced our approach to Honolulu International Airport. As the plane banked on its approach, I got that familiar sensation of exhilaration I had experienced before when returning to these islands. There is something indescribably special about Hawaii. The island's natural beauty is enthralling, with the mountains serving as a backdrop for soft, white sandy beaches and rolling waves of turquoise-blue water. From my vantage point, I could see the waves peeling off perfectly and the surfers paddling out for another ride.

The next day Steve called. His runner had no doubt also been on our flight, although he didn't share any of the details with me. The risk of being busted was over after he'd cleared customs. *Home free.* The flight to California afterwards would be a piece of proverbial cake.

Once Steve received the call that his mule had cleared customs and boarded the connecting flight back to LA, he could relax. We spent the early evening talking and watching the waves, and then grabbed dinner at the Sheraton Hotel Restaurant on Waikiki Beach. In the circle of Hare Krishna drug smugglers, it seemed that everyone knew who else was playing the game, so Steve asked me if I was still working with AJ.

Admitting that I was, he asked if I'd done a run for myself, yet. So far I hadn't. My only business in Thailand had been buying gems. Steve asked, "Why not do it for yourself? Don't you know that our friends in Pattaya (the ones who weren't home when Steve and I bumped into each other) are the main source for a lot of people? I'm buying from someone else now, but I bought my first load through them."

They had gotten small quantities for me when I was there, but I had no idea they were big time suppliers.

A lot of American drug smugglers preferred to buy from other Americans they knew who were living there, rather than seeking out their own Thai connection. Buying it could be more dangerous than getting it home. Some Thai dealers were so crooked they'd sell to you, but the moment you walked out the door, they'd call the cops on you. The police would return half of the confiscated dope for handing them the bust. Most Thai cops were corrupt and on the take, but it wasn't cheap. Anywhere between $10,000 and $50,000 was the usual range for being allowed to walk. The dollar amount depended on the quantity you were arrested with, where you were arrested, and how many others knew about it.

Our waitress came over with menus, asking what we'd like to drink. I opted for a beer. Steve was drinking one of those tropical cocktails made with rum. After his second one, Steve's tongue loosened up. He told me more about his business than I would have told him, were I in his shoes. He actually shared the trick they used to hide the heroin in their luggage. Steve added that this was his last run. He was going legit; therefore, he didn't mind sharing his trade secrets with me. He claimed that his method had never been used by anyone else.

Several guys from California I knew were running the stuff via the same route we had just taken. Flying Japan Airlines from Thailand to Hawaii via Tokyo, they would take the connecting flight to the mainland. One of them just carried it onto the plane in Bangkok, as well as through customs upon arrival in the U.S., using a false-bottom case. The other would carry his stuff onto the plane in a false-bottom case, but before the plane got to Honolulu, he would go into the bathroom, unscrew one of the wall panels, and stash it in there. Once the panel was replaced, nothing looked amiss. This could only be done if you knew for certain that the same aircraft was continuing on to California. Many *did* know.

You always had to go through customs at the first port of entry into the U.S. before continuing to your final destination. Security would search the aircraft in Hawaii after everyone disembarked, but back then they didn't dismantle the bathroom panels. Once back on the plane, safely in the air, and winging their way to LA, the smuggler would go back into the bathroom to retrieve the stash. There was also a good cover story should a customs officer notice the false bottom of his carry-on. A wallet with money would be tucked away inside. It was not so far-fetched to say it was used as a hotel hiding place for money and a passport while overseas.

However, using a false-bottom suitcase was like playing Russian roulette because the method was so well known. Then, U.S. Customs finally got wise to smugglers stashing drugs inside the planes' bathroom panels. On the Thai side, officials began to stop and search anyone who fit the profile of a drug-runner, especially those boarding flights for the U.S. The American Drug Enforcement Administration (DEA) maintained a permanent presence at the airport in Bangkok, and, along with the Thai agents, they scrutinized everyone boarding flights bound for the States.

The way Steve was transporting his stuff was ingenious. In preparation for the trip to Thailand, he would buy two new, high-quality golf bags. After removing the inner collar (a leather piece that separates the clubs inside), there is a hard plastic liner visible the entire length of the bag. This was what kept it stiff, allowing the bag to stand up on its own, as the outer material was only made of cloth or soft leather.

Once the liner was removed, the first bag would be discarded. This liner was then inserted into the second bag on top of the one already in place. Then, the club dividers and collar were replaced. There was no way anyone could tell that there was an additional liner inside the bag.

The heroin was put into super thick, almost rubbery, plastic bags that were bought in Bangkok from a stationary store. The bags were then flattened, compressed evenly by kneeling on each one, until each was thin enough to fit between the two liners. Next, duct tape was put all along the edges of the plastic bags, as well as across the middle. After removing the extra liner from the golf bag, the rubber bags with the dope were duct-taped securely to the bag's original liner.

The second liner was then re-inserted, and the leather collar was glued into place. After it was finished, you couldn't tell that it had been tampered with. If you held the bag up and looked through it, top to bottom, it appeared to be an empty golf bag. As these were high-end golf bags, an extra few pounds in weight wouldn't be noticed. The clubs would be put back into the bag, and it was ready to go!

Steve always played a golf course or two in Thailand to get some new tags, stickers, and other golf memorabilia, just enough to make the bag look *touristy*. The clubs also needed to look weathered; going to a driving range for a few hours took care of that. When the bags were checked in at Don Muang International Airport in Bangkok, they would be among countless others. There were always hordes of golfers from around the world vacationing at Thailand's resorts. Everything looked genuine, down to the dirty golf shoes and smelly sweat socks. The golf bags were topped off with dirty hand towels, which every golfer uses to wipe the sweat from their hands and brows. Everything got stuffed into the top of the bag before the cover was snapped into place.

"I'm too paranoid to be a smuggler," I told Steve. "No way am I going to check it in myself at the airport in Bangkok or walk it through customs on the U.S. side." "Kammie'll do it for you," he said. "All you have to pay him is 12K once he gets stateside with the bag."

I knew Kammie, but didn't know he was a mule. He had a job working for a business on the West Coast that imported gift items from Thailand, which meant that he had the perfect cover. "I'll call him when I get home and tell him you're going to call." Steve spoke with a reassuring tone.

The more I thought about it, the more my courage began to build. "Why not," I thought, "AJ will just get greedier and greedier. No telling how much he'll raise the prices on me next time. I might as well do it for myself." In a few days, I called Kammie and asked him if Steve had talked to him on my behalf. "Yeah," he said, "when can we meet?" We arranged to meet in Honolulu a month later. That was his next scheduled trip to Bangkok for company business. Both of us would go to Bangkok a few days after he arrived in Hawaii. We'd go separately, a day apart.

Drug task force agents were trained to look for liaisons between passengers that might fit the profile, especially for flights leaving the US for Thailand, Colombia, and other drug source countries. The only reason for taking the same flights on the way home would be just in case your runner got busted. You'd know about it, so after getting through customs yourself, you could call a bondsman to get him out once bail was set. You never expected it to happen, but if it did, it was your responsibility to get him bail and pay for his lawyer.

A month later, Kammie arrived in Honolulu. I gave him money to buy the golf bags, as well as a set of clubs, golf shoes and whatever else he needed. He also knew how to put it together, so I left it all to him. He had layovers in Hawaii. One day on the way out and two days on the way home. We agreed to meet in Pattaya Beach two weeks from then. A guesthouse that we both knew would be the meeting place.

I'd bring the stuff and he'd put it all together. We'd stay in different hotels. Kammie would only stay in the guesthouse on his last night to pack the case. He'd leave for Bangkok the following morning. Other than that, we would have no contact with each other until we were safely back in Hawaii.

Three days later, I was walking along the main drag in Pattaya amidst the smiling and beckoning prostitutes, tourists, and locals. Thailand is nicknamed the "Land of Smiles," and the Thais really do live up to it. Most Thais have a wonderful, easygoing nature about them. "*Mai pen lai*" is a phrase you often hear, meaning "Never mind" or "Just relax, and don't worry."

My love affair with the country began on my first visit. Entering the drug world changed it irrevocably, though. When you're addicted to heroin, you simply don't appreciate much of anything around you. Everything in life becomes overshadowed and overridden by heroin, turning long-term addicts into the "walking dead."

I still hadn't decided which of my connections I would use to score the dope. At first, I was going to use the American guys I knew, but then I decided against it. Too many people knew they were in this business. I chose to use one of my own connections in Bangkok. I had met Somchai through a friend who owned a well-known bar in the Patpong tourist district. Louis had told me that if I ever wanted to score big, Somchai was not only honest, but also safe to deal with. His prices were also better, although that wasn't his strongest point. Confidentiality was prime, so if nobody in Pattaya knew my business, they couldn't tell anyone else.

The day I'd arranged to meet Somchai, I took an early bus from Pattaya up to Bangkok. Somchai's son had a taxi service. I was to meet him outside a café on Sukumvit Boulevard. He would then take me to his father's house to do the deal. As I approached the café, a taxi pulled up. The driver called out to me, "Hey you! You Howard?"

Walking over to his cab I said, "Yeah! Who are you?"

"Never mind me. Mr. Tan sent me to get you. Hop in," he said as he pushed the back door open. Tan was Somchai's son. He owned this taxi, so I opened the back door and hopped in. The driver pulled quickly out into traffic. Before long, we were in a district of Bangkok far from any place foreigners ever frequent.

My driver was chubby and dark-skinned with beady black eyes and he had exceptionally well-muscled arms for an Asian. He didn't say another word, so I just slouched down in the back seat and tried to relax. In twenty minutes or so, he turned down a small street, looked in the rear view mirror at me and said, "You, Mr. Howard, get down on the floor please."

"What for?" I asked.

"No *farangs* (foreigners) ever come to this part of Bangkok. Mr. Somchai will not want anyone to see me come to his house with a *farang*. Only five minutes and we'll be there. I'll tell you when it's safe to come up."

Figuring that such a safety precaution made sense, I got down on the floor. The driver threw several blankets on top of me before continuing on. He turned this way and that, driving through a maze of small streets. In about five minutes, I felt the car slowing down. We went over a bump before coming to a stop. "OK, Mr. Howard, you can come out now." I heard the sound of a garage door closing as I got up from the floor.

We were in a tiny garage, just big enough for two small cars, and a small aisle between. Several young men opened the doors of the taxi. "Please come" one of them said. He led me up a rickety wooden stairway and down a short hallway. The ceiling was so low I could almost feel the hair on my head touching it. At the end of the hall, a beautiful carved teakwood door waited.

The young man knocked. "Come in," a voice from behind the door said loudly. The young man nodded and held the door for me as I walked into a well-lit room furnished with a turn-of-the-century carved teak wood living room set. The table had an amazing scene from the epic *Ramayana* carved into it, with a pane of glass on top to protect it. Somchai, seated there in a large recliner, rose to his feet to shake my hand and greet me. "Howard, good to see you. I hope the ride was not too uncomfortable? Such precautions are necessary, believe me. Sit down," he said motioning toward the chair across from his.

Somchai barked orders at one of his youthful minions. Within seconds, he brought a pot of tea. "Would you like a Pepsi or Sprite instead?" he asked. "No, tea's fine," I answered, "How have you been?"

Somchai smiled, his several gold teeth shining in the glare of the sunlight streaming in through the window. "Fine, fine, especially to see you now." Tea came and we talked a bit of our mutual friend, Louis, who had a very successful bar and nightclub. Somchai's son was the only taxi service Louis's patrons used.

After a few minutes, Somchai said to me, "I have two kilos for you. You want to see it now?"

"Yes, please," I answered. He motioned to one of his men, who took a cardboard box out of a closet in the hallway and placed it in front of his boss. Then he brought a scale out, placing it on the long table along one side of the room. Somchai reached into the box, and took out a large bag containing two packages. "You want to try it?" he asked me. "No, I don't do it," I said, not wanting him to know the truth. "I will test it though."

Taking a knife, lighter and some aluminum foil out of the bag I had with me, I slit the first package open and pulled back the wrapping. I made sure the product looked uniform. Digging deep inside of it, I brought out a small bit from the center on the end of my knife to test. First I tasted it. It had the unmistakable bitter taste of heroin. Dropping some onto a piece of the foil I had folded, I lit the lighter and held it underneath. In a few seconds it became liquefied and I rolled it around on the foil, allowing it to burn and evaporate.

After repeating the process with the second package, I smiled at Somchai. It was as pure as the driven snow. "Good?"

he asked, one eyebrow arched.

"Yes, very good. Just as I expected. Can we weigh it, please?"

"Of course" Somchai said, as he prepared the scale. Next, he put each package on the pan, one at a time, after resealing them.

Each of the kilos was slightly overweight, but that accounted for the plastic wrapping and tape. Reaching into my bag, I took out a package and unwrapped it. Inside was twenty thousand dollars, U.S., in two neat stacks of hundred dollar bills, which I handed to Somchai. He counted the money and then put it away in a locked cabinet while I packed the two kilos of heroin into the paper bag and then into my zipper bag.

Business concluded, I thanked Somchai and said I should be going. I had to meet someone that afternoon. Actually, I was meeting Kammie the next day, but wanted to get back to Pattaya. Somchai and I shook hands. "See you next time," I said. One of his guys bade me to follow him out, down the hallway and back down the stairs the way we had entered.

Reaching the bottom of the stairs, we were once again in the tiny garage. Tan's driver was waiting for me, drinking tea, and shooting the breeze with another guy. He stood up when we walked in and said, "Ready to go, Mr. Howard?" I nodded and he opened the back door for me to get in. "Sorry, but you have to get on the floor again. Only for a short time. I tell you when it's okay to come up." I acquiesced, getting down on my hands and knees. He threw the blankets over me, and I heard the garage door opening. After backing the cab out, he took off speeding down the street.

Soon, he told me it was okay to sit up. I raised my head, staying slouched down as I got up onto the seat. I didn't want to pop up like a *jack in the box*, just in case someone happened to be looking. "Where you going Mr. Howard?" he asked me.

"Take me to the Dusit Thani hotel," I answered. "OK, Mr. Howard." About twenty-five minutes later, we arrived at the front door of the hotel. Thanking the driver, I got out and walked into the lobby with my bag.

Once he'd driven away, I went back outside and walked about a block before hailing a taxi. None of them, not the driver, Tan, Somchai, or anyone else needed to know where I was going. I trusted Somchai enough to do business with him, but I wasn't going to expose myself to possible danger unnecessarily. Stranger things have happened. Many foreigners have been busted in Thailand because someone knew their movements and shouldn't have.

"Take me to the bus station," I told the cabbie in perfect Thai. Surprised that I spoke Thai so well, he looked up, and said, "Yes sir!" while grinning ear to ear. An hour later, I was reclining in my seat on a tourist bus bound for Pattaya.

I settled in for the less than two-hour ride, putting my feet firmly on the bag under the seat in front of me, one leg through the handles. Outside the bus station, I had purchased a fried tofu curry and a bottle of water for the trip, which I ate with gusto. All this "secret agent" stuff had made me hungry.

That evening, I didn't leave my room in the guesthouse, wanting to keep the stash both safe and close at hand. The next afternoon, I called Kammie as arranged. Answering after four rings, a sleepy voice greeted me, "Hello."

"Kammie, it's me. You all right?" I asked. "Yeah, yeah," he answered, "Just dozing. I had a late one yesterday. It was my last night out. You coming over?" "Yeah, in about an hour."

Exactly one hour later, I was at his door. Immediately, we went to work compressing and sealing the heroin in the rubbery sacks, then placing them between the liners of the golf bag. The entire process took less than an hour. After gluing the collar of the bag back in place, we examined our handiwork. It looked perfect. There was nothing to suggest that it was anything but an ordinary golf bag. Kammie put the clubs back inside and shoved his dirty golf shoes into the bag, as well as several grimy sweat towels and a half dozen battered golf balls. The bag of clubs looked just like any used by the many golfers coming to Thailand on vacation.

This was the last time we would see or speak to each other until after we returned to Hawaii. Although taking the same JAL flight, with a stopover at Nikko Narita, Tokyo, for a night, we wouldn't speak to or even acknowledge each other during the trip. Upon arrival in Honolulu, Kammie would take a taxi to Waikiki and check into a hotel. I'd go home and wait for his call. Then I'd go to meet him, take the bag, and pay him for his services.

This time, as we were banking over those familiar mountains, circling around and returning for our approach to the runway, I had butterflies in my stomach. Normally, I felt exhilarated watching the beauty of my adopted homeland as it came into view. But, this time it was very different. If everything went as planned, there'd be a celebration tonight. If not, well that would be a different story. Clearly, I didn't want to think about *that* eventuality.

Each of us breezed through customs without as much as a single arched eyebrow. Kammie called, I met him, and soon I was on my way home again, golf bag in the trunk. Bravo! My first run had gone without a hitch.

Once in the house, I locked the door and brought the bag into the bedroom. Within a few minutes, I had cut the collar, removed the additional insert, and removed the packages. I did a little bit of the heroin, immediately feeling that good old induced euphoria. Grabbing a towel, I jumped into the shower. Tomorrow, I would start weighing-up ounces for sale, but today, I'd relax.

My nerves had been on edge ever since I'd left for the airport in Bangkok. Jamie was visiting her sister on the North Shore and wouldn't be home until the next day. Life was good. I had time to think about Kammie and about my meeting with Steve, the one who had encouraged me to start doing my own runs, rather than depending on AJ. It seemed that dozens of people I knew from the Krishna movement were now smuggling drugs across international borders. Some were bringing in *coke* from South America, but the majority were smuggling in Thai heroin because the profits were better. By this time, even my old friend from Philadelphia, Andy, had started doing the stuff, meaning he was also selling it. If you did it, you sold it because there was no other way to support the high cost of a heroin habit. Heroin had seeped into both upper and middle class America, a far cry from the stereotypes of the black ghettos or the Hispanic neighborhoods where drug dealers preyed on addicts, who in turn supported their drug habits through crime. Heroin had managed to make its way into all sectors of American society. Pot smoking hippies had become coke and smack-snorting yuppies, and yuppies had money for drugs.

CHAPTER 19

Kidnapped in Laguna Beach

Heroin had sucked me into a dark hole. Everything decent in me was being extracted and dissolved. There was no more joy, no more wonder, and no more appreciation for life. It was like living in perpetual darkness because the sun never rises for a heroin addict. There I was, living in one of the most beautiful environments in the world, Hawaii, with its spectacular white sand beaches and turquoise blue water, its abundance of colorful, fragrant flowers and the profusion of fruit trees and other tropical plant life. It was a sultry paradise, an exquisite feast for all the senses. However, most of the time, all I ever saw was the inside of my apartment. Going out for dinner or shopping for food were nearly the only times I ventured out.

I sold a few ounces to my trusted regulars in Honolulu, but I intended to return to California to sell the rest because the profits were just as good. Besides, dealing with Mickey was less risky. The syndicate boys in Hawaii would be happy to take it *all* off my hands, *but* at rock bottom prices. I didn't even want them knowing what I was up to. Those guys were too scary for me. Cross them, even unintentionally, and they'd take you out without a second thought.

I called Mickey and told him I had come across some excellent *product* and asked him if he was interested in moving some for me. "Definitely, dude," he answered and followed up with "When you coming?"

Jamie and I arrived two days later, but instead of getting a rental car, we took a cab to a friend's house in LA. I decided I needed my own car while on the mainland, so on a previous trip I'd purchased a second-hand BMW from a used car lot. We kept it at a friend's place in Marina Del Rey. It was close enough, for convenience sake, to the airport for picking up and dropping off.

Once we picked up the car, Jamie and I made our way south down Highway 405 where we eventually took the Canyon Exit toward Laguna Beach. Rather than go all the way to the Dana Point Exit, I preferred taking the coastal route for the short drive between Laguna and Dana Point where the apartment was. We could stay as long as we liked, and nobody but a few friends in the area even knew when we were in town. Mickey came every two or three days for the stuff, and he paid me for whatever he had taken previously. It all seemed to go without a hitch. Until it didn't.

It was a cloudy and somewhat chilly day when I received a call from the teenage son of a Hare Krishna devotee I had known years ago in India. The kid, now in his late teens, had managed to smuggle in a kilo of heroin from Thailand and didn't know where to sell it. Although his story seemed plausible, I still had an uneasy feeling. Something I couldn't put my finger on made me nervous, but greed won over my instinct. I decided to take and sell it quickly and pay him even less than what the syndicate guys in Hawaii would have paid.

However, before I left for Laguna Beach to meet him at his hotel, something made me take my stash of dope, minus a few grams, and most of my working cash to the bank. From there, Jamie and I went to the small hotel in Laguna to meet the kid. Pulling up to the hotel, we parked on the street. It was one of those typical beach hotels where you didn't enter rooms through a lobby, but walked up a flight of stairs on the outside, and then down a catwalk. We walked up to the room and knocked on the door. He opened it and ushered us in, closing it quickly behind us.

From behind the door stepped-out another Krishna devotee I knew from years before when I first moved to LA. Brie was a Vietnam vet known for his categorically crazy behaviors. Of course, I had always stayed well away from him. Immediately, another Krishna devotee I remembered stepped out of the bedroom. He, as well, was ex-military and considered deranged by most people who knew him.

One of them was holding a 45-caliber pistol and the other a huge Bowie knife. The one with the knife, Brie, grabbed Jamie from behind, faced her toward me and put the knife to her throat. The other held the pistol, aimed at my head, and ordered me to sit down. I'd heard plenty of stories about people who made their living by shaking down drug dealers, and most were extremely violent having no compunctions about committing murder. Perhaps, since there were so many Hare Krishna drug smugglers, these crazies decided it would be easy to become premiere Hare Krishna shakedown artists. Unfortunately, I was their first mark.

What they wanted was: *Whatever I had*. I told them I didn't have anything because I had a drug habit and whatever I made went into my arm. Truth was: I was now mainlining heroin, not smoking it. Smoking it required more product to get the same high. I said that if they let us go I would go get whatever I had and bring it to them. But they weren't buying it. Brie told me to give them the keys to both my car and apartment, so they could go themselves. He warned me that I had better tell them exactly where everything was; I told them where I'd hidden a bit of cash and some weed, adding that that was all I had.

Before Brie's partner left with the kid to rob my apartment, he took Jamie into the bathroom. The other guy looked at me with cold, beady eyes and said, "Don't move a muscle or I'll blow your head off." I could only imagine what Brie's intentions were with Jamie, but with a 45-caliber pistol trained on my head, I was in no position to play hero, as either one of them could have snapped my neck like a twig with his bare hands. They were trained and accomplished killers. That's all I remembered about them, how frequently they had bragged about their numerous *kills in Nam and proud of it.*

All I heard from behind the bathroom door was Brie pleading with Jamie, "Leave this drug-dealing son-of-a-bitch, and come with me." He went on and on about what a demon I was, and how she was innocent. "I'll take care of you," he kept repeating while I just sat there listening. After a while, I decided to try to talk rationally to the guy holding the gun on me.

"Why do this?" I asked him. "You guys can't get away with killing us. People know where we were going. I'm not stupid. If I don't show up at their place ..." Bringing the pistol up to my forehead, he pulled back the hammer and hollered, "Shut up or I'll put you out of your misery!"

After a few minutes he called out to his buddy, "Come outa there, Brie. We have to *do* this!" The door opened, and Jamie didn't look like she'd been molested, at least not physically, but she looked horrified. They ordered her to sit on a chair across from me, and Brie put his knife in a sheath on his belt, took the gun from his partner, and took my keys. Brie's two partners left for my place.

For the next two hours, Brie raged on about the manner in which he was going to kill me, interrupting the barrage only to yell at Jamie, "*You are destined to be my wife.*" He told me that he was going to "*slit my throat and bleed me out in the bathtub,*" and then Jamie was "*going to leave with him.*" Brie promised her "*a life of bliss and happiness.*" Furthermore, he told her I was "*already a dead man.*" On and on he went, and judging from the size of his pupils and his wild, erratic speech and behavior, I knew he was coked-up to his eyeballs.

Next, Brie turned to me, saying that I "*should have surrendered to Swami Ramesh,*" the swami my ex-wife followed like a religious zealot. (*I guess I had missed my chance to dedicate my life to the service of a great soul.*)

Maybe, I thought, if I could convince this creep to believe I was willing to crawl on my hands and knees to surrender to *The Great One*, I might even be able to convince him to let us go. As it was, it seemed I had nothing to lose.

"You're right," I said. Immediately, I saw a flicker of surprise in his eyes. "I should have. If only it isn't too late." He turned to face me square on, as he had been facing Jamie. "Are you ready to surrender to Srila (an honorific given to great souls in Hindu culture) Ramesh?" he asked in a loud voice.

"Yes, I am, I am. I was so foolish, but I'm ready now." For the next half hour, he yelled at me, and finally said, "If I let you go, will you go to LA to surrender your life to Srila Ramesh? You'll have to beg for his mercy." He followed with a jumbled conundrum of words and epithets that made sense only to him.

I dared to hope that Jamie and I could possibly live. Whatever this madman wanted to hear, I said. Whatever promises he wanted me to make, I made. Jamie and I had to get out alive. If words would do it, I'd say anything. I hung my head, agreeing with everything he said about how fallen and decrepit I was, how glorious this Ramesh Swami was, promising to fall down at his holy feet. If only I had the chance!

Finally, I heard the sound of my car's engine as it pulled up outside the hotel. A moment later, the other two walked in. They had a suitcase I recognized as my own, but I didn't mention it. By now, the trio was becoming a bit depressed, compared to the high-energy state they'd been in. They were obviously crashing from the coke that they'd taken before our arrival.

Brie's partner looked at me, then at Jamie, and then at Brie. "What do we do with them?" Brie said they were going to let us go. Then he started in again on how I was going to surrender myself to that swami in LA. He didn't say another word about Jamie going with him. Brie's partner took the gun from him, pointed it at my head, and warned me not to tell anyone about what had happened or I was a dead man. Throwing me my keys, he said, "Get out of here!" I took Jamie's hand, got up, and strode quickly out the door and down the walkway; we hurtled down the stairs to the car. We jumped in and sped away with a loud screech of the tires.

On reaching the apartment, we just sat in the car for a while, trying to calm down. "You all right, Jamie?" I asked. Still very much in shock, all she could do was look at me. "Come on, let's go inside," I said softly. The apartment was devastated. Everything was torn apart, our stuff was everywhere, and every single drawer was overturned. I quickly took inventory: They'd taken the weed and money that I told them was there, as well as a few other possessions like some jewelry that was in a drawer.

Hurriedly, we packed some clothes and left, driving to a hotel farther south along the coast toward San Diego. We had to go someplace where nobody would know us, a place that *they* couldn't possibly find us should they decide to come after us again. We spent a few nights in a beachfront hotel. Neither of us wanted to return to either Laguna or Dana Point for fear of another encounter.

We'd had enough of southern California. By this time, Mickey had already sold most of the stuff I'd brought, and luckily all the money and all of the stuff I had left was in a bank safe deposit box. I made reservations for our return flight to Hawaii. We returned to the apartment in Dana Point and retrieved what we wanted.

I called my landlord, to tell him that the apartment had been burglarized and that we were too traumatized to live there any longer. He didn't argue with me, but I also didn't ask for my security deposit back. So that was that. After going to the bank to clean out the safe deposit box, we took the car to a used car dealer. *They* now knew my car and I didn't want to take any chances. The dealership made me an offer, and I took it, called a taxi from their office, and we were soon speeding along the freeway, heading to LA.

Since our flight wasn't leaving for another two days, we took a hotel room in Marina Del Rey. There were plenty of restaurants there, and it was out of the way. I remember sitting outside the hotel, looking out at the marina, watching people take their boats out or bring them back in to dock. "What kind of life am I living?" I asked myself. "What's going to happen next?" I had the worst feeling in the pit of my stomach, and when I looked over at Jamie, reclining on the bench and nodding off, I thought, "Poor Jamie. She was once so unfettered. Look at her now. Hopelessly addicted to heroin."

My life had become completely consumed by the drug. It was a treadmill that I didn't know how to get off of. Every day I'd swear to myself that I was going to kick it, clean up, and get my life back on track. I even let myself run out a few times, planning to quit cold turkey. Like other times, I vowed to give it up for good.

Sometimes, I'd last as long as a few days, but something would always happen to waylay my resolve. Either I'd get a call from AJ that he'd just returned with a new load, or I'd be in so much agony from my withdrawal that I couldn't take it. My self-respect was gone. Again, I felt like the walking dead.

My daughter was the only ray of light remaining in my life. But, each time I looked into those innocent brown eyes, they brought home the fact that mine was not a *life*. Every night I'd be completely nodded-out, trying to forget the horror of what I'd become. The experience of being kidnapped in Laguna Beach had shaken me to the core, but my addiction was so strong I couldn't see the proverbial *handwriting on the wall*.

CHAPTER 20

Losing My Brother

Over the years, my brother Richard and I had always remained close. He was four years my junior and a very gentle soul. My youngest brother, Brad, and I were far thicker skinned than Richard. We easily got through situations and problems without letting our feelings and emotions affect our outside dealings, or at least we thought we did.

Ricky, as our family called Richard, approached things on a deeply heartfelt basis. He appreciated each kind word you ever said to him, each thing you did for him. He was very troubled emotionally, and couldn't seem to find his place in the world. I, on the other hand, was able to shirk my emotions and somehow plough through life. When times got tough, I moved forward like a mad elephant roaring through a forest. Ricky simply couldn't. Everything impacted him on such a deep level, which caused his heart to ache, and he often sank into depression. The meanness and nastiness he saw in others, as well as what he saw as the "state of the world," seemed to weigh him down like a wet blanket of sorrow. Pharmaceutical drugs and alcohol became his method of coping with his misery.

I was probably the only person he confided in about these feelings. Ricky believed he wasn't good enough. He had no self-confidence. He was very close to our brother Brad, but he didn't believe it was appropriate to share these feelings with his younger, teenage brother. The world, as he perceived it, held no place for him.

Like myself, Ricky was a vegetarian, but not just because it was a healthy diet. He saw animals as our brothers and sisters; to him, they had an inalienable right to exist peacefully alongside us. Once, when he visited me in LA while I was living in the Hare Krishna community, we sat and talked about the subject of animal slaughter. Suddenly, Ricky broke down sobbing; tears streamed down his face. "Why are people so cruel?" he asked. "Why do they want to kill everything?" *We were both strangers in a strange land* when it came to this topic.

After high school, Ricky attended George Washington University. During this time, at least during his last years there, my parents were living in London, England, where our father headed up a branch of his Philadelphia-based law firm. Since they'd sold the family home in Philadelphia before moving to England, Ricky didn't have a home to return to. Instead, he stayed at our maternal grandmother's house in Philadelphia. Over the last few years, he'd developed a severe drinking problem. Ricky also took heavy doses of tranquilizers and sleeping pills, like Valium and Quaaludes. He became more withdrawn and no longer contacted his friends. Going to bars became the extent of his social life. His sadness continued to build and by the time he finished college, he was drinking copious amounts of Jack Daniels while taking, quite literally, handfuls of pharmaceutical drugs.

My grandmother was used to Ricky coming home late, parking the car up on the curb, and staggering into the house. Somehow, managing to let himself in, he would fall on the floor, and sleep where he lay. She would hear him come in, step into the living room, place a pillow under his head, and cover him with a blanket. In the mornings, Ricky would wake up as his old, lovable self again, and then it was back to his daily regimen of booze and pills.

One early morning, when our grandmother entered the living room, she discovered that Ricky hadn't moved an inch from where he had fallen the night before. Looking closely at his face, she saw that it was purple. He wasn't breathing. In shock and despair, she dialed 911. The paramedics arrived quickly, but there was nothing they could do. Ricky was gone.

At the time, I was living in Hawaii, Brad lived in Florida, and my parents lived in London. When we all got the call that Ricky had died, we immediately boarded flights for Philadelphia to gather together for his funeral. My parents said an autopsy showed that his heart simply gave out. He hadn't died of an overdose of any specific drug. However, there was a plethora of pharmaceuticals found in his system. The cause of death was obvious. Whatever name you wished to give it, the physiological cause was an overdose of alcohol and drugs.

Ricky's death hit me hard. I felt profoundly guilty, thinking that I should have done something to help him. But I couldn't even help myself. How could I possibly have helped him? Addicted to heroin, I had buried my true self so deeply that I was *unconscious*, still living within my body.

The last memory I now have of my dear brother is of going with my family to the funeral parlor where his body lay in an open coffin. It was horrific. I wish I'd never looked into the coffin. That memory will remain with me forever. However, I am still able to retain the many clear and positive memories of Ricky. I remember his smile, his laughter, and even his cries of defiance when I farted on his head when we were kids. Brothers do these things, you know. At the age of eight, there is nothing funnier than holding down your little brother and farting on his head. Ask any guy who had little brothers. Brothers also develop a deep love and great affection for each other. At the end of the day, no matter what happened in our lives, we will always be brothers, bound by deep familial affection. I will always miss him.

CHAPTER 21

The Beginning of the End

By now, I had tried every conceivable way of giving up heroin on my own. Nothing worked. I tried methadone as well as cutting down my daily doses, but it always happened that someone would bring heroin to my place or AJ would call me. And I'd be right back where I started.

I even went to England to stay with my parents to try to dry out. Becoming sick with withdrawal symptoms, I went to a doctor. Convincing him that I was dying of cancer and that the airline had lost the bag containing my morphine pills, he wrote me a prescription. It was the absolute lowest I had ever sunk.

By this time, my appearance was such that I was embarrassed to even go to see my gem customers. Skinny, with a ghostly pallor to my skin, I stopped selling gems. Having parked all of the gems in my bank safe deposit box, the only business I engaged in was selling heroin. I vowed to stop, kick the habit, and change my life for the better. Unfortunately, I was unable to follow through on those vows.

One evening, while I was sitting in my apartment in Honolulu, a powerful premonition of disaster swept over me; the feeling became so strong that the hairs on the back of my neck stood up. Somehow, I sensed that danger was afoot, but, in the state I was in, even if I *was* having a psychic premonition, my brain was too muddled to make sense of it. I paced from my apartment balcony to the kitchen and back. Then, something made me step out of the apartment and walk down the hallway to the door overlooking the entrance to the parking garage. Looking down from the balcony, I saw that the gate to the parking garage was up. One after another, police cars were driving in through the open gate. My heart sank because I knew they were coming for me!

Running back into the apartment, I yelled to Jamie and my friend Chris to flush everything down the toilet; we had to get out of there: Pronto! We flushed the entire stash of heroin down the toilet. But I wasn't about to waste time trying to open the safe in the closet to get my cash or anything else. Grabbing only my keys and wallet, I ran into the hallway with Jamie and Chris right behind me. Running past the elevator, I headed for the stairwell, where I ran right into a big burly cop. "Going somewhere, Howard?" he asked. Then, we were all escorted back to my apartment.

The cops were a bit gruff, so I knew better than to antagonize them. The Honolulu, Police Department (HPD) had a reputation for being forceful. The officers led me into the bedroom and started grilling me about heroin, but I kept my mouth shut, saying only that I knew nothing about it. The cops turned the place upside down, opening vents and knocking on walls, looking for hidden compartments. They looked for drugs in places I'd never even thought of!

In the end, they turned up a single gram of heroin, a half-ounce of pot, and some Valium I'd forgotten I had. In Thailand you could walk into any drugstore and buy it without a prescription. Other than that, they came up empty, but they had enough to arrest and charge me. I was taken to the police station and charged with two felonies: one for possession of the Valium without a prescription and one for the heroin. Additionally, I was charged with a misdemeanor for the pot.

The next day, I was arraigned and taken to Halawa Prison. Having called my lawyer, he showed up at court. The judge gave me a ridiculously high bail of $100,000, despite my lawyer's argument that this was my first offense. For what they had on me, it was absurd, unprecedented for someone with no record. Unless I could raise the hundred grand, I would remain in jail until my trial.

The majority of the other inmates were Hawaiian, Samoan, or Oriental-Islander mixed race. Many were very intimidating, at least to a *hauoli boy* like me. The first day, a couple of them grilled me, asking what I was in for. Within hours, one of them came back to say they'd checked me out. Not only did they know about my bust, they also knew about my drug business, including the names of some of the people I'd done business with. Whoever the head honcho in here was, he was obviously connected to "the syndicate."

A guy named Richard said, "If you want to stay alive, you're going to do exactly as we say. Got it?" He had a deeply sinister look in his eyes and a big scar across his neck. They wanted Jamie to deliver an ounce of China White (CW) to one of *their* prison guards. Obviously, the guard was in the head guy's pocket. Richard asked for my phone number and warned me of the consequences if I didn't cooperate: The penalty for noncompliance was a shank in the gut. That was it, end of story. Knifings were commonplace in high security prisons, and I didn't doubt him for a second. In prison, threats are never idle.

There was no choice but to agree to his proposal. Richard walked to the back of the dorm and out a door. A moment later, he called me back there. It was a small room with off-white painted walls and a suspended white ceiling. There was a refrigerator, a microwave oven, some cabinets, and a table and six chairs. Seated, with their eyes on me, were four enormous local guys. One was obviously in charge, and he reiterated what Richard demanded of me, adding that if I did what I was told, I would get some of it for my personal use. I'd also be "taken care of," meaning I'd be protected from harm while in prison.

There were so many stories of violence at this prison that I was terrified. "*Harm*" meant everything from being beaten, forced to be someone's bitch, or being killed. At the end of the day, I really had no choice. "She'll do it," I said. The head guy replied, "Good man," and Richard opened the door, indicating that our meeting was over. Going back out into the dorm, I waited for Jamie. I knew she'd show up before too long.

The following morning, I was called out to the visiting room. It was Jamie. At first we talked about the bail. I told her where I had hidden all the drugs and money. Asking her to call a dealer I sold to, I told her that she should give them *stuff* to sell, a few ounces at a time. Hopefully, within a few weeks, she could gather the cash we needed. As long as she told them there was a lot more where that came from, they'd pay up and keep coming back. Otherwise, they would take advantage of the situation, take the dope, and not pay her a dime. There really was nothing much I could do about anything from *Inside*. Jamie promised to call them right·away and come to see me the next day to let me know the outcome.

"One last thing," I added, "I'm being squeezed by some heavies in here. You need to give one of the guards an ounce of CW. Otherwise, they've promised to kill me." Jamie assured me she'd do everything I asked. She'd lived here all her life and knew the stories of Halawa Prison weren't based on imagination. The worst of the worst criminals in Hawaii were locked up there.

Jamie returned the next day. The guard had called her the night before, and she'd already given *it* to him. The dealer I'd told her to call was coming in the afternoon to get a few ounces, as well. We hoped they'd be able to get me out soon, but $100,000 worth is not something you can move in a day. This could only happen if we sold it all at once to one of the syndicates. No way was I sending Jamie into one of those dens of iniquity. I had to be patient.

That evening, in our dorm, there was a big meeting in the kitchen. About five guys were in there, and another one was just outside the door. When they came out after about twenty minutes one of them came over to me and said, "Robert wants to see you in the kitchen." I got up and went in. Someone closed the door behind me after I'd entered. Robert was "The Guy in Charge," and Richard was one of his henchmen. At first I was apprehensive, but after seeing the *pinned* pupils of their eyes, I realized they were all high on heroin.

"Nice job," Robert said. "Good shit, too. Here's yours," and he handed me a small bag of the dope Jamie had given the guard. "You can go now," he said. Then, he told Richard to guard the bathroom so I could take a hit. "Here, you'll need this," he said, handing me a syringe and a stainless steel spoon to prepare a fix.

Regardless of how weak I was from the withdrawals, I flew into the bathroom like a shot. A few minutes later, I was back on my mattress on the floor of the dorm. Euphoria from heroin is so powerful that even under these circumstances, I was able to forget about where I was. I closed my eyes and shut out my environment.

The next week, I spent most of my time lying down, out of it. Jamie came to visit every other day to give me a progress report. She was getting the money together, but it would take at least another week. Relieved that now I'd be left alone, I calmly waited for Jamie to collect enough cash to make my bail. Until Richard roused me one evening, to announce that the *screw* would be calling Jamie again. This time they wanted four ounces. I told him we didn't have that much at a time. Bringing his scarred, leathery face within an inch of my own, he ordered, "GET IT!" Richard's dark, steely eyes looked hard into mine for a second. Then he marched away.

On several days that week, I was back in court trying to

get my bail reduced and attending the hearing on the charges against me. I told Jamie what Richard had said. She said that she was scared of *that guy* (the guard). He'd tried to make her go with him somewhere. When she'd refused, he became angry and said she'd regret it.

"Please don't make me meet him again," she pleaded. "I promise you'll be out of here in a few days. Just hang on."

When I got back to the dorm, I told Richard we were still waiting for more to come in. He gave me an ultimatum: I had forty-eight hours to come through, "Or else," he said, dragging his forefinger across his throat. Guys like this don't bluff. My life was on the line. There was nothing to do but pray that Jamie would manage to get me out on bail before they acted.

Two days later, I was called out for a visit. Jamie and a slick-looking black guy were waiting to see me. He wore Italian shoes and lots of gold chains and rings. I figured he was either a bail bondsman or a pimp. "We got the money," she announced, and introduced me to Samuel who was all smiles. "Don't worry, Howard. We'll have you out of here by the end of the day." When I left them, I was relieved, yet nervous as hell. Hopefully, the prison thugs wouldn't know in advance that I was being bailed out. However, with inside sources like theirs, it was a possibility.

As soon as I got back to the dorm, one of Robert's henchmen approached me. He put me up against the wall and said, "You have until tonight, so I hope you told your girl to meet with our guy. He's calling her at seven, and we'll hear from him right after, bro." He shoved me aside to walk away, then whirling around he growled, "We're not messing around with you, *haoli boy*. You'll be real sorry if she doesn't come through."

It must have been about dinnertime when I heard my name called, "Beckman, let's go." Walking quickly past the *Halawa Mafioso* gauntlet, I walked out the door amid the calls, "*You'll be back Haoli! We get you then!*" When we got downstairs to where I first entered the prison, I saw Samuel outside waiting for me.

The official at the desk returned my personal effects. I signed for them, and a minute later I walked out the door into the bright Hawaiian sunshine. Never before had I been more appreciative of powder blue skies and warm, gentle breezes.

CHAPTER 22

Back on the Street

"**C**ome on, Howard," Samuel said, in his singsong accent. "Let's get your ass outa here." We got into his Cadillac and drove out of the prison parking lot, and through the gates. "Now you can go to your court hearings from home, instead of from that *damned* prison." Smiling, he added, "You can do what you like, as far as that's concerned. I got my money so I don't care if you show up or not."

I thought maybe he knew something I didn't. Soon, we arrived at his office where Jamie was waiting, wearing a colorful dress and a big smile. "Thanks for coming through, babe," I said as I hugged her. We drove home, went into the apartment, and locked the door. I practically fell onto the couch. The stress of the past three weeks had been brutal. Our drug business was now being conducted in a very clandestine fashion. Nobody was allowed to come to the apartment. We figured the cops would have it staked out. Jamie had been careful to check for *tails* every time she left to meet someone.

Over the next few weeks, we sold all the rest of our supply, except for a small amount we kept for ourselves. I even called Kimo on the Big Island and sold him some at a discounted price. He was the only one I knew who had enough cash for a big buy. I also sold as many of the gems as possible at prices no one could refuse.

After weeks of meetings with the prosecutor, my attorney finally had to say there was no way they'd agree to let me off without doing time. He tried his best to get me probation, but the prosecutor hung tough. The best deal offered was five years inside. The maximum sentence on these felonies was ten years each, plus six months for the weed. Should I not take the deal, they'd recommend consecutive sentences, meaning twenty years and six months inside. That amount of time was completely insane for a gram of heroin and a vial of Valiums!

I could be paroled in two years, but there were no guarantees. I was adamant that there was no way I was going back to Halawa! Not only could I not fathom doing time in Halawa, I knew damned well that I'd get *shanked* in short order, if they didn't beat me to death first. Robert and his guys would still be in there and decidedly would not have forgotten about me. Better to take my chances on the run.

I decided to leave the country. The plan was to fly to California and get a friend to drive me down to Tijuana, where I'd get a flight to Mexico City. From there, I'd head to Johannesburg, South Africa, after giving myself a week or so in Mexico to attempt to get myself straight. I wanted to start a new life, and I had friends in Johannesburg: two brothers in the diamond business. Both of them said that if I ever wanted to come down to South Africa to work with them, they would be happy to have me because they always needed people with "eyes" (diamond graders). When we'd first talked about it, it had just been conversation. I said I'd let them know if I ever wished to work with them.

My friends knew nothing about my sojourn into the murky world of drug dealing because they knew me from before that nefarious phase of my life. I called them to say I was thinking about coming for a visit. Moshe, the one I was most friendly with, seemed glad to hear from me. "Great! It'll be good to see you," he said. Moshe gave me his home number to call when I arrived in Johannesburg. He and I had first met when we were both going to the Gemological Institute (GIA). We became good friends and often had lunch together.

Overall, it seemed like a good plan. Jamie could travel with me to California and then on to Mexico, where we would "*dry out.*" I wanted her to be straight before I left. I was confident about me getting straight, but felt I owed it to her to help her kick the habit, too. I wanted both of us to be heroin-free prior to leaving for South Africa.

Jamie's family had lived in Hawaii for several generations, having originally come from the Philippines to work on the pineapple plantations. Unlike me, she had a home to go back to. I felt guilty for dragging her into my sordid world, but there was no use living in the past. Once free of the heroin addiction, she could go back home and try to pick her life up again. My own future was uncertain and I felt I had to try it alone.

A fugitive faces many difficulties, and personally, the biggest one was that I wouldn't be able to renew my passport. Eventually, I would have to obtain a new identity, but first I had to get out of Hawaii. Then things would fall into place. There was no way I was going to prison! My mind was made up. Whatever might lie in South Africa had to be far better than what was waiting for me in Halawa Prison.

The evening before Jamie and I were to leave, I went to see Debbie and her mother. Rhonda knew about everything that had happened, and she was even a little softer on me than usual. I played with Debbie until her bedtime, then put her to bed myself, not knowing when I would see my little princess again. I was crying when I tucked her in, cursing myself, not only for what I'd brought on myself, but on my daughter's life, as well. Tears clouded my eyes and ran down my face as I knelt beside her. For a long while I sat stroking her head, long after she'd fallen asleep.

When I left her bedroom, I sat down to talk with Rhonda. I told her of my plan to leave in the morning. Pouring my heart out, I told her I was crushed, torn apart. I felt as if I was dying inside. The thought of not being able to see our daughter was killing me. Yet, come hell or high water, I was determined to give up the dope for good, no matter what lay ahead. Taking her hand and looking into her eyes, I told her I was sorry. At that moment, I also forgave her for the treatment she had meted out to me after I finished the GIA and for her rejection of both our marriage and me when she chose to follow the swami. I let it all out. Our marriage had already been severed, but now I had to leave my darling little Debbie, knowing I might not see her again for a very long time. Completely devastated, I was on my knees before the "Lord of Fate." To my great surprise, Rhonda had tears in her eyes when she spoke, "Once you get to South Africa and get settled, why not send for us? Maybe we can start all over again."

I was floored, speechless. If she meant what she said, perhaps we could make it work. After all, we had been together for nearly seven years before any of this happened. Even though there had been problems in our marriage, the reason we split up so suddenly was because she had become a fanatical follower. I'd do anything to be with my daughter, to be a part of her life, and to watch her grow up. I didn't know if something in particular had changed Rhonda's mind, or if a powerful wave of sentimentality had taken over for the moment. I said yes, I'd call her when I arrived, and again when I was settled. Then, I'd send for them when I had a place for all of us. At the moment, though, I had to get myself out of harm's way, get healthy, and help Jamie do the same.

In retrospect, Jamie and I never had the chance to really develop a close relationship. We enjoyed each other's company and having sex, but we'd only been seeing each other for two months before I started doing heroin. From then on, we never really talked about anything except drugs and what we wanted for dinner, and that was no basis for a relationship or a lifetime partnership. Sadly, we never had a chance.

The next morning, Jamie and I took a taxi to the airport and boarded a flight for Los Angeles. The flight left on time, but when we were on the runway waiting to take off, the pilot came on and said there was a small problem. The plane had to return to the gate. He asked for our patience, adding that the delay would only be a short one. Anxious, I was sure the police somehow found out that I was on the plane, and when we reached the gate, they'd pull me off the plane and take me back to jail for violating the terms of my bail. The conditions of my bail required that I would not leave the state. Slinking down in my seat, I prepared for the worst. Many thoughts raced through my mind, from going back to Halawa Prison to never seeing my daughter or the rest of my family again.

We arrived at the gate; pretending to read a magazine, I tried to hide my face while praying. Neither Jamie nor I said a word. She must have been thinking the same thing I was. Neither of us could breathe. The door opened at the front of the plane, and a couple of guys who looked like FBI agents boarded. Slowly walking down the aisle, they carefully studied each face. When they passed us, I was so nervous I almost shook, but I kept my nose in the magazine and continued to pray.

We heard some voices from the back of the plane. A moment later, they were coming back down the aisle with a young man in handcuffs. My intuition about the reason for our return to the gate had been correct, but it wasn't me they sought! I wanted to jump for joy, but I continued to keep my nose in the magazine. Not until the plane had taken off, and the landing gear had retracted, did I put the magazine down. Jamie and I both breathed a huge sigh of relief. We looked at each other and smiled.

Later that day, we arrived in LA, picked up our luggage, and took the shuttle to a hotel near the airport where a friend was coming to pick us up in the morning. Our plan was to drive down to San Diego, then across the border into Tijuana. For now, we would try to relax. We had a little bit of stash left, just enough to last until Mexico City. We had cut our doses way down, hoping the withdrawals would be less painful.

Once at the hotel, I called my friend Ron and then room service. I'd purchased American Express traveler's checks because they were safer than carrying cash. Not wanting to take any chances, we would remain in our room until Ron came for us in the morning.

CHAPTER 23

Leaving to Begin a New Life

The next morning, the phone rang right on schedule. After checking out of the hotel, we headed out the front door. My friend Ron picked us up, and soon we were whizzing along the freeway, heading south. We made good time and within a few hours we had passed through San Diego, then San Ysidro, and on across the border into Mexico. Once we made our way through the Mexican officials, I was able to relax and breathe an enormous sigh of relief. We'd made it!

Ron took us to a small hotel, and Jamie went in to see if they had a room. Ten minutes later, she returned to the car to let me know she'd checked us in. We said our goodbyes to Ron and promised to stay in touch. Other than going to the restaurant next door for dinner, we stayed in our room all evening. In the morning, we went to the airport. Less than four hours later, we were in a cab, cruising through the streets of Mexico City. Nothing had changed since the last time I was there. The place was overcrowded and suffering from the worst air pollution I had ever experienced. But the people were nice, and we enjoyed watching them as they went about their business. In Mexico City, there is always something going on. At one red light, Mariachi players serenaded people in their cars. At others, street vendors approached with their wares as you waited for the light to change. It reminded me a little of India.

Our hotel was on Paseo de la Reforma. The room was basic, although the bed was queen-sized, a four-poster with intricately carved posts. Having used the rest of our heroin earlier that morning, we were already starting to feel withdrawal symptoms. Since smoking pot helps with nausea, I decided to go see if I could score some. After all, Mexico grew a hell of a lot of the stuff. Walking around a neighborhood square not far from our hotel, I quickly spotted a young man with a ponytail. Carrying a bag on his shoulder, he looked like he might just be my guy. A few minutes later, I walked back to the hotel with a small bag of Mexican weed in my pocket.

Back in the room, I sat down at the desk and rolled a joint. Before lighting it, we carefully sealed all the openings around the door with towels, making sure the windows were also tightly closed, because the last thing I wanted to do was stink up the hallway! After a few tokes on the joint, we both felt better.

Jamie and I talked about our immediate plans. Although agreeing with me, and understanding why I felt I needed to go on alone, she informed me that she didn't want to go back to Hawaii. She feared being unable to maintain her resolve to steer clear of drugs. If she started doing heroin again, she'd be entering an inferno, one that would surely reduce her life to ashes. Female heroin addicts, more often than not, turn to prostitution to support their habit. Even after finishing a rehabilitation program, and undergoing out-patient counseling, most heroin addicts start using again within six months, which is a sad commentary.

I came up with an alternate plan, because leaving Jamie in such a vulnerable state wouldn't be right, especially if I could help her. Maybe it would compensate somewhat for having been such a bad influence on her. We could go somewhere else. However, it had to be a place where we didn't know anyone and where we could both get our bodies and minds healthy.

Putting our heads together, we decided to go to Brazil, where the weather was nice and we didn't know anybody. Also, Brazil wasn't a source country for heroin. I didn't want to stay in Mexico where they produced heroin, not the pure white Asian stuff we were used to, but heroin, all the same. Brazil was full of cocaine, but I hated the stuff, so I wasn't worried about being tempted by it. I'd tried it before, but it made me feel nervous and ungrounded. For me, it generated no pleasure.

Jamie and I went to the Brazilian Embassy, and with a little pleading, they gave us visas the same day. That evening, we smoked some more pot, and slept fairly well that night, all things considered. The next morning, we awoke to a loud knocking on the door. Jamie stayed in bed while I got up to answer it. Two guys in sport shirts and slacks pushed their way in, showing me ID that said they were cops, but neither wore a uniform. I saw a pistol tucked into one man's waistband, so I chose not to argue. They demanded to search the room. Within a minute, they had located the tiny bit of pot that was in the nightstand drawer, along with the rolling papers. One of them said we would have to come with them to the police station. Pulling him aside, I pushed a $100 bill into his hand and said, "But officer, it's not mine." Taking the bill and quickly shoving it into his pocket, he warned, "Then be more careful. Next time you won't get off so easy." As soon as they were gone, I looked at Jamie and insisted, "Let's get out of here!"

After checking out of the hotel, we took a taxi to another hotel a few miles away. We paid the driver and walked through the front door into the lobby. Once we saw that the taxi was gone, we went back outside, exiting through the side door, where I hailed a second taxi that we took to another hotel. After waiting a few moments to make sure the driver was gone, we hailed yet another taxi, this time taking it to a hotel where we checked in, intending to stay overnight.

Thinking that my "secret agent" antics of changing cabs would have thrown anyone watching us off, I sat back on the bed and tried to relax. I still had half of the small bag of pot, and after sealing all the openings around the door and windows to prevent the smell from escaping, we smoked some and eventually drifted off.

The next morning, the same damned thing happened to us, but this time there were about a half dozen uniformed police along with their commanding officer. They ransacked our room and found the baggie of pot in my case underneath some clothes. I wondered why the hell all the cops were so interested in a couple of American tourists with a little pot. I tried to pull the officer aside to give him some money to let us go, but he declined, which was very strange because Mexican cops are some of the most crooked in the world. To not take a payoff was unheard of.

Meanwhile, while rifling through our stuff, one of them opened my little brown zipper bag stuffed with traveler's checks, all in large denominations. The cops got all excited, tearing the place apart until they had searched through all of our belongings as well as every square inch of the room. They were *Federales* (Federal Cops). Had they just been local cops, I would have been able to pay them off, but for some reason this particular officer was intent on taking us in. We were going with him to the police station, no *ifs*, *ands*, or *buts*.

They put us in the back seat of an unmarked car, and a short while later, we arrived at their station. Initially, they interrogated us both together, then in separate rooms for what seemed like hours. I wondered who the hell they thought I was. I kept saying that I had nothing to do with anything illegal, except for possessing a little bit of pot. They wanted to know what the money was for, and I told them that we planned to travel for an extended period of time, that it was for our living expenses. End of story! Since they thought they were on to something big, they had actually logged in every single dollar I had, meaning that it would have to be accounted for. At least that was some good news.

After their interrogations proved fruitless, they called the US Embassy to see if they had any information on us. At first, I was somewhat relieved. I'd heard plenty of stories about Mexican police torturing and beating prisoners, but the sense of relief didn't last long. Certainly, they would find out that I had jumped bail and was on the run. Jamie and I were put in separate cells. Mine was bare except for a steel bunk and a toilet without a seat. No mattress, no blanket, no nothing.

Late that afternoon, a different cop came to get us. Someone was here to see us from the American Embassy, a Mr. Terence. Miraculously enough, he didn't know anything about us other than the fact that we had been arrested for marijuana possession in our hotel room. The chief *federal* officer shared his theory about me being a criminal, showing him the large amount of traveler's checks I was carrying.

Mr. Terence asked to speak with Jamie and me together in private and was given permission to do so. He told us that he should be able to get us off with a small fine as long as the computer check he would make immediately at the embassy didn't turn up any warrants for us. And, tomorrow, he'd try to further sort things out for us. He made a point of telling us that no matter where the marijuana came from, we were to say we bought it in Mexico. Smuggling drugs into Mexico was a serious crime and would land us in prison for quite a while, regardless of the amount we possessed. I told him that I really had bought it here, but thanked him for the warning.

That night was awful. We were both still pretty sick, and being stuck in cold, damp cells made us feel worse. The water pipe to the toilet was leaking, creating an ever-increasing puddle of water on the floor. I shivered and crossed my arms tightly across my chest, hoping to retain some body heat. I called out to Jamie, finally getting a weak response. "Don't worry, at least you should be able to get out of here tomorrow," I told her. "Maybe I won't even be in the Feds' computer yet, and we'll both get out. Please try to relax, Jamie."

The night seemed to last forever. Nausea swept over me, and I had a major case of diarrhea. It was pretty disgusting, having to constantly get up and hold myself up to keep from falling into the toilet while an endless stream of dark liquid left my bedraggled body. I felt like a wrung-out wet dishrag.

Terence didn't arrive until about 2 or 3 o'clock the next afternoon. Was I ever glad to see him! He told us that we'd have to pay a fine amounting to about seventy-five US dollars, and then we'd be free to go. There were no arrest warrants out for either of us. The Mexican authorities had no reason to hold us any longer. I couldn't believe my ears and our luck! They didn't know a thing about my bust in Hawaii. I assumed that since I hadn't missed any court dates yet, I was not officially a fugitive. At this point, perhaps they didn't even know I'd left the island.

An hour later, we were walking out of the cop shop into a busy Mexico City street. The bright sunshine blinded me, forcing me to shield my eyes with my hands. It was like surfacing from underground. Once our eyes adjusted to the light, we picked up our suitcases (they'd taken them down to the station along with us) and began shuffling down the street. They had returned my traveler's checks, and all of our possessions except my shoelaces, which they were unable to find. I kept stepping out of my shoes!

We were both totally frazzled; simple walking required a monumental effort. Mentally and physically drained, I felt like I'd been in jail for days. In retrospect, I really should have felt blessed to be out and not on my way back to the US in handcuffs. Instead, I felt sorry for myself, silently wondering how much more shit I would have to endure. I didn't know if my next bad decision would hold such dire consequences as my most recent ones.

We went to a five-star hotel. Crooked cops tended to avoid high-class hotels. However, there was no way I intended to be stupid enough to smoke any more pot while we stayed there. Now, since the US Embassy had seen the visas in our passports, Brazil was out of the question. Once my fugitive status became official, they would be after me.

Holding my head in my hands, I sat on the edge of the bed bemoaning my fate. "So, where are we going to go now?" I asked Jamie.

"Let's go to Thailand. We can make it there. The weather's like Hawaii, and we can eat lots of fruit and good food to get us strong again," she seemed encouraged. I, however, knew that was highly unlikely. Sure, let's go to the heroin capital of the world to rehabilitate from heroin addiction, I mused to myself. Suddenly, I lost my resolve. Any initiative I had was fading. As if being directed by some unseen force, I picked up the phone and called the airlines. Booking flights leaving that night for Europe with a connection to Bangkok sealed our fate.

After bathing, we got dressed and went down to the front desk to check out. Soon, we were in a taxi on our way back to the airport. We were each lost in our own thoughts, so the ride seemed to be over in a matter of minutes. At the airport, I managed to find some cold medication to help counter my withdrawal symptoms. They had Vicks Nyquil, and I bought two bottles. Because the first flight had a lot of empty seats, we were able to lie down for most of it. The connecting flight to Bangkok was more fully occupied, but at least we had an empty seat next to us. We slept as much as we could on both flights. The Nyquil knocked me out, which I was glad for. Finally, many hours after the journey had begun, the captain came on the PA system to announce our descent into *Don Muang International Airport*.

CHAPTER 24

Return to Sin City, Bangkok

Once through immigration and customs, we made our way out of the airport and into the hustle and bustle of Bangkok. Like in India, you heard the constant droning and acceleration of motorcycles and *tuktuks* (motorized rickshaws). But, unlike India, the Thais don't have the same annoying habit of constantly leaning on their horns. The hot, sultry atmosphere smacked me in the face as we walked out of the airport, keeping our eyes on the boy pushing the luggage cart with our suitcases. Having decided where our first stop was going to be, we took a taxi into the city. I knew Bangkok very well by this time and had the driver take us to a small hotel just a short drive from the airport.

My mind was reeling, and I felt drained from the painful reversal of fortune that Fate had dealt me over the past few months. Not only the arrest and nightmare of my stay at Halawa prison in Hawaii, but having to run away from everything I knew and loved in this world. I hated what I'd become, having let down my family, and worse, my beautiful, innocent little daughter. Being rousted by the Mexican police had been the proverbial "*icing on the cake.*" I felt weak, unmotivated, and still sick as a dog from withdrawal. Depressed from the seemingly unending misery, I tried to stop worrying. My next move though was inevitable, considering where we had now, figuratively and literally, landed.

Leaving Jamie in the hotel room, I went out and caught a rickshaw. Minutes later, I was back in the room with several grams of pure heroin. Within moments, we were both high and nodding off. For now, I was able to block out all my troubles.

In the morning, we checked out of the small hotel and moved over to the Sheraton, situated a few blocks from the infamous Patpong district, on a street filled with bars and nightclubs. Men from all over the world thronged there, drawn by the many young prostitutes and international beer bars. By day, you would find men of all ages and nationalities hanging out in bars that played videos of various movies. At night, Patpong bristled with nightlife. Everything from raunchy sex shows to pole dancing was offered for entertainment. There were whorehouses where the patrons chose girls from a line-up, all of them sitting in rows behind a glass window. Some wore negligées, some evening dresses; still others dressed in various and sundry outfits meant to stimulate a man's lustful desires. The men sipped a drink at the bar while they decided which girl's charms they wished to enjoy. Once they paid the matron, the girl's number was called, and she showed her customer to a private room. Whatever a man's carnal desire was, it would be provided. For this reason alone, Bangkok has earned its reputation as Sin City.

My reason for going today was to drop in on my old friend, Louis, an American who owned the most famous bar in Patpong, The Roxy. He was a Vietnam vet who had been a medic in the field during the war. His experiences in 'Nam had tweaked him permanently, as it had countless other Vietnam vets. Plagued with frightening memories by day and nightmares by night, he simply couldn't bring himself to return to the life he'd known before the war. Living a so-called *normal* civilian lifestyle was now impossible for him. Many combat vets came to Bangkok for R&R. After the war, Louis returned to Bangkok for good.

We'd met through a mutual friend during one of my trips to Bangkok, and established a friendship. I liked sitting at the bar, listening to all the war stories. It was a great way to kill time when I was in Bangkok. Louis played videos of old James Bond movies in the afternoons (back when Sean Connery played Bond). He had every single one of them.

There were quite a few Vietnam Vets living in Bangkok at the time, and many of them came to The Roxy, since Louis was one of their own. They all had war stories. Some, I took with a grain of salt, but most you could tell were authentic. There was something about the look in their eyes when they spun their tales: Whoa! This guy has been through some ungodly experiences.

One ex-Marine, Jerry, appeared to be a real hard-ass. He never smiled; although once you got to know him, he was quite friendly. In 'Nam, he'd been a helicopter pilot. Louis said Jerry had flown the most dangerous missions of anyone he knew, and had done so for years, returning for more tours of duty than any of the other guys.

I'll never forget some of Jerry's stories. On numerous occasions, he'd flown a chopper for US Military Intelligence. The interrogators on board would fiercely grill captured enemy officers. According to Jerry, the questioning was intense. If an enemy commanding officer refused to answer questions, one of the crew was ordered to open the side door of the chopper, while another grabbed the most junior of the officers and threw him out. That usually got the senior officers talking pretty quickly. Most of these guys had seen and done things there that they couldn't live with afterwards. The majority became either alcoholics or heroin addicts. Moreover, many actually started doing heroin while they were on active duty in Vietnam.

Leaving Jamie at the Sheraton, I walked the short distance to Patpong, then to The Roxy to see Louis. At any time of the day there'd be guys inside sitting on barstools, drinking beer, and talking with the girls (none of the girls danced onstage during the day). It was pretty laid back until about six in the evening, when more girls arrived for the night shift. Then the dancing began and the music grew louder. Seeing neither Louis nor his partner, I asked the girl at the bar if he was in. She disappeared for a moment and returned with Louis, who, after giving me a warm greeting and shaking my hand, invited me into the back room. I shared with him my recent life events that had made me a fugitive. "Guess you're one of us now, huh?" he laughed.

"Guess so," I answered. Louis had a floor safe in his office, and I asked him if I could put my traveler's checks and valuables in it for the next few days. I needed to figure out what was next on my agenda, and didn't like carrying all that money on me while I did it. I knew Louis well enough to trust him. He was a lot of things, but a thief wasn't one of them.

After leaving The Roxy, I went back to the hotel to pick up Jamie and go out for a meal. There were a few restaurants in Bangkok that I liked to frequent when visiting. They went out of their way to cook a fantastic vegetarian meal for me, using tofu instead of meat. *Baan Suan* was my favorite. I was always treated like an old friend whenever I returned, so I decided to take Jamie there for dinner. Asking for Arun, the owner, when we arrived, he soon came out to personally greet us. I introduced him to Jamie, and he showed us to his best table. The restaurant had beautiful paintings on the walls, statues of Thai dancers on pedestals, and other Thai artwork placed in strategic places, all of which created a richly authentic ambience.

For the first course, I ordered green papaya salad, which I shared with Jamie. Next, we feasted on a superb green curry made with fried tofu, followed by mango with sticky rice and coconut milk. For the moment at least, I felt free from worry. After dinner, we strolled leisurely hand-in-hand back to the hotel. It was impossible to keep my troubles at bay for long though. The image of my daughter's smiling face kept replaying in my mind. Every time this happened, the feeling of panic returned. When would I see her again? What was I going to do with my life? These and other questions tortured me; I was at a complete loss for answers.

All of the big hotels had a room where they showed movies at night. It always sounded like a good idea to go and watch one, but inevitably I'd end up falling asleep, slunk down and out cold in a chair, until all of the other guests had gone. The same thing occurred on our second night in Bangkok, except this time Jamie was with me. With both of us nodded out, the likely reason for our unconscious state would have been obvious to anyone. At about 11 PM, I woke up, shook Jamie awake, and we went up to our room.

Next morning, I called down to say we'd be checking-out and asked them to prepare the bill. We arrived at the front desk and I paid the cashier. Noticing the girl at the counter looking nervously over my shoulder, I turned around to see who was behind me. Several police officers stepped up and ordered Jamie and I to come with them. I couldn't believe it! My mind was spinning, but I quickly took mental inventory of how much dope we had with us. It was in one of the smaller suitcases, but there wasn't any way I could get rid of it with two cops flanking me, two flanking Jamie, and two others walking behind us.

They took us into an empty hotel room, searched our pockets and gave us a pat down. One of the officers, a woman, searched Jamie. There was nothing on us. The officer in charge told the others to put the suitcases on one of the beds, motioning for both of us to sit on the other one. Several of them started searching through the two large suitcases. Frantic that they would soon find the dope, I decided to try somehow to get rid of it. It was a long shot, but they were going to find it anyway as soon as they opened the small case. I thought, what the hell? There was nothing to lose. I might as well try to pull a Houdini!

The small suitcases were on the floor by the edge of the bed, and I started opening them. One officer stopped me, motioning for me to place them up on the bed first, obviously to see what I was doing. I did as I was told. Next, I unzipped the first bag, removed the smaller cases with our toiletry bags, and put them on the bed next to the case. With my right hand, I was pulling clothes out of the smaller bags, and with my left I was slowly unzipping the side pocket where the heroin was. By taking things out with my right hand and placing them on the bed, I mirrored what they were doing with the big cases.

The officers carefully examined the contents of our suitcases, painstakingly going through the pockets of each piece of our clothing. At last I felt the bag; with my left hand, I took it from the zippered compartment. To cover my sudden motion, I began coughing while quickly slipping it between the box spring and mattress. Then, I continued to empty out the case. Suddenly, one of the cops bellowed an order to the others as he took the other small case. They motioned for me to stop. The officer told me in broken English, "You only sit!"

"Oh God, we're done for," I thought, figuring they must have seen me. I mean, there were six sets of eyes on us. How could they have missed it? But, they didn't tell me to get up, nor seem to have seen my sleight-of-hand. I could hardly breathe. I was so scared. After going through every single piece of clothing, opening everything in the toiletry bags, even squeezing out all the toothpaste from the tubes to see if anything was inside them, they were finished.

Finally, they simply asked me where the heroin was. "*MAI MEE*," I said in Thai, meaning, literally, *no have*. They were certain they were going to find something, but since they'd already searched us as well as our suitcases, they were in a bit of a quandary. I fully expected them to search the room and find what I'd put under the mattress. But they didn't! Considering that this wasn't the room we had spent the night in, and they had had us under surveillance the entire time, I can only speculate that, in their minds, there was no reason to search this room. They marched us out, back down to the lobby, and ordered us to sit down. While two of the cops were left to stand guard over us, the others asked the cashier for the key to the room we'd stayed in. With the key, they got into the elevator.

About ten minutes later, they returned to hand the key back to the girl at the desk. The officer in charge barked to the other cops to follow him. We just sat there. Nobody said a thing to us. A moment later, they were gone and we were still sitting there, having survived yet another close call. I'd thought we were goners for sure, but for some reason Fate was merciful that day and, once again, let us get away.

We grabbed a taxi and told the driver to take us to Patpong where I would get my stuff from Louis's safe. I went into The Roxy alone while Jamie waited in the car. Louis wasn't in, but his partner got him on the phone. I reported the latest debacle to him, adding that I'd come for my bag stored in his safe. Louis said he'd have his partner get it out for me. Thanking him, I promised to stay in touch.

CHAPTER 25

Life Is a Beach in Southeast Asia

A few hours later, we were in Pattaya, and on our way to a guesthouse where I hoped to find a garden apartment for us. I had always liked this place where the back doors of the apartments fronted vacant land, thick with tropical foliage. There were fruit trees, flowering bushes, vines, and palms. You almost felt like you were sitting at the edge of the jungle. The one I selected had a small patio with a table and chairs out back. It was April and beginning to get really hot; however, in the early morning, it was a wonderful place to sit. There was no air conditioning, only ceiling fans, but it was cheap and away from the hubbub of central Pattaya.

That evening, we went to a friend's restaurant called *Nacho Noi's,* named after my friend Wayne's Thai wife. Wayne was another ex-pat American who had made his home in Thailand. Married to a Thai, he'd easily acquired a resident visa to live here. He had a decent income from his restaurant, a nice house, and he enjoyed the paradise setting and lifestyle of Pattaya Beach.

Back in those days, Pattaya Beach had only a handful of bars, a few restaurants, a tailor, a jeweler, and a few assorted shops with touristy gifts. There were only two major hotels in town. The majority of guesthouses were widely dispersed; most were well away from the main beach road. Pattaya was no longer a sleepy fishing village, yet the beaches remained uncrowded and the fishermen continued to ply their trade as they had for centuries. For fun on the water, there was only one company offering parasailing; another rented jet skis and water bikes. There was no other commerce along the entire stretch of beach. Pattaya was very laid back in 1981 compared to what it is like today. Since I often traveled back and forth between Hawaii and Thailand, I knew most of the store, bar, and restaurant owners. Everyone was very personable, and I was always greeted on a first name basis. Since many visitors from the US, Europe, and Australia returned to Pattaya several times a year, I almost always saw foreigners that I knew when I went into town.

After a few weeks in the guesthouse, we found a nice house to rent. It was walking distance to the center of town, yet tucked away in a quiet neighborhood. It was also air-conditioned. Enduring the sweltering heat at home 24/7 had begun to get old. By now, the temperatures were in the mid-nineties, but the humidity made it feel even hotter. Jamie and I went into town in the early evening almost every day to sit at BJ's Bar for an hour or so and shoot the breeze with BJ, another Vietnam vet who had never returned to the US. He'd been here longer than any of the other Vets in Pattaya and had opened his bar some years earlier. Successful, BJ had lots of regular customers.

At BJ's, you could simply relax because it wasn't a girlie bar. Unlike the Marine Bar, where you were constantly badgered by working girls —"You want a date? You like take me with you?" — there were no prostitutes hitting on you at BJ's; he refused to allow them in his place. At other bars, the girls wouldn't bother me when Jamie was with me, but these places still weren't as comfortable as BJ's, where you could kick back, have a drink, and watch the world go by. Plus, you weren't constantly harassed into buying more drinks.

Pattaya really got crazy when the US Navy ships came in for R&R. They'd dock well away from the shoreline and come ashore in small boats. Every night, there'd be drunken sailors all over the place, in the bars and walking down the streets. Most were only interested in drinking and getting prostitutes and perhaps enjoying a little Thai weed. But there were always a few sailors who just had to try the famous Thai Number 4 heroin. Every year a few sailors died of overdoses. They had no idea what they were playing around with. Inevitably, they'd be with a prostitute in a cheap hotel room when it happened, which meant that the girl, who probably bought the drugs for them, would hurriedly leave. The next day, the hotel manager would usually be the one to find these guys, eyes rolled back in their heads, deader than a doornail.

Around this time, I began calling my ex twice a week and talking to my daughter. I told Rhonda what had happened, that I was temporarily off my plan to go to South Africa. However, her attitude toward me had already changed drastically since that last night in Hawaii. She was cold and emotionless once again, just like she'd been before I left LA.

Rhonda eventually told me that she was seeing someone else; she admitted that she had actually started seeing him before I left Hawaii. So all that talk about *sending for them when I was settled* was simply a momentary twinge of sentimentality. What could I say? I couldn't blame her. Lacking a promising future, I grew deeply depressed, and there was no one I could turn to for help. My heroin habit increased and kept me chronically anaesthetized.

About a week later, Rhonda told me to stop calling because after each conversation I had with my daughter, Debbie was overcome by grief and anguish. She'd cry and throw tantrums, screaming that she wanted her Pita. Rhonda said she couldn't take it anymore, and then she hung up on me. In a total fog of self-pity mixed with self-recrimination, I went into town to the Marine Bar and got stinking drunk.

Jamie was home all this time, expecting me to return after making the phone call. But I didn't arrive home until around 2 AM. She had been worried sick, but when she saw how drunk I was she became enraged, figuring I'd spent the night with some whore. When I told her about the conversation with my ex and how I was no longer allowed to speak with Debbie, she retreated. I just wanted to go to sleep, and asked to talk about it later. Then, I passed-out before even getting undressed.

CHAPTER 26

With Friends Like These

The next morning, another experience emerged from *The Howard Beckman Storybook of Hell*. I awoke to someone calling my name. Four Thai men surrounded me. Each grabbed one of my limbs in one hand and in the other held a razor-sharp machete. Standing at the foot of the bed were two of my old *friends* from Pattaya. Both were ex-Hare Krishna's. One of them, Kerry, had been one of the big leaders of the Hare Krishna movement. He stood there with his arms crossed and a hard look on his face. Chris, the other *brother*, stood to the side of the bed sporting a snide smirk. Jamie had been pulled from the bed and thrown to the floor.

"Where's your money?" Kerry asked gruffly. I was speechless and terrified. The Thai henchmen held my wrists and ankles so tightly that my circulation was being cut off. Their machetes were poised to chop off both of my hands and feet. "Try to be cute and you're a quadriplegic," Kerry warned with an evil laugh. I nodded toward the dresser where Chris immediately began rifling through the drawers; he found some US dollars and Thai *baht*, which he stuffed into his pockets. "What else do you have?" Kerry demanded. "Nothing," I said. "Except a little bit of stash." He'd already found that, but hadn't taken it. There was only about a gram, which wasn't worth much. Besides, they were looking for something a lot bigger. Knowing what had happened to me in the US, they figured I must have a bankroll.

Kerry and Chris had regressed into raging junkies. Previously, they had been heroin smugglers, but now they were nothing but low-life thieves. They had also formerly acted as middlemen for other foreign buyers here in Thailand, but having ripped off their last few customers, nobody went near them anymore. They had become desperate and, therefore, dangerous. When I heard what they'd been up to, I had intentionally steered clear of them. But they had found me.

Chris found some receipts for traveler's checks in the bottom drawer and asked, "Where are the checks for these?" The rest of my receipts were in a different place, in a box underneath the floorboards. The ones he'd found were actually old ones for checks I'd already cashed. "In my bank box," I answered. "But I only have about half that left, maybe less. I've been living off that money."

"Bullshit!" Kerry said, "We want all of it." I knew they wouldn't cut my limbs off at this point because they wanted my money. Turning me into a quadriplegic would make that impossible, so I stuck to my story. "Look, you can think what you want, but that's the truth."

Looking back, Chris had been the *friend* who had been at my apartment in Honolulu when I'd been busted. As far as he knew, when Jamie got the money together for my bail, it took everything I had left in the world. He said to Kerry, "I think he's telling the truth. I'm surprised he even has that much left."

Kerry said, "Alright, here's the deal. I'm going to stay here with Jamie. Chris is going with you to the bank." Turning to Chris he said, "Make sure you go in with him. Then, make him cash the checks and bring the money back here." Turning back to me, he continued, "Once we have the dough, we'll let you and your girlfriend go," adding with a sneer, "and, you can keep your hands and feet."

Kerry was tough and sinister. He and his brother had been bikers in California before they became Hare Krishna's. I knew he meant business. Chris had been indicted a few years earlier for his involvement with the Laguna Beach drug smuggling crowd. Somehow he'd managed to evade arrest. Cunningly, he had found the name and birth details of a baby who had died just after being born at around the same time of his birth. He sent away for a copy of the dead infant's birth certificate. Upon receiving it, he applied for a driver's license as well as other documents in his "new name." When he had all the appropriate documentation in place, he was able to get a passport. Using his new identity, he left the U.S.

Chris and I left on my motorcycle, a Kawasaki 175cc that I purchased soon after Jamie and I got to Pattaya. When we got to the bank I said, "Look, let's cut a deal. I need something to live on. I can't just give you everything. Why don't I give you three-quarters of it, but we'll say it was less. That way you split what we tell Kelly I had, but you'll have extra cash he won't know about." Looking him in the eye, I continued, "How about it?"

I thought appealing to his greed might work, and it did. "Alright," he said, "That works for me." Next, I told him that I wanted to go in alone so it wouldn't look suspicious. Unfortunately, that didn't fly. Chris still insisted on going in with me. I had to think fast since I had a lot more than I was admitting to sitting in the safe deposit box.

I tried to convince him again to wait outside. But, he was adamant. "Kerry will kick my ass from here to Hong Kong. He'll probably cut off both our arms and legs if he finds out I didn't go in." Resigned, I shrugged my shoulders and turned toward the bank. Because Kerry and his thugs were holding Jamie at the house, I had no choice but to cooperate.

We went into the bank and to the safe deposit department. To my great relief, the bank employee at the safe deposit desk said Chris was not allowed in the vault. Only a signer on the account could enter. If I wanted him to come in, he could come into the private room reserved for customer privacy, but not into the vault itself. He told Chris to wait until we came out.

Once in the vault, the employee and I inserted our keys, and opened the drawer. I told him I wanted to check something before going into the room. After setting the box down on a table, with my back toward him, I opened it and grabbed most of the traveler's checks. I slipped them down the front of my pants, into my underpants. Fortunately, I was wearing briefs with tight elastic. After tightening my belt, I closed the box and said, "Thanks for your patience. I'll take it into the room now." We emerged from the vault and Chris was none the wiser. The delay had been no more than twenty seconds.

The bank employee then allowed Chris to go into one of the cubicles with me. As soon as the door closed, he grabbed the box out of my hands and opened it. Inside were the checks and some papers and nothing else. Chris counted out the traveler's checks, and there was even less than I had said back at the house. "See, I told you I didn't think I had even half that amount!"

We would split half of what was there, and the other half, which was about five thousand dollars, he'd take back to Kerry. He'd say that was all there was. Luckily, I'd managed to sequester most of it. "You'll get half of that, minus whatever he's paying those goons you brought with you to scare the shit out of me," I said.

"It worked, didn't it?" Chris answered with a smirk.

"You asshole! I can't believe you went in on this with him," I had to show some bravado. Chris started explaining that it was all Kerry's idea. "If Kerry had gone to the bank with you he would have taken everything, and you know it!"

Staring at him in disbelief I answered, "So that makes it alright, huh? What am I supposed to do? Thank you? You're such a jerk! Go on, take your money, and let's get out of here. With friends like you, who needs enemies?"

I put twenty-five percent of what was there back into the safe deposit box and handed him the rest of the checks. When we emerged, Chris went outside the safe deposit area, while the bank employee led me back into the vault. Once inside the vault, I pulled the two stacks of checks out of my pants. I thanked God that American Express authorized large denomination checks. I then cashed the checks that Chris had been holding in his greedy paws, and then we returned to my house. Chris told Kerry the story, which Kerry readily accepted. Chris embellished, "I went in with him and opened the box myself. This is everything." Without so much as another word, they left. Kerry knew there wasn't anything I could do about it. At least the Thais and their machetes were gone.

CHAPTER 27

Life Goes Further on the Run

In order to escape prying eyes and another unwelcome visit, we moved into another house outside a section of town called *Loi Larn* (a hundred houses). The place was quiet with no foot traffic. The houses were mostly upscale with walls and gated compounds. By this time, I'd missed a hearing on my case in Hawaii, so my bail was revoked, and a warrant had been issued for my arrest. Trying to maintain a low profile, I stopped cutting my hair, and grew a beard.

I also needed to start making some money because what I had wouldn't last forever. Hoping to act as a middleman between my Thai sources and other drug dealers, I telephoned an old customer of mine in Hawaii. According to Louis, Lane and his brother Ty had shown up in Bangkok a few months prior. Louis related a story about two New Zealand Maoris living in Hawaii. They'd come to Thailand to score, but they'd been burned because the dope they bought was only fifty percent pure. Knowing there couldn't be anyone else fitting their description, I called Lane. When I got him on the phone, I relayed the story to him. "Yeah," he said. "It was us. The bastards gave us a gram of pure, but when we got the kilo it was cut to shit. It was maybe 50% at best. I had a hard time getting rid of it. Where the hell are you, anyway? I wish I'd known where to find you." I told him where I was living and that I'd bailed on the case in Hawaii. "They were going to send me down for five years on a first offense," I explained.

Lane said he'd deal with me, as long as I guaranteed him pure Number 4. I assured him that it would be as pure as it comes, just like I used to have in Hawaii. The Plan: Lane would be over in two weeks, and he'd call me when he was on his way. There was no phone at the house, so I gave him a friend's number where he could leave a message.

It should be noted that my Thai friends knew Jamie was Filipino, but almost everyone else thought she was Thai until she started speaking! Beyond hello, goodbye, never mind, and good luck, she couldn't speak a word of Thai. Meanwhile, I was doing my best to learn Thai, which is not easy to do because it is a tonal language, meaning a language in which a single word can have four different meanings, depending on how it's pronounced.

One night, Jamie and I were sitting at the Marine Bar, shooting the breeze with some of the bartenders. They were always glad to help me with my Thai pronunciation, and often got a chance to laugh at my efforts. Once, I tried to order my favorite curry in Thai. The way I pronounced it translated into *prostitute* curry, instead of the yellow curry I thought I was ordering. They enjoyed that one.

Most German male tourists seemed arrogant and loud-mouthed, so much so that many other foreign nationals went out of their way to avoid them. The Germans tended to frequent places with the most action, those with a lot of girls. As the Marine Bar was the biggest in town, they all seemed to congregate here. The more they drank, the louder they became. I'd often heard German voices in the Marine Bar, bragging thunderously to the girls about how big and important they were back in Germany.

On this particular evening, Jamie and I were sitting at one of the smaller sectional bars. Having to go to the bathroom, I left her alone. The music was loud and the place was packed. Guys from all over the world were there, sitting at the various bars and drinking. Clustered around them, of course, were dozens of eager young Thai women, looking for someone to solicit. On the way back to my seat, I ran into a Dutch guy that I'd met on a previous trip, so I stopped to greet him.

When I returned to Jamie, there were two Germans sitting on either side of her. Annoyed, she did her best to let them know she was here with her boyfriend. But, they refused to listen. Both of them were drunk and becoming increasingly unruly and belligerent. I walked over and told one of them that he was in my seat. At the same time, I put my hand on Jamie's shoulder. "This is my girlfriend, guys, not one of the bar girls. Leave her alone. There are lots of other girls here for you to talk to." I motioned with my hand toward the many Thai girls in the bar.

One of them stood up; he must have been at least six foot three. He had short brown hair and a moustache and goatee. Considering the size of his gut, he probably weighed a good 250 pounds. Rather than apologizing, he began berating me at the top of his lungs. "Do you know who I am? In Germany I am Big Man. I *want* this girl."

I answered him calmly while looking him straight in the eye, "To me you look like any other big, fat, sausage-eating, beer-swigging whore-chaser, but that's beside the point. You don't seem to understand that she's *not* a street girl. She's my girlfriend. Now piss off." Normally, I didn't speak like this, but this guy was a complete jerk! Watching what was going on, the bouncers began moving closer. The bartenders were also on the alert, ready to move in a split second if anything occurred.

A few seconds later, the guy grabbed the lapels of my shirt, his face so close to mine that his spittle sprayed me. As though out of his mind, he screamed, "I am Big Man. I *want* this girl. I TAKE this girl!"

That was it. Every single bouncer in the place came charging over, but the bartender closest to us arrived first. He vaulted over the bar like an Olympic gymnast and gave the guy a perfectly executed roundhouse kick to the head.

Almost as if he'd choreographed it, he delivered another perfect kick to the guy's chest as he was going down, and yet another underneath him, sweeping his legs up in the air. The German crashed to the floor like a ton of bricks. All this happened in a split second. Had you blinked, you'd have missed the whole thing.

Two of the bouncers picked the guy up, dragged him out to the street, and threw him into an open dumpster. His friend ran out of the bar as quickly as his feet would take him. Over as quickly as it began, the incident provided a topic of conversation for everyone in the bar for the rest of the evening.

A few weeks later, Lane arrived, alone. He had left his brother at home to take care of business in his absence. He took a room at one of the two big hotels in town, a five star with all the amenities. Lane felt more secure in a big hotel and liked having the use of a safe deposit box for his valuables.

On his first night in Thailand, we took him out for dinner, then over to the Marine Bar for the Pattaya Beach bar experience. Back then, the side of the bar facing the ocean was open, so patrons could watch the sunset. Likewise, we watched the sun disappear on the horizon while nursing our beer. Lane was completely enamored with all the girls, and gazed longingly at one, in particular. Addressing me, he said, "She's gorgeous."

Knowing they were all working girls, I asked him, "Do you want her?"

"What do you mean, do I want her?" he returned.

"Do you want her?" I repeated. "Yeah, I do," he answered.

I gave her 200 *baht*, the going rate of about ten dollars, which she would have to put in the till before devoting her time to him. I told her, "My friend wants you to come with him tonight."

"Who your friend?" she asked. I pointed Lane out to her. Then she said, "Tell him I love him too much," which she pronounced *maaasch*. "Yeah, yeah," I said, "Get your things and come on over," pointing to where we were seated at the bar.

Lane acted like a schoolboy with the woman. I chalked it up to a lack of female companionship in his life, having never actually seen him with a woman before. She played her part well, fawning over him and batting her eyelashes for the next few hours. When I told Lane we were ready to leave, he decided he would, as well. As I'd expected, she accompanied him back to his hotel room for the night.

The next day, he showed up at my house in a rickshaw. She was with him. I was not happy about him bringing her to my house, and I let him know. "She's a working girl, and I don't want her knowing any of my business, much less where I live, Lane." I warned him to keep his business to himself because getting busted in this country was no laughing matter. Lane was obviously annoyed by what I'd said, but he needed to learn, and learn fast: Never trust a whore with your personal business, especially when it might land you in prison for the rest of your life!

Afterwards, I calmed down and tried to ignore the girl. My expectation was that she'd go back to her job at the bar and that would be it. Then Lane and I would get down to business. We had already decided to do the deal in ten days, which would give him plenty of time to get the heroin packed for whoever was smuggling for him. His flight home was in two weeks. Making plans to meet again for dinner that night, he left with the girl.

At around eight o'clock that evening, we met at an Indian restaurant for dinner; afterwards, we went to the Marine Bar, which wouldn't have been my choice, but Lane insisted. I thought maybe he wanted a different girl since many male tourists who enjoy going there behaved like kids in a candy store: So many girls, so little time. Our business wouldn't be finished until the following week, and I really didn't care what he did as long as he didn't tell anyone about *our private business.*

As soon as we walked into the Marine Bar, the same girl from the night before joined us at our table. "Hello," she said to Lane while stroking his hand. Lane said, "Hi sweetheart," and blushed. I glanced sideways at Jamie, meaning: This is bizarre. What's he thinking? He can't be falling in love with her. Really? A prostitute! But soon it became painfully obvious that he was totally enamored with her. His name could have been Lame, instead of Lane. I had seen foreign men fall in love with Thai prostitutes before, but I hadn't expected it of Lane. Especially, since I had warned him about her being a whore. Although I had paid her 200 baht to leave her job the night before, she most definitely had asked him for at least another 500 baht as soon as they reached his hotel room. Women in the sex trade always demand their money up front.

There were plenty of poor schnooks who actually believed the girls' stories. They'd all *just started working yesterday and had come here from the countryside to get work to support their families.* To be fair, most of the girls did start out fairly innocently. A great many really were from rural areas. But once they became prostitutes, generally speaking, only an accident or old age ended their careers, unless they found someone to marry and take them abroad. Those who married out of the sex trade were in the minority. The rest were thieves. If you had your valuables with you, there was always the risk that you'd wake up in the morning to discover the girl had slipped away in the night with your money, passport, and credit cards. Some guys are unbelievably naïve, but Lane, I reasoned, had no excuse for his behavior: We'd bought this girl right out of a bar, and she'd made no bones about being a girl for hire: Pay the 200 *baht* into the till and she's yours for the evening. Having sex, whether for fifteen minutes or an entire night, cost another 500 *baht*.

After an hour or so, Jamie and I said we were going home. Lane opted to leave with his new "girlfriend." At this late hour, I was too tired to have a conversation with him about the girl. Arranging to stop by his hotel at noon for lunch, I figured we'd talk then.

When I knocked on Lane's hotel room door, the girl answered. "Oh brother," I muttered under my breath as I walked in. Lane was still in his boxers. He came up behind her, put his arms around her waist, and gave her a peck on the cheek, which was just too bloody much for me. I felt like puking. I told Lane that we needed to talk ... alone. He said that *Dok* was just getting ready to leave anyway. She picked up her bag, put her arms around his neck, and gave him a big kiss, saying, "See you tonight honey." Lane repeated what she had just said, extending the last word into "*honeeey.*" I honestly hoped I could talk some sense into him once she was gone. Considering what he was here to do, this had become a dangerous liaison by my standards, not only for him, but for me too should she know anything.

Once *the girl* was gone, Lane went into the other room to dress while I sat on the couch flipping through the morning's *Bangkok Post.* As soon as he came out of the bedroom, we ventured downstairs to the restaurant on the outdoor patio next to the pool. The tropical setting was beautiful, full of coconut palms and papaya trees.

"Lane, what's the deal with you and this girl?" I asked.

"I'm in love with her," he answered.

I wanted to grab his shoulders and shake him. "She's a prostitute, Lane, a whore! You can't fall in love with a girl that will have sex with anyone willing to pay 500 *baht* for it! It's ridiculous. If you want a Thai girlfriend, the place to meet nice girls is definitely not in the Marine Bar! They know how to play the game, but they're prostitutes, all the same. You saw me buy her for you out of the Marine Bar on your first night, for Christ's sake!"

Lane's face contorted into a scowl and he warned, "Stay out of my business. I told you, I love her. Tomorrow I'm flying up north with her to meet her family."

"Oh brother," I said, "You're crazy. She'll get you to give her family money, and then suck as much as she can out of you before you leave. Once you're gone, she'll go right back to her job at the bar, happy to go home with any guy who wants her. Believe me! Come on, man, wake up! You don't want to do this!"

Lane's scowl deepened into an angry grimace. Shaking his finger in my face, he snarled, "Say that one more time, and I'm going to punch you in the nose."

I shrugged my shoulders, thinking he was a fool, but I said, "Fine, I won't mention it again." He was obviously out of touch with reality and would have to learn his lesson the hard way. Meanwhile, he and I had business to attend to, so I chose to leave the subject of his love life alone.

In Thailand, there were plenty of dumb-asses who fell in love with prostitutes. Many of the girls could turn a lonely man's knees to jelly. After all, most of the guys who visited were lacking when it came to female relationships back home. The girls knew how to play these guys like cheap violins! You wouldn't believe how many men actually believed that a beautiful Thai woman had fallen in love with them; they were so desperate, they bought it *hook, line, and sinker*. Yet, when it came to Lane, I hadn't seen it coming.

A significant number of gullible men married the girls, getting them Fiancé Visas so they could travel to the US, Europe, or Australia. They proudly wore these gals on their arms like trophies until the girls divorced them after receiving their Green Cards or resident status. You could almost feel sorry for some of these guys, but what did they expect: You marry a woman you paid for sex and then you believe you can reform her? Not!

Wanting to finish our business as soon as possible, I dropped the subject of *Dok* and told Lane to call me when he got back from Chiang Mai. His product would be ready for delivery. Lane said he'd return to Pattaya the following week. He'd left his cash for the purchase locked up in a bank safety deposit box. At least he was smart enough to look out for his money.

Lane showed up at our house the Monday following his return from Chiang Mai. I gave him the address of a guesthouse where I'd made a reservation for him to use for our business. When he arrived at the room, I let him in and asked how it had gone. He told me that he'd met *Dok's* family and gotten her father's blessings to marry her. I should imagine so, I thought, but simply said, "Congratulations, Lane!"

After counting his money, I took the kilo of heroin out of a suitcase and handed it to him. Lane immediately took a little bit of it and asked for a spoon. I sat there while he tested it. Using a tourniquet, he found a vein in his left arm and shot up. Watching someone shoot up is always an unnerving sight.

After removing the tourniquet, Lane leaned back on the sofa, obviously feeling the euphoric rush. "Good stuff, eh?" I asked. "Pure Thai Number 4."

"Yeah, great," he muttered, "Thanks, and, uh, sorry for getting so pissed off at you last week. Let's forget about it now, okay?" "Sure," I said, "Hope it all works out for you two."

"I'll be back in a few months. I'll let you know a few weeks ahead. Maybe next time we can do two of these?" Lane sounded sincere.

"Sure, no problem," I answered. "Just let me know when you're coming."

"*Dok* and I are also going to get married in Chiang Mai next time I'm here," he said. All I could say was, "Congratulations, buddy."

A half hour later, Lane left for his hotel. After watching his taxi pull away, I left the room, dropped off the key at the office, and got on my bike. I strapped the briefcase behind the seat and slowly rode home, uninterested and unaware of the world around me. "What an idiot," I told Jamie when I got back. "He's planning to marry her."

"What about me?" she asked. "When are you going to marry me?"

"Let's not even go there," I said. "My life is in utter turmoil and I don't know what's in store for the next month, let alone think about making wedding plans. What do I do when my passport runs out? I can't just go to the embassy for a new one, can I?" Bleak reality confounded me. What WAS I going to do with my life? I could see no light at the end of the tunnel. Morose and depressed, I was in agony; I felt as if I were chest deep in quicksand and going under fast.

Once I got into the house, I did the usual. Immediately, that warm feeling enveloped me, pushing all that ailed me back into the recesses of my mind. A few hours later, Jamie and I got on the bike and headed into town for dinner. Before starting off, I put my headphones on, clipped my Sony Walkman to my belt and turned on Dire Straits' *Sultans of Swing.* Loud. Because listening to music helped me to stop thinking about my own godforsaken life. At least temporarily.

For the next few months I lived a truly meaningless existence. One minute I was calmly enjoying the easy life, the next I was overwhelmed with hopelessness and despair. I wanted to get off the merry-go-round I was on. But where could I go? What could I do? Something had to give. I kept having this premonition that what was next wasn't going to be pretty, but I was too depressed to care. Fate would reveal her answer soon enough.

At length, I decided I was going to go to the Seventh Day Adventist Hospital in Bangkok. I used to go there before returning to the US when I was doing my smuggling runs. At their outpatient clinic, you could get a prescription for methadone, no questions asked, by simply telling them you were a heroin addict and wanted to quit. After taking urine and blood samples, they'd even fill the prescription for you right there at the hospital pharmacy. Back then, the methadone had allowed me to make the flight back home without going through withdrawals. The bottle, written prescription, and receipt were kept in my carry-on bag. Should an overeager customs official find the pills, there'd be nothing they could say or do. It was totally legit.

This time, though, I wanted to quit heroin, not just for a flight, but once and for all; without quitting, I'd never have any hope in hell of creating a new life for myself. I'd tried so many times before, but something always happened to sap my resolve. Most often, it was another deal that I couldn't turn down. I was tired of making excuses. If I kept going the way I was, I'd end up in prison … or dead. Tomorrow. Tomorrow. Tomorrow, I'd go up to Bangkok and get the methadone pills. *The best laid plans of mice and men.*

CHAPTER 28

Life in "The Hole"

Unfortunately, the opportunity to go to the hospital the following day never came. The memories of the past dissipated as I opened my eyes. It took a while before it all sank in. What had happened? Where was I? Struggling to sit up, my body felt broken. Everything hurt. The blinding, searing pain in my head was worse than anything I had ever endured. Moving slowly, I attempted to check the severity of my wounds. I crawled over to the water bucket, dipped a piece of my shirt into it, and gently cleaned the wounds on my arms, legs, chest, and forehead. The bleeding had stopped, but the pain was excruciating.

Using the bucket to pee in wasn't too hard. Taking a crap was going to be another matter, but I didn't have to, at least not yet. Moving over to the wall, I gingerly leaned back, trying to find a comfortable position, which proved to be impossible. Eventually, I found a section of the wall flat enough to lean against. I sat there in a state of shock.

Sometime later, a young boy brought me food, a plate of *cow dang* (red rice) and a bowl of fish head soup. I asked him if he could go to my building and get me some food. He shook his head no.

"I can't eat this shit," I cried into the emptiness surrounding me, but nobody was there to hear. "I need to get food from my building!" I called out to any guard who might be in earshot. I heard movement in the courtyard outside the isolation cells. Still, nobody answered, and nobody came. Finally, a guard came to the door, and speaking to him in Thai, I pleaded for him to bring me food from my building. He told me to shut up.

A few minutes later, I heard the sound of keys and a bolt being drawn back. Crawling forward, I lifted my head up as straight as possible considering my confined space. The guard opened the door and motioned me forward. As soon as I reached the door, he kicked me in the face so hard that I smashed my head on the stone ceiling, then collapsed in a heap. The gash on my forehead opened up and began bleeding again. Body wracked with pain, I lay on the floor, moaning. The guard slammed the door shut, locked it, and walked away. No mercy for me.

I don't know how long I laid there. After a while, I managed to rise up onto my knees. Crawling once again to the bucket, I scooped out some water with my hands to clean my head wound. The bastard had also kicked me in the nose with his boot; I thought for sure it was broken. My face was swollen, my entire head throbbed, and my hair was completely matted in blood.

Leaning against the clammy wall, I bemoaned my fate, thinking about how close I had been to getting out of this place. Breaking down, I cried like a baby. My heart was broken, my entire *being* felt broken. I felt so completely and utterly ruined. Hidden from the world and from anyone who cared about me, I had reached the end of the line. I moved and rested on my elbows until they wouldn't hold me up anymore. Next, I tried to lean against the wall again, but ended up lying on my side, head resting on one arm.

The ceiling became a screen on which to project my thoughts. Half conscious, I gazed upwards. Suddenly, I saw a huge black and white spider in the corner. Spiders generally keep to themselves, but I had no idea what kind it was, so I kept my eye on it. The cockroaches here were gigantic, and they flew. We used to call them flying dates. You had to get used to them scurrying around, even over your body, during the night. Hopefully, the spider's web would catch a few of them.

The next thing I knew I was regaining consciousness. I'm not sure if I'd passed out from the pain or just fallen asleep from sheer exhaustion. I tried to raise myself up onto my hands and arms. Struggling, I finally managed to sit up; remembering the spider, I looked around for it, but it was nowhere to be seen.

My mouth and throat were parched and my head throbbed. I crawled over to the bucket for some water. There was a filthy cracked plastic pitcher there, but I wasn't going to put any water in it. I drank from my cupped hands and did my best to relax. It was pitch dark outside so I had no idea what time it was. It was obviously the middle of the night, but what did it matter?

For two days, I could only lay there, turning this way and that. My surface wounds began to develop scabs, but I had no idea how severe my internal injuries were. Everything hurt inside. I managed to pee and saw blood in my urine, but not a lot. I also had diarrhea. A lot. Since neither issued much blood, I figured they hadn't burst my kidneys or any other organs, but still, I knew I was hurt badly. I could do nothing about my injuries except endure them. I prayed that infection would not set in.

Twice daily, the boy brought me horrible gruel. Once a day, someone else filled my water bucket and emptied my toilet bucket. Bathing was out of the question. I wasn't allowed out of the cell for any reason whatsoever. To be honest, I don't think I could have gotten out of it by myself anyway.

I tried to keep track of the days by making lines in the dirt in the corner. On the fifteenth day, a guard came, unlocked the cell, and told me to come out. I would be allowed to bathe. Managing to roll out of the cell, I slowly and painfully greeted the outside. I was momentarily blinded by bright sunlight. Slowly, I rose to my knees, then very shakily to my feet.

The guard motioned for me to walk toward a water tank, about twenty yards away. Holding the chains between my ankles up off the ground with my right hand, I shuffled over. My pants and underwear were caked with dried blood. I took the bathing sarong and plastic bowl he offered me, but told him I needed to have the pants cut away from my body. A boy came with a knife, and while three guards stood watching, he slit my pants from the bottom to the crotch, then cut around the top of the pant legs. He made several more incisions from pant legs to waist. Before I removed the pants, I soaked them with water from the tank, hoping to protect the scabs and not cause the wounds to begin bleeding again.

Somehow I managed. The bruises on my legs were grotesque, but most of the blood that had soaked my pants had come from the injuries to my upper body. Painstakingly wrapping the bathing sarong around myself, I bathed slowly, pouring bowls of water over my head and body. By the time I'd finished, another guard appeared holding one of my T-shirts as well as a long sarong. I could only assume that they'd had Helmut get them for me.

Every little movement was severely painful, but I managed to slip the shirt over my head and pull it down. Wrapping the sarong around me, I knotted it to keep it from falling off. I had no underwear, but I didn't care. Instead of taking me back to the hole, I was led out of the prison gates to a waiting paddy wagon where other prisoners were already inside. Obviously, we were going to court. This time I had to go in chains. I wasn't the only one, but mine were the biggest and heaviest the prison had.

Walking with any sense of dignity was impossible. I had to bend over, holding the chains off the ground with one hand as I shuffled along. My back was killing me. I had back problems ever since my car accident years ago in Honolulu. Having to walk like this was insufferable. Still, I bore it. I had no choice.

Soon, we arrived at the courthouse. I had no idea if Jamie knew what had happened to me because I hadn't seen her since our last visit. I asked the guard if she'd been to see me, he barked, "No visit!" When we were locked in one of the large communal cells downstairs, I walked to the bars fronting the hallway in hopes of seeing her. I hoped she would come. Possibly the lawyer had found out what had happened to me and told her. About ten minutes later I saw her, looking distraught and harried. She asked to speak with me, but the guard shook his head no until he saw the hundred *baht* note she had folded in her hand. Pocketing the note, he let her come over to speak to me.

Seeing the condition of my face, Jamie started crying, "What happened? And why won't they let me visit you? The guard that takes the food I bring said you weren't allowed visitors anymore. I kept trying every day. I only knew you were coming today because he told me. Your court date wasn't supposed to be for a few days. What's going on?"

Her words tumbled out of her mouth all at once along with the tears that streamed down her cheeks. Poor Jamie seemed close to a nervous breakdown. At that moment, I loathed myself. Feeling completely worthless, I reminded myself that what I'd done, I'd done not only to myself, but to Jamie, too. I explained what happened, and that I was being held in solitary confinement. The worst thing was that now I had a second court case to deal with. When Jamie looked down and saw my chains, she screamed, "Oh my God!"

She wailed and wailed. It was pitiful to watch her, stooped over, sobbing, her hands grasping the bars to keep from falling over. "It will be okay baby, don't worry. It will be okay," I said, but my words failed to console her.

When she was finally able to talk, she asked, "Now what's going to happen?"

"Go call Somwan," I told her. "Tell him they're charging me with another case, which he needs to find out about. Ask him to *please* come to see me. Today's an arraignment on the new charge." Finally, looking at her tear-stained face, I added, "I'm so sorry, hon. I can't believe I've done this to us."

Then, guards called us out to go into the courtroom. One told Jamie it was time for her to leave. She listlessly walked away, shoulders hunched forward, dragging her feet. Bending over and picking up my chains, I shuffled off to the courtroom with the other prisoners. Same as last time, I had no idea what was being said. Shortly, I heard my name called out. A guard motioned for me to stand up. The prosecution read out what I assumed were the new charges against me. The judge looked at me, frowned, and said something to me, but I couldn't understand what it was. Next, a guard motioned for me to sit down again.

A half-hour later, we were led out of the courtroom, back to the holding cell. Walking to the very back, I practically collapsed on the floor as I tried to sit down. With cuts and bruises all over my body, as well as acute abdominal pain, it was difficult for me to either stand up *or* sit down. Not knowing the extent of my internal injuries, I was unsure when or if they would ever heal, especially in prison. No medical attention had been offered so it was unlikely that any would be forthcoming.

I finally began to realize how far down the precipice of life I'd fallen; the hole I'd dug for myself kept getting deeper and deeper. It was as if I was witnessing someone else's life instead of my own. My mind refused to accept that the nightmare was real; all of this had actually happened. A few hours more, and we were herded once again into the prison wagon. As soon as we passed through the doors into the compound, I was pulled aside and thrown, literally, back into The Hole. That son-of-a-bitch guard again pushed against the small of my back with his boot just as I stepped down into the cell. The kick sent me crashing to the floor, nearly smashing my head on the wall. Slamming the door shut, he muttered something in Thai, which meant animal.

My head wound had scabbed over, but it was still puffy and swollen. The climate here is so hot and humid that even the slightest cuts usually became infected. My head was tender and painful; I knew my wound was infected, but there was nothing I could do. Every morning and every night the boy would bring me red rice, gruel with fish heads, a few vegetable stalks, and God knows what else. I asked him about getting some medicine (antibiotics for infection), but he was only a prisoner and simply said, *mai loo* (I don't know). After putting some of the veggie stalks from the soup onto the rice, I poured some of the juice on it, just enough to make it soft. Slowly, I started to eat. I'd been pushing the fish heads aside, but I knew that I had to eat the rice and some of the gruel just to stay alive.

A moment later, I chomped down on a rock and broke one of my teeth. I spit the piece of tooth into my hand; it was about half of one of my molars. I knew at that moment, and for the foreseeable future, if I remained alive, I would experience even more unimaginable suffering. Although I tried to be as careful as possible while eating afterward, I ended up breaking yet another tooth while I was still in The Hole.

Two days later, I was taken out of my subterranean dungeon, and escorted up to the visiting room where Jamie and Somwan were waiting. Somwan frowned and said, "Mr. Beckman, what you have done has ruined everything. We made the payments, and you would have been getting out tomorrow with only a fine. But now the judge is going to sentence you to prison time. He says he will only give you two years, since he has accepted our payment, yet now he cannot let you go with a fine."

I just looked at him. What could I say? Every word he spoke was the truth. Turning to Jamie he continued, "Call my office tomorrow afternoon and I will tell you the date of his next court appearance."

I showed Jamie my head and told her I thought the wound was infected. She promised to get some ampicillin and bring it for me the next day. The guard she'd become friendly with would make sure it got to me. They turned and left, and the guards escorted me back toward my hellhole. Shuffling down the cement stairs, crouching like an ape as I held up my chains, I fully understood what *reaching rock bottom* means. I stooped to climb down into the hole, hoping to get in before the guard kicked me. I managed to dodge his boot, but slipped, banging my head against the edge of the gate as the iron door slammed shut behind me.

The Twilight Zone. Nothing about my life seemed real. The image of my daughter's face flashed before my mind's eye and I cried my heart out, sobbing until my stomach cramped. My life was over. I would never again see Debbie's smiling face. An hour later, the boy brought the rice and gruel, but I couldn't eat. The hell with it, I thought. I don't care anymore. Or so I thought for the moment, but somehow, we human beings manage to adapt to most situations we find ourselves in, no matter how horrible. Almost anyone will choose life over death, no matter how untenable *life* may be.

Large spiders and other insects had begun making their home in my water bucket, shaping patterns on the surface of the water as they moved. I had no idea what all was in there. I not only had to use it to clean myself after using the poop bucket, but it was my drinking water, too. There was no choice. Drink it or die. If I died from drinking it, oh well. Without drinking water, death was certain. Besides those in my water bucket, there were also plenty of spiders, cockroaches, and other insects crawling about on the walls and ceiling. They were my only companions. Before long, I became immune to it all, resigning myself to whatever Fate had already decided. Whatever diseases I might get, or whatever other travails awaited me, even death, at this point, it was all in the hand of Fate.

Time stood still. The outside world ceased to exist. In my private hell again, I thought about the life that I'd led back in Hawaii. How I'd ruined all the opportunities presented to me. The realization came that no matter what excuses I made, everything that happened to me was due to the choices I had made. Nobody else was to blame. I had known better than to go down this road, yet I went there, willingly. A verse from the *Bhagavad-Gita* came to mind when Krishna asked Arjuna, "How have these impurities come upon you?" I remembered the words of my teacher, "*In this world, we are each flying our own planes. Krishna (God) never usurps our free will, so we are free to serve Him, or to serve Maya (illusion)."* Without question, I was fully in the clutches of Maya. She managed to soundly trounce me because I had made myself vulnerable. Waves of sorrow and regret washed over me. I felt sorry. Sorry for those I had hurt, sorry for all my failings, and sorry for myself.

Falling into a disturbed sleep, I dreamt of my daughter, Debbie. I was with her in the park playing on a seesaw. She was laughing gleefully. When I awoke, I couldn't remember much else. Sadness enveloped me like a dark cloak of all-encompassing despair.

Day after day, week after week, I languished in my subterranean chamber. At first, I was so weak I slept constantly, day and night, waking only for short periods of time. It was a temporary escape from the grim reality that had become my life. One day, when the boy brought me my allotted portion of gruel and rice, I noticed the absence of fish heads in it. There also seemed to be more vegetables than before. I'd recently told him that I was a vegetarian when he asked me why I never ate the fish. The boy was the one to scoop-out my meal from a larger container and I suppose he was showing me some kindness by leaving the fish heads out and attempting to get as many vegetables as possible.

I began pushing the rice to one side of the plate, taking a small quantity from the pile to spread it out. I did this in an attempt to remove the rocks before eating. It took time, but time was the only thing I had plenty of. Eating slowly, trying not to break another tooth, I began to gain a little strength, physically, at least. Contemplation was certainly my only friend. All I did was eat, excrete waste into the bucket, and think. I began to assess my entire life. The question that constantly haunted me was: Why had I taken this road to nowhere? Remembering the mantra that was so dear to my previous spiritual regimen, I tried to concentrate on it, repeating it over and over in my head and concentrating on the vibration. I chanted softly so that I could hear it. Day after day, I battled with my mind while chanting the mantra:

HARE KRISHNA, HARE KRISHNA

KRISHNA, KRISHNA, HARE HARE

HARE RAMA, HARE RAMA

RAMA, RAMA, HARE HARE

By now, I was allowed out of the dungeon once a day to bathe. Holding up my chains, I would slowly shuffle over to the water tank. Taking my time, I delayed the inevitable return as long as possible. Every day was the same. Besides bathing and eating, I would chant my mantra. Otherwise, I was either trying to sleep or think. I'd realized where I'd gone wrong, but had yet to understand how to go *right*. Honestly, even with all my previous attempts at walking the spiritual path, I finally determined that I had read the book, but missed the plot.

On the morning of my court date, I was taken out to bathe as usual. An hour after being locked back in the hole, one of the guards returned and unlocked the door. It was time to go to court. After the short drive, I was taken down to the holding cell. Somwan came down to see me shortly after I arrived at the courthouse. "You will receive a two-year sentence," he shared without emotion. "I'm sorry, but this is the best we could get after you were arrested in prison." Frowning, as usual, he walked away and back up the stairs. Before long, I was taken into the courtroom, along with the other prisoners. When my name was called, I stood up as the charges were read. The judge quickly said something and brought the gavel down. Done! The guard motioned for me to sit down again. Afterwards, back in the holding cell, I saw the guard who had let Jamie see me at my last court appearance; he whispered to me *song pee* (two years). He held up two fingers, adding *choke dee* (good luck).

Jamie showed up just when we were about to leave, but the guard let her speak to me, anyway. "Where were you?" I asked, "They gave me two years." She looked at me and started to cry. She was having an extremely hard time. She hadn't been able to get a ride to the courthouse. She had to take the bus, and it arrived late. All I knew to say was, "I'm so sorry, hon." Jamie only nodded her head and, crying, turned to walk away. When the guard motioned for me to go, I had to follow the line. Numb and disbelieving my fate, I was soon back in isolation inside a living grave.

The next day, Somwan showed up to see me, and I was glad if for no other reason than it got me out of the hole for a while. I asked him what would happen to me now. "Soon they will transfer you to Bangkok. You will go to *Lard Yao*, to Klong Prem Prison," he answered, "but you still have the matter of the other case. There is also another problem which may affect the sentence you receive on that charge."

"What's that?"

"Someone is saying you were part of a heroin syndicate and the American DEA has been talking with the Thai police."

Flushed, panicked, and needing answers, I asked, "What's that about?

"This is over my head," Somwan answered. "Only if they bring additional charges against you will I be able to find out more, but that is what the prosecutor told me when I went to speak with him about your other case."

"What could happen?"

"No use worrying about it now. I hope they don't have enough evidence to prove this allegation, because if they do, it can mean a prison sentence of fifty years ... or more. You would then go to Bang Kwang Prison to serve your sentence. However, even if they do not, just for this second case from inside the prison, it is likely you will receive a minimum of ten more years. Any sentence under twenty years usually means you stay in Lard Yao." Somwan just looked down, "I am very sorry, Mr. Beckman."

CHAPTER 29

Alone Behind Blue Eyes

The sheer hopelessness of it all was overwhelming. Any hopes I'd had for the future had been extinguished. It was highly likely that I'd be imprisoned in Thailand for at least the next twelve years. The judge had the latitude to give me as much as 20 years should he be so inclined. I most likely would be kept like an animal in a cage, constantly fearing torture and abuse. Would my story end on this note? How could I survive? This couldn't be happening to me! I wanted to wake up and find it had been a bad dream, but that wasn't going to happen.

Over the next month or so, I was physically assaulted numerous times. Most of the time, it was after I'd been let out for my daily bath and was attempting to climb back into the hole. No matter how hard I tried to jump down as soon as the door was opened, I was never fast enough. I was kicked in the back, hips, thighs, and even the back of my head more times than I could keep track of. Tired and worn out, my body grew thinner and thinner, my mind grew more and more depressed. Sometimes I felt like giving up; death would be better than enduring this treatment.

Yet, something made me hang on. More than a few times, I was either beaten with a baton or subjected to a volley of kicks for failing to walk quickly enough back to the hole or for tripping over my chains. Those "offenses" brought vengeance down on me at least four or five times a week. Always at the ready with their batons, the guards took any opportunity to crack it across my back or to knock my legs out from under me. One of the guards, the one we had named Hitler, was the worst. He always wore a look of glee on his face as he beat me or kicked me into my cell with the bottom of his boot. Like a dog at the hands of a cruel and sadistic master, I endured all my beatings without protest.

One of my assaults, in particular, stands out as the single most terrifying encounter I experienced in Chonburi Prison. A guard came to my cell one night, unlocked the door, and motioned for me to come out. I knew it was after midnight because only the croaking of frogs interrupted the silence. He ordered me to climb out of my dungeon and follow him to another area of the prison. Not knowing why he was taking me out of my cell, I hoped that maybe I was going to be taken back to my former building. That was not the case.

Pac Man, a name he'd earned because he had a round head that seemed too large for his body, showed me a small bottle of heroin. Speaking in broken English he said, "I give you. You make with me," putting his finger in his fist to crudely illustrate what he wanted. He tried to make me get on my hands and knees, but I refused. I cringed when he raised the baton to strike me. Fearing for my life, I decided to charge him. I slammed into him with all my weight, knocking him down. Trying to run, which was really impossible due to the mammoth shackles, I screamed, "Noooooo! Help! Help! Help! Somebody! Help!"

I was screaming at the top of my lungs, in both Thai and English, knowing that both the guards and the prisoners had to hear. We were outside, so I knew that my loud cries would carry all around the compound. *Pac Man*, back on his feet, swung his stick at me with all the force he could muster. I lunged out of the way, but he landed blow upon blow, hitting me repeatedly on my legs and back. Falling to the ground, I curled into a ball and cradled my head protectively in my hands and arms. But one blow managed to hit me in the back of the head. Everything faded, my vision blurred, and

I couldn't hear. Everything seemed to be happening in slow motion. Eventually, *Pac Man's* boot came at me and found its mark in the small of my back. The pain was so excruciating, I thought I was going to pass out. Throughout the beating I tried to scream, but nothing came out. Too weak to resist, I finally lost consciousness.

I faintly heard approaching voices and running foot-steps; it was the night officer in charge and some of the other prison guards. The guard who attacked me could not explain why I was out of my cell because, obviously, someone had to let me out.

"This shit head was trying to rape me," I said in Thai, as two of the guards grabbed me under my arms and began to lift me up from the ground. The officer barked orders to the guards. Two guards, each holding me under an arm, carried me back to the hole. They didn't say a word as they helped me down into the cell. This was the first time, in a long time, I had gone in without being kicked through the door.

I was dazed and racked with pain. I figured I would be dead before the sun rose. There was a large swollen contusion at the back of my neck, and I couldn't turn my head. I considered that my neck might be broken because of the way *Pac Man* had struck me mercilessly with his baton. His kicks had all but crushed the life out of me before the other guards rescued me. The welts all over my chest, arms, and back were swollen and discolored. My head throbbed so much that it felt like it might burst. I thought death was imminent. My left ring finger must have taken a hit when I tried to block the blows; it was swollen to at least five times its normal size. Clearly, I was shaken to the core and I most likely had a concussion. Going to sleep might mean I wouldn't wake up, but I couldn't stay awake. Finally, I surrendered myself to the will of Providence. I didn't like the idea of dying in such a cursed place where I would be forgotten by the rest of the world.

Praying, I begged for forgiveness for the pain and hurt I'd caused Debbie, Jamie, my family, and my ex-wife. I was fully cognizant of the pain to others I had caused by my descent into the sordid world of drugs. This was where it was all going to end, alone in a dark dungeon in Southeast Asia. My life seemed to have come to its woeful conclusion. Finally, no longer able to keep my eyes open, I lost consciousness.

The next morning, one of the guards came to my cell and opened the door. I remained still and watched, but rather than entering, the guard backed away. I thought I was supposed to go out to bathe, but I wasn't sure that I could get up, let alone get myself out of the cell and over to the bathing tank. Slowly, I tested my limbs and felt my head and neck. I tried to turn my head, but I had little range of motion and the pain was agonizing. It was so hard to get up with my battered and swollen legs, but eventually I managed to get on my hands and knees. Slowly, I crawled to the door. Getting my hips up to ground level, I rolled out of the cell. It was difficult to lift my arms much less hoist myself up the step, but somehow I did. Once my torso was outside the door, I sat up and lifted my legs out of the cell. The chains felt like they weighed a hundred pounds. Once I cleared the cell door, I rolled onto my side and pushed myself up to a crouching position.

I remember stooping over and holding the chains with one hand as I shuffled along just inches at a time. Painfully, I reached the water tank, where I scooped out half-filled bowls of water and poured them over myself with one hand while holding on to the side of the tank with the other. After a few feeble attempts to wash, the bowl dropped from my hand. I collapsed onto the ground and then leaned against the water tank. Several guards had been watching me; one of them barked orders at the prisoner who had been bringing my meals every day. He told the man to help me. Over and over again, he poured water over my head while I remained seated on the ground. I tried to clean myself, but I couldn't lift up my arms past my ribs. Piercing pain shot through my stomach, ribs, and groin. My head and neck throbbed, and my left ring finger was the size of a small banana; the top digit was bent and immovable. The only appendage that wasn't totally battered was my right hand.

Bit by bit, I managed to get myself cleaned up, using only my good right hand. Afterwards, I wrapped my sarong around my waist, expecting to be taken back to the hole. As I started to shuffle back to my underground cell, the guard yelled in broken English and pointed toward the building where the other prisoners were housed, "Stop! You go back with foreigners today!"

He walked me back to the building where Michael, the first to see me, gasped, "What the bloody 'ell happened to you, mate?" He put his arm around me to help me walk into the building. Having to carry the iron shackles fastened around my ankles, I was horribly stooped over. Michael practically carried me inside where I collapsed on a wooden sleeping platform.

Many of the foreigners came in to see how I was. All they could say was, "Man oh man!" or "Holy shit!" But, in time, the guys started asking me, "You alright, man? What'd they do to you?" After hearing the story of my recent *Near Death Experience by Bludgeoning*, they were speechless. Nearly everyone incarcerated there had been hit or smacked at one time or another, but nothing like what I had endured. None of the foreigners had ever been put in chains or locked in The Hole.

One American, returning from the canteen, took one look at me, whistled, and then hollered, "Howard, you look like shit!" which made me smile, although it hurt.

"Thanks, Eddy. Good to see you, too." Others began filling him in on my recent traumatic experience while two of the guys helped me over to my place on the platform and unrolled my mat and blankets. I should add that my things were only available because Helmut had taken responsibility for keeping my possessions safely under his bunk.

In contrast to the hard dirt floor of the hole, my new accommodations seemed somewhat luxurious. I was grateful for the change. Besides the wounds from the beatings, my ankles also had infected sores, especially along the backs of my Achilles tendons, a result of wearing rusty iron shackles.

At some point, someone went to the canteen to get antibiotics for me. Fortunately, Louie sent some over, and within a few days the infection started to clear up.

Within a few months, my chains were removed because I was being transferred to Bangkok. The scabs on the back of my feet remained for a while before clearing up. The scars proved to be permanent. The worst one still looks like a keyhole on the back of one of my Achilles tendons. My left finger remains permanently bent since I never was able to see a doctor or get a proper splint. I had taped a small piece of wood to it, hoping to keep it straight, but the kick had crushed the bone at the topmost joint. When it finally healed, I could move it slightly, but to this day, I can't straighten it, and it has a permanent hump at the top of the joint. My permanent injuries/scars were *mementos* to remind me that what I had been through was not a bad dream, but reality.

Jamie continued to come to see me twice a week. She had moved into a small one-room apartment; she was the only foreigner living in the building. "How you making out?" I asked when I saw her.

"Alright," she answered. I could tell that she was not all right, but I didn't press her, knowing that there was absolutely nothing I could do to help her. I was deeply thankful that she still continued to visit me. After giving some food to the guard for me before leaving, she turned back momentarily to throw a kiss. I did the same as she walked through the gates. With a sigh, I slowly returned to the prison compound. Climbing up onto my bed, I stared solemnly at the ceiling.

By this time, the realization had sunk in that Thai prison would be my home for a long time. Day after day, I spent countless hours lost in my private thoughts. I had sabotaged myself, not only with the second drug possession charge, but also with all my bad decisions over the past three years. If only I could reverse time. However, we only have 20/20 vision in hindsight; I had to accept my fate.

For the next few weeks, I spent my days either sitting on a bench outside or lying down inside my single-room building. Miraculously, on a positive note, my body actually began to heal. Since my digestion was still working properly, my bladder, bowels, and other key functions followed suit. The kicks I had received to my kidneys left the most painful internal bruises, but everything was slowly healing. Michael noted that I was lucky to be alive after the thorough thrashing that bastard had given me. *Pac Man* was nowhere to be seen after that night. Maybe he'd been transferred, or maybe they did everyone a favor and got rid of him. Frankly, I didn't care.

One afternoon, I was called out for a visit. Expecting to see Jamie, I was surprised to find Somwan. "How are you getting along, Mr. Beckman?" he inquired.

"Oh, I've been better," I replied, managing a smile because he cared enough to visit me. He didn't say anything about the recent beating I received and that led me to assume he didn't know about it. I chose not to mention it. I simply didn't feel like retelling and reliving my ordeal.

"In a few days you will be transferred to Bangkok to serve the rest of your two-year sentence," he told me. When I asked him about the status of the other case, he explained that there were many cases pending in the courts, so many that he had easily gotten mine pushed back. "If we are lucky, you will finish serving the two-year sentence before it comes up. Then, maybe, we can get you out on bail."

"Did you find anything else out about what the prosecutor told you?" I asked.

"No, but no news is good news, as you Americans say. I don't think they have enough evidence to charge you in Thailand. If they did, they'd have done so already. But, the judge is almost sure to give you at least ten years on this other charge since it is a second offense." Whatever it is, it is, and that meant I couldn't do anything about it.

"I will come to see you in Bangkok as soon as I know something," Somwan said as he stood up to leave.

That night, I awakened sometime around midnight to a blood-curdling scream. It sounded like a woman screaming for her life. It went on for what seemed like several minutes.

The chilling sound made me shudder. When I first heard it I bolted up, thinking someone was being tortured. Loud and shrill, the screams were ear-piercing. The terror in the woman's voice brought a dark feeling to my heart, and I began crying. It sounded as if some demon was cutting her up, slicing off one limb at a time, delighting in the most sadistic and terrifying acts that a person could do to another person.

The next morning when I went to visit Louie, I told him what I'd heard and asked him if he'd heard it also. He had. The source of the blood-curdling screams was neither woman nor man. They were the fearful screams of terror and agony emanating from a pig as they held it down for slaughter. Remembering those terrible screams, even now I shudder.

If only I hadn't. If only I hadn't was the game my mind constantly played while it raced through the various scenarios that had transpired during the past year. But, life doesn't have a rewind button: *You make your bed, and then you lie in it.* I had made mine into a bed of nails. And, there I'd lay for at least the next few years ... quite possibly longer.

CHAPTER 30

Klong Prem Prison
"The Bangkok Hilton"

A month later, I was transferred to Klong Prem Prison, more famously known as The Bangkok Hilton. I couldn't believe it had been eight months since that fateful day of my arrest in Pattaya Beach. It had happened in October of 1981, and now here it was the summer of 1982, and I was the only foreigner being transported to Bangkok. Boarding the prison paddy wagon, I joined a group of Thai inmates who were also being transferred to Klong Prem Prison. The trip would take an hour and a half.

Upon arrival, all I could see was a massive wall. The truck pulled through a set of large double doors leading into a gigantic garage-like holding area. After the doors had closed behind us, the truck doors were flung open and several guards ushered us out. We were ordered to line up facing several officers. I had no idea what they were saying, so I just watched what the other prisoners were doing and followed suit. I'd been processed into a prison twice before so I had a basic understanding of the drill. Everyone had to empty their pockets and place the contents on the ground. Next, we were subjected to a thorough search. After being ordered to strip naked, we piled our clothes on the ground in front of us. Guards went through each prisoner's clothing in search of contraband. They made us bend over, one at a time, spread our butt cheeks wide, then lift up our testicles, so they could see if we were concealing anything.

Actually, the butt cheek check wasn't foolproof, I'd learned. Many prisoners hid drugs up their ass. Using a small plastic vial with heroin tightly wrapped in plastic inside, they would slide it up inside their butts. Once the vial got past the sphincter muscle, it was no longer visible. Using this method, even a cavity search would not reveal the hidden stash. Some men tell stories of smuggling as much as six to eight ounces of heroin out of the country this way. One at a time, they'd insert the compressed heroin, tightly packed in condoms, well inside their bodies and hold it there for as many as forty-eight hours or longer.

When the search was finished, we were told to get dressed again. Next stop was Building 6. Some prisoners stayed there if their sentences were a year or less, but most were transferred to another building within a month. To start off, I was shown to a cell in Building 6. Four men shared one cell. The cells were no more than cement block cubicles with steel doors. I brought my bedroll from Chonburi Prison, so I put it against the wall where three other bedrolls were already placed. My cellmates were out in the compound. The buildings were off-limits during the day, unless you were in solitary confinement. Without exception, inmates spent their days out in the compound.

I was escorted out to the compound where we would stay until the whistle blew in the late afternoon, signaling prisoners to enter their. I decided to take a walk and explore the compound. Thai prison society is very cellblocks different from European or US prison society because Thai convicts don't segregate themselves into racially divided groups. Thailand has had immigrants arrive throughout the centuries, like anywhere else, but most of the country's residents are Thai, Chinese, or a combination of the two. You hardly ever hear of racial bashing there. Race is not the contentious issue it is in prisons in Western countries. Wherever I went, other prisoners greeted me, mostly by nodding. There was no undercurrent of fear amongst prisoners due to bullying or abuse from other inmates. It was the guards and their physical and mental torture that were feared. Rarely did inmates have reason to fear other inmates.

Before long, I started running into other foreigners. One in particular, another American, invited me to sit down for a while. Ronnie was also in for heroin possession, the same as 90% of the other foreign inmates. He had received a two and a half year sentence.

Although the Thais had to work, foreigners were basically allowed to just hang out. None of us were forced to do anything in terms of work or duties. I spent the first week walking around, getting used to the surroundings, as well as meeting most of the Thais who ran the place. Not the guards, mind you, because the less you dealt with them, the better off you were. Thais are generally a friendly people, and the Thai inmates were no different. They enjoyed conversing with foreigners, probably because their paths rarely crossed with foreigners when on the outside.

There was plenty of contraband for sale inside, but at this point, I wanted to keep my nose clean, which was easier said than done. All three of my cellmates were in for heroin, and two of them, both Frenchmen, were doing it every chance they could. The third, Bobby, an American, was just plain weird. I couldn't really put my finger on it, but he was strange in a schizophrenic kind of way. He seemed to live in some kind of alternate world, sometimes giggling to himself, sometimes morose and angrily muttering. In here, you could choose your friends, but not your cellmates. As for me, I tried to get along with my cellmates.

I spent my days walking around the compound speaking mostly to the Thai inmates I'd befriended. It was a good exercise in linguistics. They got to practice their English, and I got to practice my Thai. Twice daily, I had my meals at the "restaurant" next to the Chicken Death Camp, where unspeakable acts of "food preparation" were performed. The free prison cuisine here was the same vile gruel and red rice that had been served in Chonburi. However, the food at the restaurant was a gourmet delight in comparison, and a blessing worth counting.

In the evenings, I began doing breathing exercises along with some yoga postures. I have to admit, though, that my heart still wasn't really in it. Knowing what's best for you and actually being able to discipline yourself enough to practice what you know is best are two different things. Equally true is the difference between abstaining from temptation because you have been forced to and abstaining from temptation because you have changed your former mental and physical constitution. The latter truism became painfully evident all too soon.

After about four weeks, early one morning, the two Frenchmen and I were told to gather our stuff. We were being transferred out of Building 6. We were marched over to the Foreign Section, accompanied not by a prison guard, but by deputized prisoners called *Blue Shirts,* a name based on the color of their uniforms. Bobby wasn't included in our transfer from Building 6. His sentence was twenty years, so he was transferred to Bang Kwang Prison where there were a significant number of foreigners with lengthy prison sentences, more than a few were serving life sentences.

The Foreign Section, as it was called, was a fairly clean-looking compound. Anytime a foreign embassy asked to see the living conditions in the prison, they were brought here; they were never permitted to see the entire compound. If a politician or a VIP was coming to see the place, all the prisoners were confined to one building's indoor area. The Thais who worked in the foreigners' compound were also removed until after the visitors left.

The building I was housed in had two floors. The ground floor was mostly taken up by a large day room. In it, one area had cabinets and shelves to store supplies, equipment, and cooking paraphernalia. In the Foreign Section, almost everyone had food brought in. Most of the prisoners had either paired off or formed themselves into slightly larger groups of three or four, for cooking and sharing meals, except for the Italians, who ate together as a family would. The arguments and heated discussions they had over meals often sounded like they were about to have a brawl, but they never did. No matter how much they screamed and yelled at each other, they always quickly set their differences aside.

I ended up pairing for meals with a Frenchman named Henri. For some unknown reason, the other Frenchmen didn't like him very much. My guess was that it was because he was Jewish and none of the other Frenchmen were. In some European circles, such prejudices remained strong. Henri was a funny little guy, in for heroin like most of us. He had impeccable manners. He would fold our napkins a certain way, and make as nice a presentation as possible with the plates of food, and he'd always say *bon appetite* before we ate. As soon as he realized my cooking was less than desirable, he decided to do all the cooking himself, which worked for me. In the end, Henri was happy to have someone to eat with, and I was happy to wash the dishes. We split the cost of the fresh vegetables, tofu, and rice, which were our main staples.

The cells were on the second floor, which housed up to eight inmates per cell. There were sleeping platforms, the same as those we had in Chonburi, along with the usual squat toilets, which came with a pitcher and water trough for cleaning and flushing. As soon as the guards opened the cells in the morning, they were kept off limits until we were herded back in the evening. We spent our days either on the ground floor or outside where there were a handful of Thai prisoners working around the compound. Some even lived there, but most came from other buildings in the morning and returned to their cells at the end of each day.

Being assigned to the Foreign Section was a very desirable position for a guard. Officer salaries were low, but the bribes they got allowed them to significantly improve their lifestyles. We'd been told that the Building Chief owned a huge house and several cars. The main reason for this was apparent: He oversaw the heroin racket inside.

Most of the foreigners were doing heroin, bringing it in through the visiting room concealed in food, much the same as had been done in Chonburi. It could also be purchased inside. One or two of the day workers sold it to the inmates, but they were selling it under the auspices of the Building Chief. The prisoners did the business and the guards just looked the other way. Some of them were probably the ones carrying it into the prison. The Building Chief stayed removed from such dealings, but I was told early on that he controlled all of it.

I had every intention of staying clean from that point on, but my resolve proved extremely difficult to maintain. As soon as we got into the cells at night, the guards would do a head count and leave. Then, immediately, out came the heroin. Almost every single inmate would be fixing a shot for himself. As for me, I lasted just five days before succumbing.

There was never any sexual violence in the prison, at least not in the Foreign Section. In American, European, and probably many other countries' prisons, sexual violence occurred on a daily basis. It's a way of life in high security installations, where the worst offenders are incarcerated. Weak or effeminate men are usually forced to become *bitches*, either claimed by one inmate or used by a number of them. However, they were often protected from other acts of violence.

Sometimes men who were not effeminate, but small or otherwise unable to adequately defend themselves, were raped. Once that occurred, the victims either chose to submit to becoming someone's *bitch* or continued to face violent beatings or rape on a regular basis. Most will submit. High security prisons, especially in the US, are the most fearsome *societies* in the world. Brutal violence is a constant. There are always plenty of homemade weapons, especially knives. Being *shanked* (stabbed) is commonplace in prison life. In Thai prison, however, there are always a substantial number of *Katoys* (He-She's or transsexuals). Most *Katoys* had been prostitutes on the outside who were sentenced to prison for offenses ranging from theft to drug possession. In prison, they continue to prostitute themselves freely. Their presence meant other inmates did not engage in violent behavior for sexual gratification, so prison authorities chose not to interfere.

Since most of the foreigners were on heroin, they weren't really interested in sex. But, if you were, you always had access to it. There were two Thai *Katoys* who lived in the back of the compound in a small hut, both of whom were pre-op transsexuals, named *Moi* and *Noi*. *Noi* truly looked like a woman in every aspect. She had a fantastic body with nice breasts, wide hips, and a thin waist. Her face was also beautiful, and had I seen her on the street, I would never have guessed that she was biologically a male.

Moi was not as pretty, but she still looked like a woman. However, if you looked at her long enough, you would notice certain characteristics that weren't quite so feminine, like her hands. But *Moi* had one particularly exceptional characteristic: gigantic breasts. Think Dolly Parton. Nobody who went to her for a blowjob could possibly have cared less about her large, manly hands. From what Michael, an inmate I'd first met in Chonburi Prison who was transferred here sometime after I was, told me, "She could suck a tennis ball through a garden hose!" And, the cost for a blowjob was only two packs of cigarettes, well within the means of most inmates.

As for the Italians, they were a bunch of pricks that collectively were the exception to the rule of no violence among inmates. Like Mafioso running a protection racket, they would strong-arm you for drugs or cash. Most of this activity came from three of them who were loud-mouthed, pea-brained assholes: Pietro, Stephano, and Luciano. Pietro was tall and had a huge nose. His nickname was *Naso* (Italian for nose). The ringleader, as well as the diplomat of the group, *Naso* interacted with the other national groups on the pretense of keeping the peace. Stephano swaggered around, forever bragging about his exploits on the outside. If you believed him, he was God's gift to every Italian woman in Rome as well as the most feared Mafia enforcer in Italy. Once, when I was stoned, he walked up to me in the dayroom and hit me so hard across the face that I went flying off my chair. "Next time you better give me, you understand! You understand?" he screamed. I had no intention of giving him anything, but neither did I feel like fighting with him because he was built like the proverbial brick shithouse. Luciano, the third Italian bulldozer, walked around calling everyone foul-mouthed names and trying to extort whatever he could from them. He had twice the bulk of Stephano with huge weightlifter muscles, even though he was only about 5′ 8″. None of us were big or mean enough to defy them, so they were able to strut around and perpetrate their protection racket without much opposition. Whenever they had their own stuff, they were stoned and didn't bother anybody. But when they didn't, you either gave them some of yours or contended with their harassment.

After the Stephano incident, we all coexisted "peacefully" for a few months because they seemed to have a steady supply of drugs. Since they weren't hassling me, I didn't pay any attention to them. I stayed out of their way, and tried my best not to let them know any of my business.

Taking the bus up from Pattaya Beach, Jamie came to see me faithfully, once a week. I figured she was probably going through the money she had left, spending it on heroin. But when I asked her about it, she was evasive, so I left the subject alone. Clearly, I was in no position to lecture her about lifestyle choices. I asked her numerous times to buy a plane ticket and go home. Whatever my fate, there was no life here for her. At least in Hawaii, she had a chance of getting rehabilitated. But Jamie always refused, saying she had nothing there and no reason to return.

One of the other Americans, Tony, had a lawyer named Aroon, who had already managed to get a few other guys out and was working on Tony's behalf. His case was much bigger than mine, and although he'd been sentenced to twenty years, he had appealed the conviction. Meanwhile, Aroon was trying to get him out on bond. Tony introduced me to Aroon one day in the visiting room while Jamie was there. I told him about my situation, including all the details of my idiocy in screwing things up by getting busted again inside Chonburi Prison. Before leaving, he said he'd check on the status of my case.

Aroon came to see me the following week. He had all the details and said that my second charge from Chonburi Prison could be bailed, but the problem was that the American Embassy had a special interest in me, which meant they had to be contacted if bail was requested. He said this was unusual, and that it most likely meant there were charges pending against me in the US. He asked if that was true in my case, so I told him my story. "I still think it is possible," Aroon said. "We need to have a hearing and try to get you out while you are in court, instead of from jail."

"I don't care how you do it," I said. "I'll do whatever I have to do in order to get out."

Naturally, I was waiting for Aroon to put a price tag on my case. His answer came quickly enough. "I will need twenty-five thousand dollars, US," he said, "However, I am sure I can get you bail. But, nothing can be done until after you serve your two-year sentence because the time period for appealing that sentence has already passed."

Turning to Jamie, I asked, "How much money is left?"

"I don't think there's anything close to that amount," she shrugged her shoulders with her response.

I thought there was more money than that, but I hadn't counted it after getting ripped off by my *friends*. What could

I say? There was still a year to go on my original sentence before I'd even be eligible for bail on the second case. If that case came up, then I was screwed. Without a substantial amount of money to pay the judge and prosecutor, my additional time would be at least ten years.

When Jamie came back the following week, she said we had only six thousand nine hundred and sixty dollars left. I had no way of knowing if she was telling me the truth. She still needed money to live on and to continue to put something into my prison account every month. It came as a shock, although it really shouldn't have. The bulk of the money had been given away quite some time ago in an attempt to gain my release. The sheer hopelessness of my situation took me to a dark emotional place once again. The thought of another eleven years in prison was far too much for me to accept. However, the thought of getting twenty years was worse; more like *incomprehensible*. Up until that moment, I had stubbornly clung to the hope that somehow there would be a way to get me out once I had served two years. However, without money, my hope of securing my freedom was on the edge of impossible.

The next week Jamie didn't show up. Another week went by and she still hadn't shown up. Every time a *Blue Shirt* came in to call someone out for a visit, I looked up, hoping to hear my name. But, she didn't show. I tried in vain to get messages to Jamie or to others who might know something about where she was or what might have happened to her, but I never received any answers. A few months later, another inmate's Thai girlfriend with relatives in Pattaya said she would try to find out about Jamie. **Sometime** later, she returned and relayed the following story: A policeman had murdered Jamie and dumped her body. *No evidence, no crime.* Eventually, when we began having visits from the US Embassy, I asked if they had any knowledge of a Filipino-American woman from Hawaii being found murdered in

Pattaya Beach. They checked, but came up empty. To this day, I don't know for sure what happened to Jamie. She simply disappeared, and I never saw or heard from her again. Feelings of guilt and sorrow inundated me.

CHAPTER 31

Desperation and Permanent Loss

At the depths of despair, and drowning in a sea of self-recrimination, thoughts of Jamie never left my mind. She'd stuck by me, even though her life had become as much a nightmare as my own. She had been helpless with no one to protect her, and a predator had taken her life. *When its heavy hand is set against you, Fate can be brutal.* I wanted to believe she'd gone home to Hawaii, but I knew better. Jamie would've let me know she was all right. Heartbroken, I fell into a dark well of despondency. I'd lost Jamie, and would carry that guilt in my heart forever. The prospect of leaving this hellhole alive was growing dim, which only heightened my distress.

Wanting to numb my anguish, I bought a gram of heroin from one of the prisoners peddling it. Getting Tom, another American, to keep a lookout on the other side of the large water tank we used for bathing, I took off my clothes and wrapped myself in a sarong. This was the way we hid ourselves out in the open. We'd crouch down behind the bathing tank so the guards couldn't see, and should one approach, a lookout had plenty of time to warn us. Other prisoners would be bathing around the perimeter of the tank, so nothing looked out of the ordinary.

Within a few moments, that familiar warmth and euphoria permeated every cell of my body. I handed the stash to

Tom. Not having any money himself, he was our cell's *bag-man.* He'd hold everything in exchange for a daily share. Standing up slowly, I bathed by pouring bowls of water over my back and chest, and then dried off. Feelings of depression and despair had been driven away, at least for the time being. Retreating to the dayroom, I reclined and nodded off. Sometime later, Henri roused me. I told him what I'd heard about Jamie. He was very sympathetic, but I didn't even hear his full response before getting lost again in my anguish. Not hungry for dinner, it seemed only moments before it was time to return to our cells for the night.

The next morning heralded a new event. After bathing and getting dressed, I sat down to pull on a pair of socks. Just as I was getting up from the chair, Stephano approached me. He looked terrible. His eyes were bloodshot and tearing, and his nose was running — two of the most obvious signs of withdrawal from heroin. Getting right up in my face, he yelled. "*Fangulo,* what did I tell you, you son-of-a-bitch! I saw how high you were last night, and you didn't even offer me any!" Then, with his thick, heavy hand he smashed me across the face, and I found myself in a mental blizzard. A whirl-wind of uncontrollable anger overcame me and I reacted like a cornered animal. Picking up the nearest chair, I smashed it over Stephano's head. He went down. Possessed by fear and rage, I repeatedly smashed him over the head with the chair. Out of the corner of my eye, I saw someone coming to his aid; not even looking to see who it was, I swung the chair around and smashed it into the side of the intruder's head. Then, in one sweeping motion, I raised the chair again and continued to beat against Stephano's head and shoulders.

The other guy I hit was an Italian named Alberto. Fortunately for me, the rest of the Italians were still outside. By the time they came in to see what was going on, the guards had already interceded and were actively engaged in taking me to the Building Chief's office. Everyone else was imme-diately locked down to prevent a riot. In time, my breathing slowed and returned to normal. All my pent-up anger, fear, and despair had surfaced, exploded, and manifested in the most savage way.

I'd completely lost it. Animal instinct had taken over, and for a few ragingly inflamed moments, I was a very dangerous opponent. It caught Stephano completely by surprise because he'd never expected it from me. Luckily, the other Italians failed to reach me before the guards. Reverse their order of arrival and I would surely have been killed.

That episode marked my last day in the Foreign Section. I was transferred to Building 2 that afternoon. Building 2 was the only other building in Klong Prem Prison that housed foreigners. One of the guards told Tom to gather up all my belongings and deliver them to the Building Chief's office. I was taken directly to Building 2 with one of the Thai prisoners assigned to work in the Foreign Section. Several guards accompanied me and one pulled a wagon that held my stuff.

Only now did I realize how massive the prison actually was. It had high, dark gray, foreboding walls that separated all of the buildings and compounds. Each wall had large iron gates at their entrances, guarded by armed sentries. We passed numerous buildings, and finally took a pathway I recognized. It was the one leading to Building 6. We passed it and penetrated deeper into the maze of the prison before arriving at Building 2. My escort showed documents to the sentry at the gate to confirm that I was being transferred there. The huge gates were opened and we entered.

The compound with its array of buildings reminded me of Chonburi Prison, but this section alone was as large as that prison altogether. Medieval looking, the dark stained outer walls of the cellblock building stood ominously just inside the gates. I saw hundreds of prisoners, but no other foreigners. Only a few groups of Thai prisoners were working on the grounds. As we passed by, they looked up at me and quickly turned away, as if frightened of being reprimanded for casting a glance in my direction.

Soon, we arrived at the Building Chief's office, where my escorts remanded me to the custody of a guard who told me to wait while he took my papers into the adjacent office. After a moment, he returned and motioned me to go into the Building Chief's office. I noticed he had stars on his lapels. He must have been a high-ranking officer. I wondered why he was only a Building Chief in a prison. Later, I got my answer. He made a far better living here than he would have anywhere else. The Building Chiefs of Building 2 and the Foreign Section reaped more graft than any of the other Building Chiefs in the prison. Why? Foreigners were only housed in these two buildings, and they had more money for bribes than the Thai inmates.

Because this Building Chief didn't speak fluent English, he spoke to me in Thai. Later on, I was told this was a pretense. He spoke angrily in a loud voice. With a scowl on his face, he said, "Any fighting here, you will be beaten and locked in the hole. You understand?" Maintaining his stern expression, he continued to read me the riot act, while a Thai prisoner who spoke fluent English simultaneously translated every word he said.

In a small section at the back of the compound, foreigners were segregated from Thai inmates, unlike in Building 6. The translating inmate was ordered to take me there. The foreigners were kept there during the day. No Thais were allowed in the area, except with special permission from the Building Chief. The reason, explained to me later, was that the Building Chief didn't want foreigners having access to contraband from any of the Thai inmates. Any money foreigners had for such things went through his network, thus, a good portion of the money found its way directly into his pocket.

Building 2 had none of the clean, spruced up atmosphere of the Foreign Section. It was dirty and had an ancient feel. The stone buildings and inner retaining walls were moldy and stained. You could never forget for a moment where you were. Everywhere you looked, there was barbed wire, high walls topped with gun towers, and prisoners in chains. Violence was a daily affair in this section, but not usually among the foreigners themselves. The Italian bullies in the Foreign Section had been the exception. They were the only ones I ever saw during my time in Thai prison who picked fights with other foreigners. In Building 2, the bulk of the aggression came from the guards: sadistic bastards who had free rein to beat up anyone they wanted. And, they were always up for venting their unabated wrath upon hapless prisoners.

Heroin was as readily available here, as it was in the Foreign Section. If you had money, you could score within minutes. A number of guards would accommodate you, but you had to be wary. Sure, they'd get it for you, but few could be trusted. They could, and sometimes did, tell another guard to bust you afterwards, so that they could both squeeze more money out of you.

The Building Chief was allegedly one of the most corrupt in the Thai prison system, which suited foreigners just fine. You had to be even more careful of him than the guards though. This man was a sadist in the worst possible way. He loved to order beatings and have prisoners tortured while he watched and hurled insults at the unfortunate victims. If you got on his bad side, or if he were simply in a bad mood, he'd have you searched and brought before him.

Most of the foreigners were Caucasians. Half a dozen were American, a few Canadian, five were Italian, and about the same number were French. There were a couple of Australians, one Englishman, and a smattering of Europeans, Germans, Swiss, Belgian, Danish, Swedish, and Fins. Also in the mix were a few Asians from Pakistan, Indonesia, and Singapore.

Everyone pretty much got along. The Americans tended to hang together in their own groups, as did the Italians and the French. The northern Europeans all seemed to understand each other even though they each spoke different languages, and they tended to group together. There was a large pavilion that we crowded under during the day to shelter ourselves from the searing sun. It was equipped with wooden platforms and had just enough room for all the different groups. When the first foreigners came here, there was nothing but concrete, so they paid the Building Chief to have the pavilion built.

Although it was a dirtier, smellier, older, and a far more decrepit place than the Foreign Section, at least there were no predators among the inmates. In this building, the Italians minded their own business, same as everyone else. The foreigners were allowed to walk around the compound, and since there were hundreds of Thai inmates, I figured I could practice my language skills. **At first,** I would walk around the compound, stopping to strike up conversations with Thai inmates. After a while though, the guards became suspicious, thinking I was buying drugs from them. As soon as I started walking back to the foreigners' area, they would stop and search me, which got old real fast. Eventually, I gave up on any further improvement to my Thai language skills.

The guards were constantly on the prowl, looking for any chance to give a prisoner grief. The Building Chief, especially, took great pleasure in intimidating us. At least once a week, he summoned all the foreigners into the courtyard in front of his office. Here we were forced to watch some of the most savage beatings imaginable meted out to unfortunate Thai inmates. I had never in my life witnessed anything as heartless and appalling. First, the inmate was made to squat, hands clasped behind his neck, in front of one of the guards. The Building Chief would stand beside him and begin verbally attacking him. His insulting diatribes were vile. They always included a denigration of the inmate's mother, after which the inmate was expected to respond, "Yes, sir!" But, whether he did or not, another guard would be standing behind him wielding a large thick baton. He held it at the ready, like a four-foot long baseball bat. Before the prisoner could answer, the guard would swing it with all his might, landing the blow at the base of the inmate's spine. Then came the screams.

The hammering blows forced the inmate to tumble forward to the ground. Immediately, they were ordered to get back up and assume the squatting position. It should be noted that most Thai inmates who were beaten this way wore leg chains like those I wore while in Chonburi Prison. The beating would continue until the Building Chief called for it to stop. Afterwards, the brutalized inmate would be carried away because he was physically unable to walk. Many inmates were crippled for life; some even died.

One fortunate thing about the timing of my incarceration was that guards were supposedly no longer allowed to beat prisoners from the US, Canada, Australia, or any European country. I was told that just six months before I arrived, guards had beaten two European prisoners to death. Subsequent to the deaths, an enormous uproar ensued from Western embassies. Formal complaints were lodged. From then on, the Thais were not *supposed* to beat foreigners from Western countries. However, the mandate failed to include Asians. If you were Indian, Pakistani, Indonesian, or from any other Asian nationality, you were in danger of being beaten to a pulp with the same impunity as the Thai prisoners.

Still, we all took some form of physical abuse from the guards. Everyone was subjected to being punched, kicked, or hit across the back of the legs with a wooden baton, some more than others. Since that fatal European incident, no other foreigners had been killed, but the guards continued to abuse us. What could we do about it? Tell our embassy and risk being thrown in the hole? *Hello!*

The best course of action was to keep your head down, kowtow, and do your time. There was no point in complaining. It would only make your life worse. One incident, the most savage and sadistic beating I witnessed during my years in Thai prison, involved three inmates in leg chains. The prisoners were squatting at the feet of the Building Chief while a guard with a high, shrill voice screamed at them in Thai. In this instance, most unfortunately, I understood his words.

The guard verbally degraded them in a fashion unlike any I'd ever heard one human being speak to another. Each of the inmates summarily received resounding cracks from the huge baton at the base of their spine, just above the hip, and directly to the ribcage. The beatings went on for so long that I was overcome by nausea. By the looks on their faces, some of the other foreigners were sickened by it as well. The Building Chief turned to us with his lackey translating his words into English. "This is what we'll do to you if you are caught with drugs or if you break the rules! Don't forget it!"

At last, the horrible spectacle was over. The three young men were lying on the ground, their bodies contorted in unsightly positions. I couldn't fathom what kind of pain they must have felt. Not one of them could stand, much less walk. One by one they were picked up by their hands and feet, carried to the edge of a grassy area used for sports, and abruptly dropped to the ground. Once they were lying at the edge of the field, they were told to roll until they reached the far end. Based on the damage they must have suffered to their spines, kidneys, and other internal organs, they couldn't turn over, much less roll. Two of them somehow managed to roll once, maybe even twice. The third lay motionless. The Building Chief laughed along with his guards. We were all told *the show is over, folks,* and ordered back to where we belonged. I kept a blank, emotionless look on my face, but shuddered inside. Faceless expression is an acquired survival skill that, if you were lucky, evolved into an instinct. It was always best to keep your feelings hidden. All they needed was an excuse.

By the time we went up to our cells that night, the heavy monsoon rains had begun. Walking past the field, I saw the three men lying in the mud. Not one of them moved. I'll never forget the horrific expression on one man's face, frozen in death. Once inside the cellblock, we talked about what we'd witnessed. It was another day we knew we'd never forget; unfortunately, there were many.

In the morning, when we left the building to enter the compound, the bodies were gone. One of the blue shirts confirmed that all three men had died. After a while, you learn to let it go. Dwell on it, and you risk losing your mind.

What doesn't break you makes you stronger ... maybe.

CHAPTER 32

Surviving the Final Lesson

By winter, my cellmates had changed. Now I shared my cell with Brian, an Australian who was in for twenty years, and Tom, the American I had previously hung out with in the Foreign Section. Tom had been sent here when they busted him and several others for heroin in their cell. Nobody *copped to it* (declared ownership), so they transferred them all out of the Foreign Section, which was probably better than being hit with another court case like I had been. Somehow, Brian had managed to stay in Klong Prem Prison to serve his sentence rather than going on to Bang Kwang.

By now, I had been in Klong Prem, Lard Yao Prison for six months and in custody a total of fourteen months. I was frustrated and depressed at the dismal outlook for my future, as the case from Chonburi Prison still hung over my head. I had to be called back to court, but without money to pay anyone off, I knew I would be sentenced to at least another ten years in Klong Prem. Only a miracle could save me, and there is little hope for miracles when you are locked up in a Southeast Asian prison. The feeling of impending doom hung over me like a dark cloud. Witnessing the most sadistic and deviant behaviors, undergoing constant berating from guards, and living in fear of being singled out for a beating, or worse, was all I had to "look forward to." Day after day, I was just *there*, existing. The days rolled into weeks, then into months, and finally into years.

What kind of hope could a person hold onto in such a situation? Only faith in God within my own heart gave me the courage and strength to endure. The phrase *God helps those who help themselves* came to my mind, but we get what we deserve in life, no more, no less. We are not, as some recovery groups say, *powerless as addicts*. We cannot blame God, nor expect God to control our actions. We always have free will. Actions shape destiny. My own choices had brought all this about. I felt I was sinking in quicksand with nothing to grab onto, and no one near to throw me a lifeline.

The American Embassy was terrible about sending anyone to visit its citizens held in Thai prison. I don't even know if they knew that I had been in Chonburi because nobody had ever come to see me there. In contrast, European embassies were always bringing supplies to their citizens and made sure they had a little money in their canteen accounts. They also kept in close contact with inmates' families to keep them abreast of their family member's health and status. The Italian and French embassies regularly brought care packages for their own. All of the other Western embassies showed more concern for their citizens than the US Embassy did for us. And, by comparison, the British Embassy wasn't as attentive to their citizens as the Europeans were to theirs, but at least they sent someone on a regular basis to check up on them.

Many months after my arrest, the US Embassy finally got word to my family that I was in Klong Prem. Although I wrote to them, I felt ashamed and didn't know what to say. I had also written to my ex, Rhonda, who responded by cruelly reiterating that I would never again see my daughter, adding that she hoped I would, *rot in that Thai prison for the rest of my life*. Emotionally, I was at my lowest. It was hard to look to the future because I wasn't sure I had one, at least not a foreseeable future. My money was completely gone. The only reason I was able to survive was thanks to my parents who had begun sending a few hundred dollars a month through the US Embassy, which was then deposited into my prison canteen account. This enabled me to buy food, and I could also use some of it for whatever I might want, like cigarettes, which I could trade for other items. By this time, I'd totally quit using heroin. I would like to say it was based on a conscious decision, but the truth was: I simply couldn't afford it.

I heard that one of the Americans had obtained some heroin via a visitor. When the Visiting Room was crowded and practically every inmate was getting cooked food and rice in plastic bags, the guards hardly felt like searching with genuine scrutiny. Tom was the one who received the heroin, and that evening after head count, he offered to *give* Brian and me some. He'd already given some to our friends in the next cell and to a few others. I figured it must have been a sizeable stash for him to be sharing so much of it.

Watching the syringe being emptied into my vein was the last thing I remembered. I had overdosed "Big Time." The only reason I didn't die was because Tom and Brian held me up and kept me walking for hours in our tiny 6 x 10 foot cell. They also intermittently poured water over my head from the water tank next to the toilet. When the guards came in, in the middle of the night to do their head count, my cellmates yelled to them, "Come quickly." I was barely breathing, and they lacked the stamina to continue to hold and walk me. To their amazement, the guards took the situation seriously, and opened the cell door for two Thai inmates with a stretcher. As a rule, the authorities really didn't give a crap about prisoners who were sick, injured, or dead. Much to everyone's surprise, I was already turning purple. I was rushed out of the cellblock building and taken to the nearby prison hospital. However, there were no doctors present at this late hour. The hospital orderlies tried to revive me, but they were unsuccessful and finally gave up, leaving the hospital ward to inform their supervisor.

I recall being outside my body, hovering above the bed and looking down at myself. It was surreal, to witness the last moments of my own life. I sensed a powerful presence in my company. I was not alone. There was no pain, only a feeling of release, like I was about to turn and enter another world. So many thoughts and memories from my life flashed through my mind. A feeling of deep compassion washed over me. Was it for myself? I am really not sure.

Suddenly, a fire of determination swept over me; a spiritual wave that empowered me. My life wasn't supposed to end this way, and something was drawing me back from an ignoble demise. Then, I saw the face of my teacher, my beloved guru, Srila Prabhupada. This was not an apparition. I saw him in the sense of Conscious Awareness. His eyes radiated with abundant love. The thought that there was still something important for me to do in this life was the *last thought* that came to me.

And then, I was waking up. Spasms wracked my stomach and I coughed up a ton of liquid mucous. Eventually, the spasms subsided. Gathering my strength, I managed to partially sit up. I clearly remember being outside my body, watching the interns working on me. It had been like watching a movie. One minute I was looking down at my dead body. The next minute I was back in it, hacking and coughing. I struggled to stay upright. Looking around the room, it was obvious that I was in a hospital ward. There were a dozen or so other beds, but nobody was in them. Then, the memory of doing that shot of dope with Brian and Tom came back to me.

The next thing I noticed was a group of Thais crowded together at the far end of the ward; they were staring at me with eyes as big as saucers. They were also patients, but they had managed to vacate their beds and sequester themselves in a corner. Sheer terror was etched on their faces. Several of them kept saying something I couldn't understand. Later, I was told they were saying something like *pee noke* (ghost). They had all seen the orderlies try to revive me without success, so they were now absolutely convinced that a *pee noke* inhabited my body. **However,** at this point, I really didn't care what they believed. I sat up fully on the bed. My chest hurt so badly that it was difficult to breathe. My cellmates, Brian and Tom, had definitely helped save my life by performing some type of artificial respiration on me. The hospital orderlies had continued doing the same. But neither had actually "saved" me.

I was confined to a locked hospital ward for the rest of the night and the next morning. The following afternoon, I was escorted back to the prison. As soon as I arrived at Building 2, I was immediately placed in solitary confinement, "The Hole." Months later, when I was finally allowed back into the prison population, I was told just how badly I had overdosed. Nobody could believe that I had lived to tell the tale. "You were a dead man; you were purple," Brian swore, "when they carried your ass out of here." Tom said that my eyes had rolled back into my head just before they carried me out. One of the guys in the cell next to ours had also overdosed, but he hadn't been so lucky. Yukka, an inmate from Finland, had died that very night of an overdose from the same stuff.

As for me, I was convinced that this was the epitome of divine intervention. Remembering everything about my near death experience, I continued to dwell on it for days. Somehow, a renewed confidence rose up inside me that suggested this terrible chapter of my life would eventually end. Fate had decreed that I still had something to do here in this world. For the first time in a year, I dared to hope again. *There are no accidents in life.* But, I also knew that, once again, it was up to me. Whether I would sink or swim depended on the choices I would make from this day onward.

Alone in a solitary cell, I resolved to begin working on both my body and my mind, knowing that their wellness went hand in hand. Without bringing my body into a healthier state, my tortured mind would never become fully healed. However, at the moment, I was still extremely weak. Exercising would be next to impossible. I chose simply to be quiet, to close my eyes and see what came to me. Silently, I prayed for guidance from within. I began to meditate. There I would sit throughout the day and long into the night, and pray for the strength to heal and then to change my life's course from the utter disaster it had become. I sat in undisturbed contemplation day after day, communing with my body and my mind within the confines of my little cement cell.

It seemed like a higher power was forcing me to relive every event I had ever experienced. I saw all of the foolish mistakes I had made, and the wrong turns I had taken at the crossroads of my life. All of them had led me down the wrong path. What turned me away from the path of truth that I had been searching for? Guiding myself through the years of my marriage, I re-experienced the hurt and betrayal that was still raw within my heart. But, there could be no blame attributed to my wife or anyone else for my fate. Of my own free will, I had made my own choices. Contemplating endlessly, day after day, I suffered in silence, experiencing the pains, trials, and tribulations of my life. In the stillness, I learned to view the thoughts in my head as though I were an observer rather than a participant. Imagining they were like a river, I simply let them *flow on by*. I continued to venture deeply into all that had been buried within the hidden recesses of my subconscious mind.

My higher self urged me beyond my self-imposed boundaries so I could clearly see the reality that I was facing. I had always been quick to place blame for my bad choices on God or Karma. As I delved into my past, reliving my life from a higher perspective, I began to discover my true psyche; this was progress in every sense of the word. Some memories invoked sadness, others bore feelings of dejection, and some showed the confusion that had haunted me. Yet others brought elation, a blend of momentary happiness. Still, I detached myself from all of it and continued watching and experiencing, as one might experience an emotional and heart-rending documentary. At times it tore me apart, for I am human, yet my inner voice told me this was the only way to heal my wounded psyche. Without healing from the inside out, lasting change and subsequent development into the person I wanted to become would not be possible.

Meditation like this was something I had not fully understood before. My mantra yoga practice was something that had inspired and helped me to direct my mind in the years when I was attentive to the discipline. But, the goal was always liberation from the outside world, freedom in the future, going to a better place. My goal had been quite similar to other religionists who had been looking toward entry into heaven, toward inhabiting someplace beyond the mortal world. Everything from my past, the thoughts and impressions that led to my actions, had been swept under the rug previously. But change has to begin with deep self-examination. I realized that from the time of childhood, my experiences had begun to mold my thought patterns. Everything we see, everything we experience, and every thought that enters our mind serves to develop our sense of self-identity.

Finally, after a few weeks or so, the weight I'd been carrying for so long seemed to lift, along with the pain that I had held within me. I actually felt lighter. Emotional burdens and sorrows that I had been carrying around for so many years — like my brother's death, drug addiction, failed marriage, high crimes and misdemeanors, betrayals, beatings incurred, etc. — were now being lifted from my shoulders. It felt liberating, this new freedom from anxiety. It was something I'd never known or experienced before.

A psychic change happened, a paradigmatic shift in my awareness and perception of my self, and my consciousness. I saw the truth plainly and it wasn't pretty. My problem was not just being an addict. It went far deeper than that. I had never understood how to live peacefully within my heart, without fear, without worry, and all along, I had been trying to escape from my very *self*. "The world breaks everyone," said Ernest Hemingway. Broken maybe, but I was finally determined to become whole again ... or maybe, for the first time in my life.

This process was no easy undertaking for me. It was physically tiring and mentally exhausting, yet I continued on, day after day, week after week. There could be neither pretense nor room for excuses. There could only be "The Truth," no matter how painful it was for me to accept. The future would take care of itself, once I accepted responsibility for my past actions and transgressions. Solitary confinement was the perfect environment for such a meditative exercise. There were no interruptions. There was no outside stimulus except for the times when twice daily the boy brought my meals. Once again, the dirty, red rice and broth had become my diet. However, this time, it didn't faze me. Rather than lamenting over it, I meditated on being grateful for being given something to sustain my body, which I had almost given over to death. Chewing the rice slowly and gently, I was able to remove the rocks and pieces of foreign matter without breaking any more teeth.

Years later, when I saw a television program on Vipassana Meditation, I was astounded. The process that the teachers were putting the students through was almost exactly what I had gone through. But I had done it alone. There was no one in my prison cell to teach, monitor, or prepare me, nor to take me slowly through the stages. It all seemed to flow from somewhere in my soul, guided by Providence within my heart.

CHAPTER 33

Rebuilding Myself from the Inside Out

One day a guard opened my cell. My period of solitary confinement had ended. Walking out into the sunlight, I felt like I'd been in the cell for years, but it had only been three months since the night I *died*. Since that night, I had died another kind of death, one that stripped away countless layers of emotional pain and torment. All the memories were still there, but they no longer controlled me. I walked around slowly, taking in my environment as if for the first time. I smiled at some of the Thai inmates as I walked by them, nodding my head, getting a reciprocal greeting from most. Finally, I reached the path to where the foreigners stayed and walked up to the pavilion's entrance.

"Oh Howard, have they let you out, *mon ami*?" one of the Frenchmen, Jean Michel, asked. A few new foreigners had been assigned to our building in my absence; after greeting almost everyone, I was introduced to one of the newcomers. His name was Bob Word and he was in for heroin, like most of us. His wife, Shelly, was inside the women's prison, right next to the men's. He was a big guy, very friendly, and he had a great sense of humor. I liked him instantly, and we quickly became friends. Bob was avid about exercise. He did calisthenics and lifted weights. While I was in The Hole, a second pavilion had been built. It seemed that some of the foreigners had paid the Building Chief to have it erected. One new inmate, who still had significant resources outside the prison walls, also paid for a set of weights. Additionally, chinning bars had been erected from pipes welded together and sunk into the ground. Bob had also built some pushup bars out of wood.

Bob and I started working out together every day. I started doing pushups, sit-ups, leg lifts, squats, and various other exercises. Bob coached me in the correct method of lifting weights. I was his spotter while he did his bench presses, and he did the same for me. I really got into it, and within a month my body started going through a significant transformation. For the first few weeks, I was really sore, but I doggedly kept at it. Within three months, I was buff, which gave me a sense of accomplishment in having changed my body. At this time, I also began jogging around the compound. In the beginning it was Bob who had instigated my motivation, but after a while, I found inspiration from within, just as I had experienced in my meditation practice.

We had a routine for several hours in the morning and again in the late afternoon, alternating exercises for different muscle groups. We had two separate workouts, meant to strengthen and develop different muscles; each one was done every other day. After working out, I would bathe and go alone to a quiet corner of the compound to meditate. I spent at least two to three hours a day, first doing the silent meditation I had begun while in solitary confinement, then the mantra meditation I had learned from my teacher years ago. I came to realize how the first step of the practice made the second so much more meaningful. Slowly but surely, I felt that I was becoming someone I wanted to be, someone I had never given myself the opportunity to become. I had never before been so reflective and so painfully honest with myself.

For me, the meditative process of self-analysis has never stopped. There's no *end* to it, no time to sit back and say, *I am there, so there is no more to be gained.* As human beings, life constantly presents challenges. I have learned to deal with each challenge as it comes along. Those challenges that once seemed insurmountable are now only small obstacles to work through.

We're all on this everlasting search for love, peace, and harmony, but sometimes we lose our way. We revel in love when we find it, and die a thousand deaths when it is lost. We mourn the loss of all we once knew and loved. Birth, death, decay, and finally death ... such is the natural progression of life. But all of the world's philosophical paths speak of, or give a hint of, the hope for rebirth. Now it was time for me to be reborn within my heart.

I resolved that I'd never again wallow in self-pity, nor blame others or the world at large for what was lacking within me. Given a second chance, I was determined to savor every single moment of life. I had gained faith in myself and faith in my destiny. I was NOT going to rot in prison for the rest of my life. *"Man proposes and God disposes,"* my greatest mentor used to say. My proposal was to be able to make retribution for my mistakes. I wanted the chance to do something worthwhile, not to waste a single moment from this point on.

Soon, a Pakistani man, Sohail, who was in for an immigration violation, was assigned to our cell. Our other cellmate had been released, leaving only two of us, myself and Bob. Upon arrival, Sohail asked if he could cook for us in exchange for being able to share the meals, as he had no money. "Sure!" I said, "But first let's see what your food tastes like, okay?" The following day, we bought tofu, vegetables, and rice. By this time, Bob and I had already started pooling our resources for food. I told Bob that Sohail had applied for the position of personal cook for us.

"Sounds good to me," Bob grinned, and we gave our new cellmate a license to prepare our evening dinner that night. Sohail turned out to be an excellent cook. He would prepare the evening meal for the three of us, which we would eat later in our cell. Because we spent so much time in our cell, it seemed prudent to have our biggest meal there.

Unexpectedly, and completely out of the blue, the American Embassy started sending an emissary to see us regularly. Until this time, it was often months before anybody came to check up on us. A new employee at the American Embassy, a Christian minister named Calvin, was a wonderful person. He made us feel that he sincerely cared about us. When he asked if there was anything we needed, I asked if he'd get me a copy of the *Bhagavad-Gita*. I also asked for a strand of rosary beads called *japa mala*. He was delighted to fulfill my requests and not at all prejudiced against spiritual paths different from his own. He became the liaison for our families, as well. We could send letters home directly from the prison. Of course, they were censored. Some never arrived at all. Soon I started reading again, something I had done regularly before heroin had taken over my life.

Calvin also brought other books that I asked for, most on the subjects of Vedic astrology and astronomy, as well as Ayurvedic medicine. He went out of his way to fulfill my requests. He brought me notebooks, and I began writing both poetry and short stories. All of this had a profound impact on not only my healing, but on my mental, emotional, and spiritual growth. I began spending every waking minute doing something constructive, be it physical exercise, yoga, reading, writing, or meditation. In contrast, I didn't have outer freedom, but I did have inner freedom. Most of the other inmates were only waiting for the day they would be released so they could again begin doing exactly the same things that got them in here. Drugs were what most of them talked about, as if drugs were their Great Goal in Life. Inmates talked about doing deals together once they got out and about ways to avoid being arrested again. Most would likely either return to prison or they would die untimely deaths. There were no other alternatives for people like them, and until recently, I had believed this of myself. I now vowed to *never forget, never repeat* the actions that had ruined my life.

Was it easier now to keep myself from doing heroin? Easier, yes. *But never easy.* Beating back the demons when they reared their ugly heads and tempted me required constant effort. Temptation was always lurking about. The heroin rush was the perpetual goal for most prisoners. They would do it at every opportunity. Every time I had a moment of weakness and wondered if my life in prison would ever end, I remembered the night I had *died,* and that revelation helped me maintain my new and fresh perspective. Change is always about perspective.

There was still abhorrent violence and continual beatings that we were forced to witness. Inside prison, we lived in a sick, demented world, but it had become my external world, a world less relevant. I continued to rebuild myself, both physically and mentally. I didn't know how it was going to happen, or when, but I would leave this place!

Oh, I had my moments of struggle when witnessing pain and suffering all around me. Sometimes, when forced to witness an inmate being tortured by a sadistic guard, anger poured over and through me. Learning how *not* to hate torturers would come later, but in the meantime, I would manage to endure and navigate through the hard times. I had learned to remain silent, stay out of the oppressor's way, and have hope. I told myself that I would never again lose hope. It may seem hard to imagine, but while incarcerated in such a hideous place, *I finally had a better life waiting for me in the future.*

My writing began to become more prolific. I kept my poems in a journal, but shared my stories with a woman named Jolene in the women's prison. I met her at the courthouse during a hearing. She was an American, and we became pen pals. Our pen pal relationship filled a void in each of us. Poems were easy to share because they were not so long to copy like my stories. Anyhow, she wanted to read them, and ended up with all of them. I wish I had them back to read now because they reflected my psyche's deep imagination at the time.

My stories were about worlds within worlds within worlds. At the time, I suppose, I desperately needed to share my emotions. I still believe that my deepest emotions were embedded in those stories. Because my meditation had become more intense, my emotions became an instrumental factor in my writing. I taught myself how to go into an altered state of consciousness where I found calm and peace. I developed deeper realizations of having past lives and how they influenced my present life. How? It was as if this ability was always there inside me in a dormant stage, and as I accessed it, I began to grow. I really have no other way of explaining it: The teacher within was calling to me and I heard his voice!

I titled one of my stories, *Amazing Journey*. It detailed the adventures of a young man who traveled in his astral body to other worlds and other planes of existence, leaving his physical body suspended in a deep meditative state. None of the stories I wrote in prison were about being in prison, nor were they about experiences from my recent past. However, some of my recent memories emerged in my poetry.

CHAPTER 34

Light at the End of the Tunnel

As of yet, I hadn't heard anything about my pending court case, but knew that it had to be coming up soon. One of the guys in my building had a lawyer named Josephine who managed to get several other foreigners out on bail, as well as out of the country. Although I had no money to pay her, I asked if he would have her call me out the next time she visited. **The moment I met her,** I sensed that she wasn't like the lawyer I previously had. She seemed down to earth, and she had a wonderful infectious laugh. Josephine instilled a sense of confidence in me that she could actually do something proactive for me. If, of course, I could somehow come up with the money.

In a letter to my parents, I let them know that there was a possibility of bail after serving my two-year sentence. However, I would have to pay the judge, the prosecutor, and an attorney in order to get bond. My father, an attorney himself, refused to believe that this was how things were done. My Dad had never traveled to countries like India or Thailand, where corruption is the norm. Therefore, his assumption was that an unscrupulous lawyer was trying to cheat desperate foreigners in Thai prison. That is, until an American attorney I had known many years earlier in Philadelphia showed up in the visiting room one day. He had come along with Calvin to see the American prisoners.

The American government and many European governments were discussing prisoner exchanges between their countries and Thailand. Dick Atkins was the attorney heading up the US effort to secure a prisoner exchange treaty with Thailand. He was a lawyer from Philadelphia who had represented the Kohn brothers, notorious pot and acid dealers I had known in my teens. When he introduced himself to us, I recognized his name immediately. "Didn't you used to defend Murray and Sammy Kohn back in the late 60s and early 70s?" I asked.

Surprised to hear these names, he smiled and replied, "Yes! Do we know each other?"

"No, but I *sure knew them*, and I remember your name as their attorney," I quipped. Our initial exchange launched a special relationship between us, at least a different one than those he would have with the other prisoners. He explained to everyone who he was, adding that he would be the liaison for a possible prisoner exchange program between the US and Thailand. Following his talk, Dick asked me to remain for a few minutes.

When Dick asked what I'd been arrested for, I was completely honest with him and told him the story of my incarceration, including the second case I had brought upon myself while in Chonburi Prison and how the two-year sentence for my first offense had already been served. Currently, I was waiting a disposition on the second case. Unless I managed to make bail and leave the country, the sentence would likely be an additional ten years or more. He listened attentively, then asked about the status of the pending case. I told him that I had heard nothing regarding a hearing date. I also told him about Josephine and how she had helped other foreigners to buy their freedom, but I had run out of money a long time ago. Dick nodded in agreement, "Yes, that's the only way in this country. Can I help?"

I related that my father simply refused to believe that we could just pay the judge and prosecutor to grant my bail. Josephine had said she could get me out for ten thousand dollars US, including my passage out of the country. This was a pittance compared to what the other lawyer had taken from me. Dick knew my father, and said he would see him when he returned to Philadelphia. First, though, he wanted to meet Josephine so he could assess her. He said he would return within a month or so, but would talk to Josephine in the next few days before leaving. "Thanks, Dick" I said, "You can't imagine what that means to me. You've given me renewed hope!" We said our goodbyes and I returned to the sweltering compound.

It had been raining for days. Sometimes on a particularly bad day, there would be floods *inside* the prison, which generated a stink so foul it made your eyes water. The sewage system was ancient, and the stench from it was something you had no choice but to endure. This happened numerous times throughout the rainy season. After almost two years inside, I'd become numb to it. I no longer had to shield my eyes like a child who couldn't watch a horror movie. Thai prison life was a horror movie in many aspects, and I had witnessed far too many of them. The atrocities were too numerous to count.

About one month later, I was summoned to the visiting room. On the other side of the cage was Josephine, and she was positively beaming. You hardly ever saw anyone smile in prison. Just seeing her was uplifting. She told me that she had good news. Mr. Atkins was back in Thailand and had brought money to get me out on bail. She had even spoken by telephone with my mother!

Dick had arrived the night before and had called Josephine. "He says he'll come to see you today or tomorrow," Josephine said in her singsong English. She continued to smile as she spoke, "Don't you worry, Howard. I can take care of this problem. You try to be happy and I will be here to take you out soon."

Completely floored, I must have simply stared at her with my mouth hanging open. Suddenly though, I jumped to my feet and said, "Really! Oh Josephine, thank you, thank you. I'm *so* grateful!"

Feeling as if I was walking on air, I nearly ran back to the building compound. I couldn't believe it! I was finally getting out, I joyfully told myself. Entering the building, I blurted out the news to Bob and the others. "I'm getting bail! Josephine just came to tell me!" Many of the men congratulated me, but others made no comment, silently wishing they were in my shoes. I recall hearing poor Brian wistfully mutter, "I'm never going anywhere."

I was healthier physically, mentally, and spiritually than I had been in years, more than I'd ever been in my entire life and I was bound and determined to stay that way. I continued my exercise regimen, along with Bob, and continued my private meditation practice. I had also immersed myself in the study of both Vedic astrology and Ayurvedic healing. My writing had become more profound and prolific. I had been turning out three in-depth short stories a week while writing poetry every day. Firmly convinced that these practices would prepare me to live a more fulfilling life, I felt confident and enthusiastic about the future. Although I understood that it was one thing to do all that I had been doing to rehabilitate myself while confined in prison, it would be quite another when I was finally back in the world where there would be an abundance of distractions and temptations.

Dick arrived the next day to update the Americans about the prisoner exchange treaty. We were all brought out to the visiting room from both Building 2 and the Foreign Section. He said that those with long sentences might be able to get them reduced once they were back in the US federal prison system, but there were no guarantees on that point. He was hopeful the treaty would be signed within the calendar year and implemented within the following eighteen months. **Again,** he asked me to stay after the others left. He asked the guard on his side of the cage to tell the guard on the inside that he was my US lawyer and needed to speak with me. "I assume Josephine told you the good news?" he asked smiling. "She figures she'll have you out on bail in a matter of days.

"Thanks, Dick," I said. "I can't thank you enough. My Dad never would have believed it could be done had it not been for you."

"Karma, right?" Dick asked with a wink of an eye, adding, "Nothing happens by accident. I'm glad I was in the right place at the right time to be able to help." I felt like Dick and I must have been friends in a past life and that he was here to save me in this lifetime.

Over the course of the next few days, I was somewhat distracted during my meditation. My head grew full of worldly thoughts. I had to figure out what my next steps would be once I was actually out of prison and safely out of the country. I couldn't concentrate on anything else. Where would I go? I didn't have any money and couldn't depend on my parents to support me once I was out. I thought of South Africa and what I would say to my friends there. *Hey, sorry I didn't call, but I just stopped off in Thailand for three years, and now I'm on my way to Johannesburg.* I had too many thoughts whirling around in my mind. *First things first*, I reminded myself because, essentially, I knew I would have to wait and see what options presented themselves to me.

Finally, late one afternoon, I was called out for a visit. When I got to the visiting room I saw Josephine, but her signature smile was missing. My heart sunk. I walked over to sit across from her and listen to her news. "There is a problem. Someone is trying to block your bail. We will get around it, but we are being delayed because we need some help from a higher official. Don't worry. It will take just a few more days." She smiled and got up to leave.

Naturally, I was devastated. Hopelessness tried to take hold of me, but I resisted. I knew it had to be the DEA. Why did they care so much about a state case in Hawaii? It didn't make sense. Certainly, they had bigger fish to fry, there were no federal charges pending against me, and the feds never served as bounty bunters for state criminal courts. My mind was reeling while that too familiar feeling of helplessness tried to overwhelm me. The Blue Shirt escorting me back to the building was speaking to me, but I couldn't hear him. It was hard not to worry. *What if the Feds succeeded in foiling Josephine's efforts to get me bond?* All I could do was reassure myself that Josephine would be able to work through the obstacles and get me out.

When I got back to Building 2, I entered and walked toward the far end of the compound. Enveloped in a mental fog, I wasn't watching where I was going. Out of nowhere, I tripped on something and pitched forward onto my left arm and shoulder. A sharp pain in my big toe pulsated my whole foot. I'd tripped on a small stump from a bush that had been chopped down, ripping apart the top of my big toe. Sitting up, I looked at my toe while it bled profusely. My arm was scratched and my shoulder was killing me because it had taken most of my weight when I hit the ground. *What an inauspicious omen,* I thought, while struggling to get up. Wiping tears from my eyes, I limped back to the foreigners' pavilion and sat down beside the water tank to wash my foot and arm.

Bob and another guy came over to see what was up. One of them went to get first aid ointment and a bandage for my toe. After attending to my wounds, I walked over to the bench to sit down and relate to Bob, and a few others, what Josephine had just told me. They grimaced. Someone else walked by and asked, "Howard, not out yet? What's up, man? I thought they were coming to get you today," which made me feel worse when I had to answer by saying, "Got some delays, but hopefully, in the next few days."

This was all one big emotional test for me. Gathering my strength, I was determined to not lose hope. Walking over to my favorite spot in the compound, I began practicing my breathing exercises with deep intention. I inhaled deeply, expanding my diaphragm, and then I exhaled slowly until my lungs were empty. This is how I practiced the yogic breathing techniques, and they now had a calming effect. I then contemplated on what today's unexpected turn of events might mean. Eventually, I came to the conclusion that I had to *Let Go*. That Fate would have her way with me. What was to be would be. I began to consciously meditate on my desired results. Picturing Josephine, I saw her receiving signatures from several people. Then, with a smile on her face, I saw her driving to the prison to see me. Then, I saw myself being called to gather up my things, and at last walking out through the prison gates. Over and over, I replayed this scenario in my mind.

For the next two days, I meditated for longer periods of time. I did my yoga practice, continued to exercise with Bob, and I prayed. I prayed and prayed and prayed. I didn't do any writing though, preferring to channel all my creative energy into proactive visualizations. Sohail cooked the evening meals, as usual, and I waited, trying my best to remain calm and be patient. I told myself: *This is just another test.*

At about eleven the next morning, I was called out to the visiting room, where Josephine was waiting. This time she stood up and greeted me warmly with her big smile; the one I had come to like. "It is all done!" she exclaimed. "The papers have been signed and bail has been granted. I will be here between 4 and 5 PM to take you out and away from here." I couldn't believe it. My heart soared!

"Thank you Josephine," I responded, adding emphatically. "I was a little worried, but I had faith that you could do it!"

"Be ready," she said. "It is *loi* percent (100%) this time!"

I eagerly told Bob and the others the good news. Within minutes, they were congratulating me. They even offered me drugs, but I was determined to NEVER take another hit of heroin. I told them that I hoped they were also out soon.

CHAPTER 35

Thailand, the Final Days

At 4:15 in the afternoon, two Blue Shirts came to get me. I was being released. Overwhelmed with exhilaration, I hugged Bob and a few others, and then I said my good-byes to everyone, thinking *I'm really getting out. It's not a dream.* I took a small bag with some clothes and very little else. Of course, I took my poetry notebooks and mantra beads. Whatever else I had, I gave to Bob.

Walking out of the compound, and down the walkways toward the front gates, I clearly remembered the day I'd first entered Klong Prem Prison. What a different man I had become since then. When I had entered, I was a skinny drug addict with a very dysfunctional mentality, and now I was twenty-five pounds heavier and arguably in the best physical shape of my life. Mentally, I was sharp and I was determined to do something significant with the rest of my life.

My meditation exercises had changed not only the way I thought, but also my entire outlook on life. Years before, I had thought of myself as a spiritual person. But today, I was light years beyond those immature perceptions that I had of myself back then. Now I would have to prove it to myself. At the end of the day, that is all that really matters. It's your *Self* you must answer to.

The gates I was now walking through were not only freeing me physically, but emotionally and spiritually. Striding out of the outer gate, I paused for a moment of reflection.

Turning slightly, I glanced back at the prison walls and then toward a police wagon with two cops and Josephine. Briefly, she filled me in, "We have to go to the police station first, and then you will be able to leave with me."

I didn't like the idea of having to ride with the cops, but I did as I was told. Josephine followed behind in her own car. As soon as we arrived, I was taken into an office and told to sit in front of a desk. After a few minutes, an officer came in and sat down behind the desk, opened a drawer, and took out a folder that appeared to contain all of the documents, including my release order stating that I had been granted bail. "I need to see your passport before you can go," he said, adding, "I have to check that your visa was valid when you were arrested. As long as it was valid at that time I can let you go with your lawyer. You will then have to come to court when your case comes up."

"I don't have it! I don't have it because the police took it from me when they arrested me in Pattaya Beach in October 1981." (It was now late January, 1984.)

"You wait!" he insisted, and got up.

Josephine came in and spoke with the policemen. She explained to me that they were calling the Pattaya Beach Police Station as well as Chonburi Prison to determine what had happened to my passport. "Don't worry, soon we'll be able to go," she assured me. I sat there for more than an hour until the cop finally returned to tell us that no one could find my passport. Incredulous, I began speaking, "I had it when I was arrested. Had my visa been expired, I would have been charged with a visa violation, as well as the drug charges!" My tone was insistent and steadfast.

"We still must see that your passport shows a valid visa when you were arrested," he persisted. I continued to protest, but it was no use. Josephine also argued on my behalf and eventually went into someone's office and shut the door. When she came out, she said that she would try to straighten this out; meanwhile, they would be taking me to the immigration jail where people were kept before deportation or when they were arrested for immigration violations. I sighed, and said resignedly, "My Fate is in the hands of God. Please, Josephine, do all you can."

"I'll be back soon," she promised before leaving.

They put me in an empty cell at the police station. Within an hour, I was back in the paddy wagon and on my way to the immigration jail. After being processed, they put me in one of several huge cells that held more prisoners than I could easily count. There must have been at least 100 in the cell, maybe more. Sitting down against the bars in the back, I prayed that Josephine would quickly be able to get things sorted out. It was getting late and the sun had set, so it didn't surprise me when she failed to show that night. Reluctantly, I told myself that she probably needed to talk to someone who had already left for the day.

Abruptly, I was shaken out of my reverie by several figures looming over me. Looking up, I saw a couple of very gruff looking guys. They were darker skinned than I, and spoke in an accent that was unfamiliar. It sounded something like a Russian accent, but not exactly. When they didn't sit down, I stood up to look them in the eye. "You American?" one asked. "Yeah," I said. "You got money?" he asked. I had, only because Josephine had given me money before she left so I'd have it to buy something to eat or drink if I needed to. However, I answered "No."

"I think you got money," he said, and his friend quipped, "Yeah, he have money." "I don't have any money," I repeated. "Leave me alone, alright!" They weren't very big, and outside of the odds being *two to one*, I wasn't feeling at all intimidated by them. But when the one who was doing the asking grabbed my shirt pocket, I remembered what Bob had taught me about self-defense: How to head-butt, smash someone in his Adam's apple, put your adversary in a chokehold, and break his neck with one swift motion! Although Bob hadn't taught me enough to make much of a fighter out of me, his teaching was helpful. With one quick movement I reached forward, firmly grabbed the lapels of the guy's shirt, and pulled him forward while I smashed my forehead into his nose with all the strength I could muster. It was easy then to swing his body forward and off to one side, letting go so he went headlong onto the floor. Then, I kicked the other scumbag in the balls, thinking: *Screw fighting fair!*

The first guy's nose gushed blood all over the place, spewing it on several guys he'd fallen on when I threw him down. They, in turn, started kicking him and pushing him away. His smaller buddy had also fallen against another detainee who began punching and kicking him. The little guy got his ass kicked. As for me, I took advantage of the chaos and scampered away to another section of the cell. There were so many people in there that the guards couldn't see what was going on, but the guy whose nose I smashed was yelling while his sidekick was screaming in pain. Within seconds, several guards came charging in, and everyone made way for them. They grabbed the bleeding guy and took him out of the cell. By now, all heads in the cell were turned to see what the ruckus was about. At least a dozen or more guys had seen what had happened, but nobody said a word. The guards barked in Thai, asking who was involved and responsible, but they were met with blank stares and a collective shrug of shoulders, which **meant** I'd become an instant celebrity, of sorts.

There were no other Americans present. The only Westerners were a few Europeans, while the majority of our cellmates were from other Asian countries. Guys were coming up to me, saying, "Good work, man," or "I like your style." The two that accosted me clearly were not well liked, and everyone loved seeing them get their butts kicked. People started offering me things to drink. One guy told me to give him my T-shirt and he'd get the blood from the nose bashing out for me. I spent the rest of the night uneventfully, and in the morning gave one of the guards some money to get me something to eat.

Josephine showed up around noon. She said she'd found out what was going on and was now one hundred percent

TEMPTING THE DEVIL IN THE NAME OF GOD

positive that the American Embassy had my passport. She had called them, and they were sending someone down to the immigration jail to see me that afternoon, and she would return after that. The idea was that I could get my passport and stay in Thailand until I was called to court. However, Josephine would actually be putting me on a train bound for Malaysia ASAP. She also had money for onward plane flights, which she would give me before I left.

That afternoon, when a representative came from the embassy, I was called out of the cell and led to a room where he was waiting along with cops and immigration officials all milling about. He introduced himself as Bill Manning and shook my hand. Manning sure didn't look like what I had expected. He looked like a stocky, well-built cop, not at all like any embassy employee I'd ever met. "Let me get straight to the point," he said. "We can arrange for you to be set free, but only if you are willing to go back to the US to face charges."

"What charges?" I asked him. "Since when did you guys start coming to get someone in a foreign country and take them home to face state charges?"

"These are federal charges," he insisted. "Three counts of distributing a controlled substance and three counts of conspiracy. Have you ever heard of the RICO Act?"

Floored, I asked, "When was I charged with these?"

"About a year ago," he said.

"On what evidence?" I persisted.

"I can't tell you that, but you have already been indicted. Here's your choice: You can either agree to be accompanied by agents from the US Federal Marshalls' Office on a flight back to the US where you will face charges in a US Federal Court of Law *or* you can stay in this immigration jail until your case here goes to court."

I glared into his eyes as he continued. "If you decide to stay here, you'll probably get twenty or thirty years. You'll go to Bang Kwang Prison, not Lard Yao. If you thought that prison was bad, wait until you get to Bang Kwang!"

"Son of a bitch!" I shouted. My words were not directed at him, but toward the *powers that be* who had orchestrated this nasty setup. Still looking straight into his eyes, I acquiesced, "I don't really have much of a choice, do I? Take me back."

"You're making the right choice, Howard. We'll see you soon," Manning said, as he stood to leave.

After he left, I was led back to the cell. Josephine showed up a little while later, and a guard allowed me out of the cell, but continued to keep a close eye on us. She asked what had happened; the embassy wouldn't tell her a thing, only that someone had been sent to see me at the immigration lock-up. I told her what had transpired and how I knew I was wedged between a rock and a hard place. "I'm so sorry," she said in consolation. "This is obviously why I've had so much trouble getting you out in the first place. But, I didn't know what the problem was." She asked me if there was anything she could do for me, and I said, "No, but I thank you so much for what you have done. Better I go back now to face this in the US than have to stay in a Thai prison for who knows how many more years. Besides," I smiled, "It is the will of Buddha, yes?"

She smiled at me and said, "Yes, all is up to Buddha. You take this," handing me a wad of US currency. "Your father sent it for you to get out of Thailand and for your travel onward. It is not mine to keep."

We stood up and hugged. "Thank you Josephine, may Lord Buddha bless you always. Thank you for all your help."

"Maybe I will see you again someday," she nodded. As I saw tears fall from her eyes, she reached into her bag for a tissue.

"Not here, I'm afraid," I said. "Maybe you'll come to the US someday and we'll see each other again."

Then she was gone and I was taken back to the cell. Josephine was a rarity. She could have easily kept the money my father had sent her on my behalf. Certainly, I will never forget her and will always be grateful. Who knows where I would have ended up without her help.

At this point, I was almost relieved. At least I knew where I was going and what I had to deal with. I didn't know what the outcome would be, but I wasn't about to lose heart after all I'd gone through. I wasn't even sure what the charges stemmed from, but I had a good idea. Somebody must have been busted and decided to involve me. It was very convenient to have me languishing in a Thai prison. Otherwise, how could there be charges of conspiracy much less charges under the RICO Act, which meant there were others alleging that I conspired *with* them. Sighing, I resigned myself to whatever Fate might have in store for me next. At best, unlike in Thailand, in the States, I had a chance of getting a fair sentence. Calling the guard and giving him cash to buy some food, I sat down to think about the past few years of prison life. No matter what happened, the realizations that I'd gained during this period of growth, and the healing that resulted, would always remain with me.

The following day, two officers from the embassy came for me. They identified themselves as US Federal Marshals, telling me they'd be accompanying me back to the US. Only too happy to get on with it, I signed the papers for the Thais, stating that I would return for court on such and such a date for my next hearing, then the three of us left. The embassy had issued me a temporary travel document valid only for this trip. It would allow me to leave Thailand and to enter the US as a US citizen. The Marshalls wasted no time once they had me in their custody. We went straight to the airport and directly to the gate for our flight. We were going to Hawaii, which was where I had been indicted on the federal charges. Passing quickly through security, the next thing I knew we were boarding the plane. Before long, we were taxiing on the runway and the plane took off on its way to Tokyo.

Once we took off, I exhaled. I knew that, if nothing else, I wasn't going to see the inside of a Thai prison *ever again* and that it was better for me to take my chances on US soil. Whatever destiny awaited me, I was confident that the end of this terrible saga was in sight. There was a light at the end of the tunnel, at long last. The marshals were fairly friendly and willing to let me travel without handcuffs, even in Tokyo Airport between flights where I assured them I wouldn't try to bolt. Finally, after two extremely long flights, we were banking over that old familiar mountain range in Honolulu. Even though I was apprehensive about what awaited me, the sight of the mountains still gave me a thrill. I loved Hawaii. I still felt deep affection and nostalgia for the place. There had been so many good times in paradise, before it all fell apart, ending in a personal hell at Halawa Prison. Before landing, I said a silent prayer, "Please, God, please don't send me back into Halawa."

CHAPTER 36

Facing the Music

After clearing immigration and customs, I was taken to the Honolulu Community Correctional Center. It's a state facility, but the Feds had one wing designated for federal prisoners, because they didn't have their own holding facility in Hawaii. After being thoroughly searched, I was taken to the jail and placed in a dorm. It was a large dorm with bunk beds as well as mats and mattresses on the floor to accommodate an overflowing inmate population. It was a jail for people awaiting trial, and for those with short sentences that did not exceed a year. Since I had state charges pending, the ones I'd jumped bail on three years earlier, I was put in a state dorm.

I had been told that I would be housed in the federal wing, so I protested. I figured the federal charges would take precedence over the state charges, so the Feds would deal with me first. After that, the state would get its turn. My protests fell on deaf ears; I would have to wait for my attorney to sort it out.

Most of the inmate population was locals, meaning they were native islanders like Hawaiian, Samoan, Japanese, Filipino, or mixed race. We *haoles* (whites) were a minority group because there were so few of us in the dorm. Being a young white man in prison in Hawaii might be compared to being one of only a few black men in an all-white prison in rural Alabama or being thrown into a cellblock housing the Aryan Brotherhood. You were likely to experience severe prejudice and have your ass kicked severely, more than once.

After being assigned to the large dorm and told to *find a bunk in the back*, I had to run the gauntlet, so to speak. Trying to act distant and appear perplexed I made my way slowly toward the back, passing many inmates sitting on their bunks. Others stood around talking and nodding to those who were watching me. Some of the greetings that were thrown my way were not very hospitable.

Concerning the prison environment and culture, inmates are constantly using expletives of an obscene nature during their verbal discourse with others. Crudeness and vulgarity are the norm among inmates and any sign of cultural refinement or decency are usually viewed as weakness and would normally generate some unwanted and violent reaction. Among my first greetings were: *"Eh, haole, F*** you!"* and *"Eh, haole, you like one knuckle luau?"* Deciding it was safer not to answer, I ignored their taunts, knowing more were coming my way. I recall a guy shouting, *"Haole, we give you welcoming later, brah."* Finding the bunk where I was directed, I threw my blanket on it and sat on the edge. Eventually things calmed down. Nobody had made any moves on me. Not yet.

As soon as I was allowed to make a phone call, I called my lawyer, Earl, who had been an Army lawyer. When he first came to Hawaii, he worked for the law firm of a well-known, very hip attorney named Jack Swisher. I knew Jack because he had been the attorney for the Krishna Temple in Honolulu when I lived in the area. Jack was a different kind of attorney than I had met before. He was very laid back. As for Earl, he promised to sort things out and get me moved into the federal wing. Because it was the weekend, he wouldn't be able to do anything until Monday when he would see me about my hearing.

Returning to my bunk, I hoped to avoid any altercations before Earl could get me out of the state dorm. Some of the guys were over six feet tall and weighed in at a good 250–300 pounds. A large, powerful body and a bad attitude guided by the intellect of a pigeon make for a very dangerous combination, especially if they disliked you. There were a few other *haoles* there. A couple of them were quite big and gnarly themselves, so I made friends with them. The weekend passed without any serious incidents.

When I went to court on Monday, I was remanded without bail on the federal charges. I hadn't expected to be granted bail, nor was there a question of getting bail on the state cases because I'd already absconded before. Without means, it would have been a moot point, anyway. The state hearings were put on the back burner until the Feds were finished with me. When Earl and I sat together at the courthouse, he held a folder that contained all the details of the charges against me. From it, I learned that Lane, the friend who had fallen in love with the prostitute in Pattaya Beach, had been busted. He named me as his source in Thailand, saying I'd also provided him with heroin to sell when I was living in Hawaii before I jumped bail on the state cases.

AJ had also been busted. Even though he was the one who smuggled the heroin into the US, and gave it to me to sell, he named me for involvement in the smuggling operation, which was an out and out lie. AJ had been smuggling heroin into Hawaii via the Philippines with his partner, Tim. Furthermore, they each had homes and a factory in Cebu where they made rattan furniture. First, they had smuggled the heroin into the Philippines from Thailand, and then they had it packed into the legs and frames of their rattan furniture. Subsequently, they shipped it all to Hawaii where U.S. Customs finally caught a shipment, but let it enter so they could follow the whole operation to snag a few more participants for their case.

Conveniently locked up in a Thai prison, I couldn't be called to answer to any of the allegations at the time the charges were made. AJ and Lane both made plea agreements, agreeing to testify for the prosecution if I was ever brought back to face charges. Based simply on *their word*, the case had been lodged against me with no supporting evidence other than their testimony. Because I had jumped bail on the state charges, the Feds believed I had been actively involved.

By the time I arrived back in Hawaii to face the music, they were all in prison serving other sentences. They had cooperated with the investigation by naming me as a primary player in the heroin smuggling operation. I had no idea who else they may have testified against or given false information on. Although, it really didn't matter much at this point because there was no way for me to contest their testimony. Their cases were all said and done. *Finito.* They would gladly testify against me just to get out of prison for the day, and I knew it. *No honor among thieves!* People will say anything if it means getting a reduced sentence. Considering I was stuck in prison in Thailand at the time, placing the blame on my shoulders was easy and expedient.

At the hearing, I pled not guilty as per my lawyer's instructions. He still needed to speak with the prosecutor to see what he might agree to in a plea deal. The odds were stacked against me as far as getting a not guilty verdict, so this was our best bet. We knew that the guys who named me as being complicit would be called to testify for the prosecution if we went to trial. Courts in the US move much more quickly than they do in Thailand, but it can still be a slow process.

I was taken back to the jail, where later that afternoon, I was transferred to the federal wing, Corridor D. There were only about fifteen or so prisoners in this wing, which held a mixed bag of *haoles*, locals, and a few foreigners. There was one policeman named Joe, from the Honolulu Police Department, who was up on corruption charges. Joe would likely be in danger in any of the state dorms, so they elected to put him in with the federal prisoners. A conspicuously gay young man came in shortly after I did, and Joe managed to have him assigned to his cell. No violence occurred, but the guy had to perform oral sex on Joe every day. I remember going to the showers early in the morning, seeing the guy on his knees between Joe's legs. If there wasn't any violence involved, who cared? Not the guards, much less the prisoners.

There were also a few Hawaiian brothers in there from a famous crime syndicate on the Big Island. The boss had already been sentenced and was on his way to a maximum-security prison on the mainland. One of the brothers, Sonny, was a friendly guy who laughed a lot and hardly seemed like the syndicate guys I'd known years ago. Sonny was up on several felony drug charges. However, his brother was creepy; he had been charged with around forty hits (murders) for the syndicate. He had an evil and extremely daunting look in his eyes. Not that he bothered anybody, but then again, who would have been stupid enough to mess around with someone like him? A cold darkness surrounded him; I felt it intensely anytime I was in close proximity to him.

Another interesting guy there was a Japanese *yakuza*. He was short and stocky, and had four of his fingers cut off, which made me speculate that he had messed up at least four times. Another memorable guy, Juno, was an absolutely crazy, young, eighteen-year-old Samoan kid with a pea brain and an enormously muscled body. To boot, he was extremely volatile. Juno had a very high voice, which reminded me of Mike Tyson's. Sometimes he'd just go off on someone for no reason, also reminding me of Tyson. He was always beating the crap out of somebody. He had hurt several prisoners, one of which was my cellmate, Paul, whose eyes were swollen shut and face remained bruised for weeks after Juno made a punching bag out of him. Eventually, the kid was removed from Corridor D.

There was also a fairly young guy of Portuguese descent who hassled me when I first came in. There are many people of Portuguese descent in Hawaii; they are called *Portigee* in local pigeon language. This guy was always mouthing-off at me. Usually, I would tell him to *take it to the can* because he really didn't frighten me. One day, about a month after I had arrived, Mr. Portigee started getting particularly abusive with me. I really couldn't have cared less what he thought, but he just wouldn't leave me alone. At this point, I was simply tired of his crap. I'd been to court that day and had to deal with decisions on pleas and what sentences I might receive. No matter what recommendations the prosecutor makes to the judge in a plea deal, you don't know the outcome until the sentence is passed. He could choose to accept or reject the deal, although they generally went along with the prosecution. I was tired and feeling emotionally unsettled. It was impossible to meditate in here, except in the early morning hours. Conditions were better where I was, but there was less space for getting away from the jerks that were always in your face.

Finally, I told Mr. Portigee to take his act somewhere else. I guess he figured I would never react to his words with my fists, so he continued to bully me without anticipating any opposition. Puffing up his chest, he walked over to me and pushed my shoulders, throwing me back and slamming my head into the wall. That was a bad move on his part. He picked the wrong guy at the wrong time. Ironically, my lawyer had just warned me that because I'd jumped bail it was possible for me to be sent to a maximum-security prison to serve whatever sentence I received. Being sent to a place like Marion Federal Penitentiary was unimaginable to me, even after all I'd already been through in Thai prison. Portigee's move was the straw that broke the camel's back. Grabbing the hair on both sides of his head, I head-butted him, just as I'd done to the clown in the immigration jail in Bangkok, except this time I was furious; it was more like the time I had beaten Stephano with the chair in Klong Prem Prison.

When I started pounding Portigee's head into the bars of the cell, it caused a big commotion among the inmates. Sonny and another guy finally managed to pull me off of him. I let go and he slumped to the ground, bleeding. There was blood all over the place. Barely conscious when the guards came in, they took him directly to the hospital. They were about to take me to solitary confinement when Joe intervened on my behalf. He told them that the guy had deserved his beating because he had been badgering me and I only reacted as I did when he physically attacked me. It was a simple case of self-defense. They left me with only a verbal reprimand. *No more fighting*. The next day Portigee was returned to our wing; he never even looked at me cross-eyed after that.

Directly upstairs from us was Corridor B. The gay wing. Many of these guys were also transsexuals. We were allowed out in the yard for an hour each day, along with the inmates of Corridor B. Maybe they figured we were the least likely to bother them, and apart from Juno, they were correct.

As for me, my attorney did a great job. He had me evaluated by psychologists, and had letters written to the judge on my behalf by family members and others. The result was far better than I had expected. I agreed to plead guilty to two of the conspiracy charges, so they dropped the rest. My case had been before the best judge possible, according to Earl. The morning of my sentencing I was up at 4 AM trying to meditate, but I couldn't. Too distracted, I prayed until it was time to leave for the courthouse. After breakfast, I was called out of my cellblock and handcuffed, then put in a van with a half dozen others who were going to court that day. After a short time in the holding cell, I was called into the courtroom, as my name was first on the docket. Earl was waiting for me, and I walked to the front of the room, where he stood beside a table. Once the judge entered, we were ordered to *All Rise* and then to *Be Seated*. I sat in nervous anticipation behind the table; after a few moments, my name was called. I stood up along with my attorney, Earl, who spoke on my behalf, after which the judge asked if I had anything to say. "Yes, your honor," I offered, licking my dry as sandpaper lips.

I did my best to make a good impression on the judge. I truly was a changed man. Nothing about me remotely resembled my former self. I had also written letters, one to the judge and one to the prosecutor. I reiterated that I'd spent two and a half years in a Thai prison before coming back to the US to answer these charges and I had altered my way of thinking. My entire outlook on life had genuinely changed. Throwing myself on the mercy of the court, I asked that I be given an opportunity to become a contributing member of society, not another long-term prison system statistic. In conclusion, I thanked the court for allowing me to speak and asked for its kind consideration.

Then the judge spoke: He said that at his discretion, my sentence could be anywhere from a minimum of eighteen months to a maximum of twenty-five years on each of the charges. He said that he believed my words were sincere and that he was going to give me a chance to prove it. I was on pins and needles, waiting for his judgment. He sentenced me to two concurrent eighteen-month sentences for the conspiracy charges (the maximum could have been *a fifty-year sentence*). In addition, a three-year special parole would be imposed on me after my release. This meant I would serve eighteen months in prison with the possibility of time off for good behavior followed by another three years on parole. The other charges were dropped. Needless to say, my attorney and I were extremely happy!

Next, we had to deal with the state charges. For those, I had to go back to state court. Although the state judge sentenced me to ten years in prison, he suspended my having to serve any more time. I was to be released with "time served" and then *paroled to the Feds*, which meant I was, at that moment, on parole from the state of Hawaii and released into the custody of the federal government. Therefore, when the Feds released me from prison, I'd be on both federal and state parole. As well, when the term of special parole was over, I could apply to the state for release from their parole. I couldn't have hoped for a better outcome. I promised myself that the rest of my life would bear no resemblance to what it had been in the years before my *Awakening*.

Earl tried to get me sent to a camp, the lowest security facility, to do my time. These prisons don't even have fences around them. This is about the least stressful place to do prison time in terms of the sorts of inmates and facilities inside, but our request was denied. The reason was due to my having skipped bail back in 1981, which the court viewed as being no different from a prison escape. Therefore, the lowest security prison I was allowed to go to, according to federal guidelines, was a Level Three. (Camps are Level One and the prisons are more secure as the number gets higher. Level Six is the highest because, of course, these maximum-security prisons house the most dangerous criminals.)

The judge sentenced me to serve out my sentence at Pleasanton, a prison in northern California, which was, believe it or not, actually a co-ed prison back then. This sounded like it wouldn't be too bad a way to do my time. Maybe I would forget my angst at not being able to go to a Level One camp. The biggest worry that I had was being sent to a maximum-security facility, where someone like me might not survive to tell the tale. Now that I knew that wasn't going to happen, I relaxed and prepared to bide my time until my release the following year.

CHAPTER 37

Pleasanton Federal Correctional Institution

One day, without any notice, the Feds picked me up from the jail in Honolulu and took me to the airport. Two Federal Marshals and I, boarded a regular commercial flight bound for Tucson, Arizona, which was the first stop on the way to Pleasanton, California. By evening, I was at the Metropolitan Community Correctional Institution, Tucson (MCC), where I remained for the next two weeks. There were some heavies in there, so fights, rapes, and a variety of altercations within the prison population were not uncommon. However, I managed to steer clear of trouble in my short time there.

The cells were more like two-man dorm rooms, which afforded a bit more privacy than cells with bars. They had concrete block walls with a heavy steel reinforced door. The facility was fairly new, so it really wasn't too bad, considering my accommodations over the past three years. I found adequate time to resume my meditation in the evenings, and my cellmate was quite respectful of my practice.

The prison was one where you were given prison-issued clothes to wear. Upon arrival, you went through the usual strip search and then were ushered to a window where you received your *attire*. Whatever the closest sizes in underwear, T-shirts, and jeans they had was what you got. This is where the style of young men wearing their pants so low that their butts hang out was derived. You're not allowed belts in prison, for obvious reasons, so if they didn't have your size, you got something larger. Often the pants are so big in the waist that they fall down or the legs are too long, so much so that they are scrunched up on your shoes. The *prison look* became a style for gang members on the outside.

There were plenty of facilities for exercise. They had free weights and chinning bars, which allowed me to resume the same exercise regimen I'd begun in Thai prison. This place was like a boarding school compared to the one in Bangkok, as far as facilities and basic cleanliness were concerned. In Thailand, the living conditions were filthy. You were exposed to a myriad of infectious diseases, and putrid sewer smells constantly assaulted your senses. In comparison, the living conditions here were almost sterile. In U.S. prisons, however, you have to be wary of violence coming from other prisoners, yet not so much from the guards, at least not until you pissed them off. Going along with the program, I did what I was told and kept to myself as much as possible. I had nothing to prove to anyone. I just wanted to do my time and get out ASAP.

In two weeks, the federal transport plane came for the next leg of my trip. A group of us, all in transit and waiting to be transferred to other prisons, were taken to a military airfield. For this flight, we were not only handcuffed, but we also wore waist chains attached to the handcuffs, plus every-one had on leg chains. This was *just standard procedure*, the Marshals said. It didn't matter if you were in for a year for a minor offense or doing a triple life sentence for murder: Everyone was transported in the same manner.

The plane made several stops along the way until we finally arrived at Vandenberg Air Force Base, which was adja-cent to Lompoc Federal Prison. Anyone going to Lompoc was taken there without delay. Most of the other prisoners had to go into a county lock-up until their next transport plane was scheduled, except for those of us going on to Pleasanton. There was a van on the runway waiting for two of us. Also waiting in the van were a few female prisoners, so you could only imagine what the two of us were thinking.

Within a few hours we arrived, and the actual induction process was fairly quick. We were taken to the men's building. The dorms were like college dorms, except they were made out of concrete blocks and had heavy reinforced steel doors. They were locked from the outside at night. The windows were made of such thick glass that it would take a sledgehammer to break one; they couldn't be opened. A bunk bed, dresser, toilet, and sink were inside each cell, and they were clean and more than sufficient. My cellmate, Jesse, hailed from the mountains of Oregon. He had been working as a logger prior to his arrest. His crime? Burning out a mine with a Molotov cocktail, something that he had been paid to do. In any case, he was pleasant enough to be around and wasn't at all bothered that I wanted to be left alone to meditate in the evenings. Most inmates preferred to watch TV in the Common Room rather than stay in their cells. Anyway, he gave me plenty of space to read, meditate, or simply contemplate life.

Pleasanton was an interesting mix. The men were housed on one side of a main courtyard and the women were housed in their dorms on the other. For men, your security level couldn't be higher than Level 3, which meant you were a nonviolent offender. The only exceptions were inmates who had been in for a long time and had earned a reduction in their security level, which allowed them to eventually transfer out of a high security prison. Usually, this only happened when they were within a year or two of being released. It's worth mentioning that there was a high fence around the perimeter, but no wall.

On the women's side, the security classifications went all the way up to Level 6, the most serious and violent offenders. Quite a few were in for murder or an assortment of other felonies. Some had notoriety, like one who had murdered all four of her children by throwing them off of a cliff. Others had been convicted of crimes ranging from assault with a deadly weapon to armed robbery. There were also a significant number in for drug offenses. An entire contingent of Thai women were housed here, every single one of them convicted for attempting to smuggle heroin into the country. They had all been mules — women given packed cases of heroin in Thailand to carry on a flight bound for the U.S. *Not one of them made it past Customs.*

In most men's prisons, especially where the inmates have higher security classifications, there are frequent incidents of sexual violence. In Pleasanton, however, none of that stuff went on. Gay men would be left alone, not forced to perform sex acts. Most of the guys actually had girlfriends, but this is where the rules got *really silly.* Men and women were allowed to hold hands, but nothing more. No kissing, sex, lying down together, *or whatever.* Therefore, inmates were always finding innovative ways to have a "quickie" beyond the vision of the guards' ever-watchful eyes. Most of the guards weren't really interested in busting inmates for having sex anyway. If you were the least bit discreet, you could get away with it. For one or two guys, though, it became an obsession. They were the kind of men who seemed never to have been with a woman. You know the type. The type that girls turn their backs to while making that *stick-your-finger-down-your-throat*, gag me sign to their friends.

On the women's side, it wasn't so clear-cut. There were a number of really tough lesbians. Obviously, they were not interested in men, but with some of the others you were never quite sure. We all ate meals in the same cafeteria and the sexes mingled freely. Definitely not what most inmates would have expected in a correctional facility. Nobody complained.

One day, while I was talking to a very attractive blonde gal in the cafeteria who was maybe twenty-two years old, a super butch black lady interrupted us. She looked me straight in the eye and warned that if I didn't stay away from her woman, she'd kick my ass. And, she could have! This Amazon was over six feet tall with a cropped flattop that stuck straight up on her head. She had long, muscled arms and biceps that would have cracked my skull like a walnut inside the crook of *either* arm. She was like something out of a horror movie. Needless to say, I stopped talking to the blonde and apologized. I never so much as looked at her again.

Everyone had to work. All inmates had jobs and worked for about six hours a day. There were both industrial jobs and office work, while others worked in the kitchen, laundry, or on the grounds. My job was taking care of the grounds around the men's dorm. I would mow the grass and water the bushes and flowers, something I enjoyed doing, especially since it allowed me to be on my own.

The favored place for couples to spend time together was on the track field. The track was sizeable, at least a quarter mile or more. There were a number of exercise pit stops along the way, much as you'd find in public parks in cities like LA or NYC. For instance, one stop had chinning bars; another, a place to hook your feet under; and another one, to do sit-ups. At each exercise pit, there was a sign with instructions on how to do a particular exercise. Each sign was just large enough to hide the midsection of a person's body, and if you stood behind it, it provided a perfect sex station for a "quickie."

There was also a game room complete with pool and Ping-Pong tables. They even had a movie room. At least once a week, we would have movie night. Like naughty pubescent teenagers, many men cut out the bottoms of their sweatpants pockets to allow a girlfriend to reach in and give him a handjob during the movie while the lights were out. Some women did the same, allowing their partner the same access, in an X-rated National Lampoon movie script sort of way.

Most couples spent a good deal of their free time walking around the track holding hands, which really looked more like something you would see at a junior high school rather than at a prison. The only time I remember anyone getting caught was when a guy simply *had* to give his girlfriend oral sex. He and his partner had tried to be discreet in a corner of the game room behind some tables. On his knees, he made slurping noises as she cried out, "*Oh, Oh, Oh.*" Last we heard, he was being transferred to a high security prison. He probably went on to give oral sex for the rest of his sentence, but the recipients were more likely to have names like Tyrone or Big John.

I don't believe that co-ed prisons are a very good idea. On the one hand, you're allowed to hold hands, sit together at meals, and watch movies while huddled closely together in a dark room, but on the other, you're forbidden to have sex. It's absurd. Pleasanton's no longer a coed prison, though. Someone working for the Feds must have finally realized that *it doesn't work!* I have to admit, though, it wasn't a bad way to do the rest of my prison time.

CHAPTER 38

Back to the Real World

My time at Pleasanton was relatively short, only eight months from the day I arrived to the day I was released. At long last, I *almost* walked out a free man after serving a total of fourteen months out of the eighteen-month federal prison sentence. I say *almost* because I still had to fulfill a three-year term of special parole. My brother Brad had arranged for a limo to pick me up outside the prison gates on the day of my release. After giving the driver my bag and sitting down in the back seat, he asked me, "Where do you want to go? You have the limo for the whole day."

"Take me to the airport," I replied.

"But you have the car for the whole day," he protested.

"I don't care; just take me to the airport. You can take the day off and enjoy the limo." Sitting in the back seat while looking out the window at American suburban life, it was hard to believe my long nightmare was finally over. This day not only began my parole for the Feds, it also began my parole for the state of Hawaii. I couldn't help reflecting on the last 4+ years and that I was now 31 years old. I had my life back along with an opportunity to create a new one. Doing exactly what? I asked myself. I knew there'd be *a long and winding road* ahead, but I was ready.

In the meantime, I appreciated being able to watch the scenery go by through an open window with a breeze blowing on my face. My first destination was Los Angeles, where I planned to stay for a few days. After more than four years, my first order of business was to see my daughter. How would she react? What would I say? Would my ex treat me with the same cold, cruel attitude? These questions were foremost in my mind. But I'd have my answers soon enough. I was nervous, with a sense of trepidation about seeing my ex. Rhonda knew I was coming to see Debbie, so hopefully there wouldn't be any explosive scenes. I couldn't afford any crazy 911 calls saying that I was making threats or something worse.

They weren't expecting me at the parole office in Philadelphia until the following week, which gave me a little time to visit with my daughter in hopes of reestablishing our relationship after so many lost years. Meanwhile, my parents had generously offered me a room in their home in Philadelphia while I attempted to rebuild my life. Upon reaching the San Francisco Airport, I thanked the driver.

"Sure you don't want a tour of the area?" he asked. "The car's yours for the day." I smiled *No thanks*, closed the door, and walked into the terminal with my small bag. I found a pay phone and placed a call to Rhonda to let her know to expect me the following day. My brother had already called her to announce my intention to visit. I hadn't seen Debbie for four years. Rhonda had no legal grounds to deny me visitation rights, but when her husband answered the phone and handed it to Rhonda, the disdain in her voice gave me the shivers. She was curt and cold as ice. That she could still feel so much animosity toward me was disheartening. I prayed she would not create a scene when I arrived.

I took a cab to Brenda's, an old friend who lived just a few blocks from my ex's apartment. She had offered to let me sleep on her couch while I was visiting, but I spent a long and sleepless night thinking about the next day, trying to imagine what it would be like to see my daughter.

Finally, it was time to walk the three blocks to their apartment: Down Regent Street, left on Watseka Avenue, and on to the apartment building in the center of the Hare Krishna

Community. Memories flooded back from when I had lived there before, but I pushed them aside. I was about to walk through the door into the courtyard when a group of four young men stopped me. The men were well-groomed with close-cropped haircuts, and they were wearing sports jackets. The beads on their necks identified them as Hare Krishna devotees. "*Hamsavatar!*" (my Sanskrit name: one who descends as a swan), one of them exclaimed.

"Yes?" I answered.

"We're here to escort you to *Sita's* (Rhonda's Sanskrit name) apartment," another stated.

"Why?" I asked, "I'm here to see my daughter, and I don't require an escort, thank you very much!"

"Well, you're not going without us, so don't try anything" the first goon challenged. While speaking, he pulled back his sports jacket ever so slightly, revealing the handle of a holstered pistol. Scanning the others, I saw that they all had bulges in their jackets.

"What are you going to do, shoot me?" I asked in disgust. I had lots more going through my mind to say to them, but managed to hold my tongue because I was on a mission and wished to get as far away from these people as I possibly could.

Surrounded by the *Hare Krishna Mafioso (HKM)*, I walked up a flight of stairs to an apartment door. One of them knocked. Rhonda's husband, John, opened the door and nodded without saying a word. The *HKM* started to go in with me, but I stopped them, "You're not coming in! I'm here to see my daughter, and you're not invited!" John nodded a second time and suggested that the men wait outside the door. Trying to keep my composure, I walked into their apartment. Nothing could have prepared me for the reception I received. The air was thick with anger, hatred, and animosity. Debbie was sitting on the couch next to her mother. To me, the look in her eyes spoke volumes. She was obviously terrified. I tried speaking to her, simply saying, "Hi Debbie," but she hid behind her mother. Then I asked if they would please be kind enough to leave me alone with her for a while. Rhonda's response was to scream, "Absolutely not!"

John chimed in, "Who do you think you are anyway? You're nothing but a criminal and a drug addict! You have no rights here."

In truth, I did have the right to be there. Our divorce had been an uncontested one. There were no conditions that I had to fulfill other than to pay child support, and my parents had kept the payments up during my incarceration. We shared legal custody, and although she had physical custody of our daughter, *I had visiting rights*. Rhonda wasn't supposed to make decisions about Debbie's schooling, or make any other major decisions for that matter, without consulting me. However, my ex always did her best to snip me out of the picture. Her eyes were now spitting venom.

Their heartless words cut me to my heart's core. Didn't they know? Could they not imagine what I had been through for the past four years? Had they not a single grain of compassion? After all, Rhonda knew how much I loved our daughter. I had never been anything but a loving father toward her, and whenever possible I was patient and attentive to her needs. As I tried to talk to Debbie, Rhonda's dark eyes burned and John just sat there with a smug look on his face, arms across his chest. Every time I'd speak to my daughter, Rhonda answered for her, not giving Debbie a chance to speak for herself. In a loud tone of voice, just shy of shouting, she said, "She doesn't want to see you. She doesn't want anything to do with you. She just wants you to leave us alone!" Rhonda and John were emphatic. I was devastated. Beaten and battered from all I'd been through, my sole desire was to see my beloved daughter again, to rekindle our relationship and have the chance to somehow make things up to her.

Tears streamed from my eyes as I continued trying to speak to Debbie while Rhonda disallowed it. She raised her voice and grew more cruel and vile with her insults. All I seemed able to do was to cry pitifully. I was heartbroken. The most important person in the world to me had always been my daughter and now she was completely terrified of me. What had they told her? What kind of a mother would make her daughter so afraid of her father? Rhonda had poisoned Debbie's mind against me, and there was nothing I could do about it. My long awaited dream of seeing my little Princess again had become a nightmare.

Defeated, I finally got up to leave. Obviously, there was no point in sitting there only to be berated by my ex and her husband. I realized that I couldn't force myself on Debbie, although I shared legal custody. My intentions had been to never traumatize my daughter by dragging her through court proceedings. I had to accept Fate's decree in this matter, just as I had in everything else. Debbie was young, barely eight years old, and I had no idea what kind of lies and horrid stories she had been told. Whatever Rhonda and her husband had told Debbie of me, their words had obviously scared her. I had expected my initial visit to be a difficult one, but I never anticipated the sight of sheer terror on my daughter's face. I looked once more into Debbie's frightened little eyes and said, "I love you, Princess. I always have and I always will."

Getting up from the chair, I walked to their door, took one last look at Debbie, and stepped out past the *HKM* who were waiting outside the door. I made it down the flight of stairs, through the courtyard, and past the door leading out to the street. Ignoring the four men as they hurried along behind me, I turned and slowly made my way back to Brenda's house.

CHAPTER 39
Returning to Where It All Began

The following day, I flew to Philadelphia where my family gave me a warm welcome. My father and I both had tears in our eyes as we hugged. I hugged my mother closely and told them both, "Thank you, I can never repay you for all you've done to help me get out of that terrible place."

In the evening, my brother met us for dinner downtown. We embraced each other, glad to finally be together again. Ever since Ricky had died, Brad and I had become extremely close, and of course there had been a time when I thought I'd never see any of them again.

My first order of business was to check in with the Federal Parole Office, only a fifteen-minute walk from my parents' apartment. A parole officer had already been assigned to me. Naturally, he read me the Riot Act. All the rules and regulations of my special parole were explained in excruciating detail. Any infractions meant my parole would be revoked, and I'd spend the next three years in a federal penitentiary. I promised him that I would follow every stipulation. Absolutely! Gainful employment was one requirement, so I had to find a job, which is not an easy task for an ex-convict. Somehow, I had to find work. I would also have to take weekly drug tests, which meant providing a urine sample in the presence of my parole officer. My movements were restricted to the state of Pennsylvania, unless granted permission to travel elsewhere. Once I found a job, I would have to present my pay stubs every week to prove I was truly working full-time.

Without notice, a parole officer could visit my home and demand a urine sample. They could search my person or my residence. Basically, my life rested upon the whim of my parole officer. Remember that old Dustin Hoffman movie, *Straight Time* when Dustin's character chained his parole officer to the dividing fence on the highway, pulled his pants down, and drove away in his car? That movie was the closest thing to keeping company with a parole officer I'd ever experienced, until this day! Whatever I had to do, I would do. I'd bite my tongue and do my time on parole just as I had done my time inside. Even if he were the type who wanted to harass me, I was determined not to allow myself to be shaken. *This Too Shall Pass* became another of my mantras. My parole officer didn't seem like too bad a guy, although I was wary. Agreeing to everything he said, I assured him that I would be there to see him without fail every week. I would fully comply with all the rules and regulations, and I would somehow find a job.

Dick Atkins, the attorney who had been so instrumental in getting me out of Klong Prem Prison, lived and practiced law in Philadelphia, so I gave him a call to thank him once again for all he had done on my behalf. He was thrilled to hear that I was finally out of prison. He heard what had happened after my release on bail in Bangkok, and he also knew that I had done more prison time here in the US. We made a date to get together. I wanted to thank him personally for the immense assistance he had offered me in my darkest hour. Had he not been willing to explain the realities of the Thai legal system to my father, I surely would still be imprisoned in Thailand for another ten to twenty years.

I met Dick at his office and related the events of the past year and a half. He commented that I must have had *someone watching over me*, considering how the sentence I'd received from the federal judge was so extraordinary. Dick had a client who owned a store on the local Jewelers' Row who he said might be able to help me find a job. Why? Because Dick had recently helped the man's son get out of some *very sticky* legal drug-related problems. Perhaps the man would be willing to return the favor by helping me since I was a Graduate Gemologist, fully qualified to work in a jewelry store. Not only that, I had plenty of experience in the wholesale trade.

Meanwhile, I continued my daily, early morning meditation practice. I joined a health club, as there was one right next door that gave a discount to residents of the apartment building my parents lived in. I also did a lot of walking, hoofing it all over Center City, Philadelphia. Walking helped me think and was also good for me, physically. It would take a while to fully normalize myself internally after years of incarceration. By day, memories flooded my head, and by night they entered my dreams. The scars of Thai prison life would remain with me for many years, possibly for life.

Within days, Dick called to say his friend came through; a jeweler he knew actually needed someone. Since I was a qualified gemologist, he was willing to interview me for the position. Immediately upon receiving the contact, I went to the jewelry shop to introduce myself. In turn, they gave me a short interview and seemed satisfied. I was to start the following Monday. *I did it!* I told myself, then quickly revised my self-congratulatory thought to: *No, the universe has given me another chance to prove myself! Thank you.* Walking home through the city streets at a lively pace, I bought a bite to eat, then called Dick to share the good news. Pleased for me, he said he would thank his friend. I said that I would also thank him personally, which would be easy because his shop was right across the street from where I would be working.

My next parole visit gained me quick approval from my parole officer who hadn't imagined I would be able to get a job so quickly, let alone get one working for a jeweler. He accompanied me to the bathroom for the "urine sample shuffle" and reminded me to bring my pay stub after I received my first check.

Monday through Friday, 8:30 AM to 5:30 PM and Saturday 8:30 AM to 1:00 PM were my work hours at the jewelry store. The lowest man on the totem pole, I was delegated all the menial tasks. But I was grateful to have the job, knowing that most cons have to take jobs at a local car wash, almost the only places willing to hire them. I waited on customers if the other salespeople were busy, but I was also expected to sweep the floors, empty the trash, and clean the glass display cases.

Whenever it began to get to me, I reminded myself, *this too shall pass*. I did what I had to do. I got through every day and every week without any serious problems in any sphere of my life. Without friends to socialize with, I began frequenting a local health food store & café. Sitting there on Saturday afternoons in the cafe drinking tea or juice, I would often find someone to share a bit of conversation with. At the time, beyond the reach of my work, the gym, daily walks, meditation practice, and the café, this was my life. It felt so strange.

One day, in late spring of 1985, Dick called and asked if I would be interested in being a guest on a local Philadelphia radio show to discuss what it was like to be arrested in a foreign country. They wanted guests who had actually gone through the experience. Since I had survived the infamous Bangkok Hilton and lived to tell the tale, they were eager to have me on the show. The other guest was Billy Hayes, the man who had written a very successful book titled *Midnight Express*, which detailed his escape from a Turkish prison. Later, a movie was produced based on his book. During the radio show, each of us spoke on the horrors of having been incarcerated in foreign countries: Turkey and Thailand. The host, Bernie Herman, prodded us with questions we answered by sharing our experiences. I actually did the interview using my parents' kitchen telephone.

Showing up at work every day was no problem. I had long ago learned to become disciplined. What I found difficult was constantly being *talked down to*. All day, it was "Beckman, if you're not busy do this. Beckman, clean the floor if there are no customers," even when the floor had already been washed and didn't need washing again. Working at a job where I was accorded little respect and working for peanuts became frustrating. But never mind, I reminded myself, *this too shall pass.* After spending all those years in prison, I knew I would do whatever it took to complete my legal obligations. Once off parole, I was certain I would find something more fulfilling to do. Meanwhile, I learned yet another lesson in humility.

Something else very important was missing from my life at this time, female companionship. But what woman wants to go out with a parolee? I was starting to meet women I was attracted to and who seemed naturally attracted to me, but I wondered how many of them would still be interested in me had I told them I was on parole, living with my parents, and hadn't a *pot to piss in.* **Then,** I ran into Tracy, an old friend from back in high school. She ran her own business, manufacturing maternity clothes and was divorced; she wasn't currently in a relationship. Having known her for a long time, I was able to be completely honest with her. Know what? She didn't care, so we started seeing each other. Before long, I was staying at her house more than at my parents' place. Another month passed, and she asked if I would like to move in with her. Her house was in New Jersey, a short drive over the bridge from Philadelphia. If I wanted to change jobs, she offered me one running her office. I would keep the books, payroll, accounts-receivable & payable, and whatever else needed to be done. Basically, I would handle all the paperwork, freeing her to concentrate on the manufacturing and sales aspects of her line of clothing.

"Hmmm, let's see," you're probably thinking, "Live with your new girlfriend who not only has her own house and business, she also gives you a job that covers you with the parole board. Or, work as the gopher at a jewelry store while living in Mommy and Daddy's apartment." Sure, using that line of thinking it is a no-brainer, and I was genuinely fond of Tracy. She accepted me for who I was without any pretention.

Knowing I needed to clear it with my parole officer first, I wasted no time seeing him. Since things were going so smoothly with him, I wanted to maintain the status quo. He permitted me to move in with Tracy and work for her because I could still use my parents' address as my legal residence. The next morning, I gave notice at the jewelry store, and two weeks later I spent my last day on that job. That afternoon, I packed up my belongings and moved into Tracy's house. Working in her office was easy for me, but I didn't want to make a career out of it. However, for a while it was like being released from *another kind of confinement*. But, being together around the clock began to adversely impact our relationship, so I began to seriously ponder ways to get back into the only business I really knew and loved — the gem trade.

I started doing visualizations every day, picturing myself selling gems. Knowing all the ins and outs of the business, it was easy to meditate on the specifics. I would *see* myself with a bag filled with goods travelling to places I had already been to on business. Every day, my visualizations progressed as I concentrated on how I would *feel* rather than on the sales and business aspects. To me, my interaction with others and the satisfaction of doing something I enjoyed were the two most important factors. Of course, visualizing financial success didn't hurt either.

CHAPTER 40

Opportunity Knocks at the Holiday Inn

Over a year had passed since I was released from Pleasanton. Fulfilling all of my obligations, I remained in good standing with my parole officer. When I checked in, I asked him if he had a few moments to talk. Sitting across from him in his stuffy little office, I presented an idea to him. With his permission, I wanted to go to the annual wholesale gem trade show in Tucson, Arizona. My aim was to find an opportunity to work for a gem company as a sales representative. To make a long story short, he agreed. "Yes, I'll give you all the rope you need. Either you'll use it to pursue a meaningful career or you'll hang yourself with it. I'll tell you frankly, Howard, I'm going out on a limb for you, but for some reason, I actually believe in you." With a fixed eye on me he added, "Just let me know when and where you intend to go. I'll give you documents showing that you have my permission to travel there."

I was exhilarated as I drove home to New Jersey. The universe was giving me the opportunity to create the life that I wanted. Tracy thought it was a fantastic idea, and I think she was also happy to get me out of the house for a few days. Besides, with me becoming financially independent, our relationship would be healthier. In a few weeks, I was sitting on a plane bound for Tucson with 150 business cards showing my old company name and my current phone number and address in New Jersey. My plan was to go to the two biggest wholesale gem shows in the county and see who I would run into. After arriving in Tucson, I picked up a car, took the scenic mountain-view drive to the hotel, and checked in. First, I planned to go to the American Gem Trade Association's Show and then on to the Gem and Lapidary Association's Show, the biggest and most well-known gem trade shows in the United States. They were held twice annually, and at the February shows, I would most likely see people I knew. These shows were famous the world-over because there were so many going on simultaneously throughout the city.

First, I went to the American Gem Trade Association (AGTA) exhibition at the Holiday Inn. Walking around leisurely, I observed the booths and display cases from dozens of gem companies. It didn't take long before I met someone I knew. Isaac had been an emerald dealer for many years. He sold Zambian emeralds rather than Colombian, the source country of the emeralds I once sold in Hawaii. I told him that I was looking for someone who needed a business representative. He said he didn't need anyone, but would be happy to give me a good reference if I needed one, which I took as a good omen. I saw a few other people I knew, but most of them were one- or two-man shows and didn't hire reps, which was not unusual in the business. Feeling hungry, I decided to go to the hotel restaurant for lunch. Carrying a menu, the hostess took me through the restaurant to a table on the far side of the room. After being seated, I looked at the menu and then looked around for a waitress. That's when I noticed who was sitting at a table near me. I couldn't believe my eyes! There, sitting by himself having lunch was John Baines, the Texan for whom I sold emeralds when I first returned to Hawaii from LA. "John!" I called out while walking over to him.

"Howard! How the hell are you? Good to see you!" He jumped up and extended his hand to shake mine, "Are you with anyone?" he asked, looking behind me.

"No, just me" I said.

"Well then," he offered. "Sit on down. It's been years!"

We talked over lunch, and for a good hour thereafter. After telling me about his business and personal life, he asked about mine. I told John I'd been living overseas and had recently moved back to the States, adding how I had made some bad investments, which cost me my shirt. My version of what had happened was not much of a stretch from the truth. I also told him that I was here looking for an opportunity to *rep for somebody*.

Looking at me earnestly, John asked, "Why don't you sell stones for me again?" He told me that he had two partners now, but *if I could still sell like I used to*, he was sure they would be interested in having me work with them. I noted the way he had said *with them* rather than *for them*. His word choice told me that he respected me and felt that if I were to come *on board*, I would be an asset to their company.

John quickly took me to meet one of his partners. George was manning their booth at one of the shows, and we immediately hit it off. Their other partner was the primary buyer and was rarely stateside. He tended to remain in Colombia. We made arrangements for me to visit their office in Dallas in a few weeks to discuss the particulars. Mission accomplished!

Elated by what I had accomplished, I decided to return to Philadelphia the following day because there was no reason to bother going to the other shows. In a few weeks, I would fly to Dallas, spend the weekend with John, and get reacquainted. We had been good friends back in 1979, and he now seemed happy to have me back on his team.

I didn't wait for my next scheduled appointment to speak with Dick, my parole officer. Hoping to get him on board, I called him the minute I got home. "I found a great opportunity!" I said, excitedly. Later the same day, I went to his office and related everything exactly as it had transpired. "I'll need to go to Dallas in two weeks" I said. "And, then I will need your permission to travel to whichever states I can claim as my territory."

"If you can prove to me that what you say is true, I'll go along with it. But, you have to be one hundred percent straight with me, Howard." He was used to interacting with lying and conniving ex-con druggies, so I wasn't offended. It was obvious that he had faith in me; otherwise, he wouldn't have let me go in the first place. Dick Hill had never had a parolee who was even remotely like me, and he readily admitted it. He truly wanted me to succeed. It must have been refreshing for him to have somebody he felt worthy enough to go the extra mile for.

My trip to Dallas went well, and I was "on board," as John had put it the day we'd bumped into each other in Tucson. Pennsylvania, New Jersey, Delaware, Maryland, and Washington, DC became my territory. They didn't have anyone else on the East Coast selling their goods. Every day I would contemplate where to go by researching all of the jewelry stores in the area. A member of the Jewelers Board of Trade, John gave me a copy of their directory. All I had to do next was to make contacts and close some sales!

My visualizations became very pointed: Picturing exactly what I desired to achieve, I would *see* my success unfolding. At first it was rough sledding while establishing new contacts, but I worked tirelessly with patience and confidence knowing that success would come from my endeavors. Within a month, I had customers in Washington, DC; Baltimore; Philadelphia; New Jersey; and Wilmington, Delaware. Working six days a week, I figured anything worth having was worth working hard for.

Dick was more than pleased with my attitude and the headway I was making. He said I was his top success story. While in his locked office, I showed him some of the gems I carried so he would know I wasn't embellishing. After showing him invoices from my sales, as well as copies of checks that had been made out to me for commissions, Dick encouraged me to expand still further. By the time another three months passed, he said I only needed to report once a month. He gave me documents allowing me to travel all over the Northeast, giving me the leeway I needed to increase my client base. The work wasn't easy. Traveling constantly takes a toll, and anyone who has ever been a traveling salesman knows that catering to the whims of store buyers is a profound lesson in patience and humility. Yet, I never let the bad days sap my resolve or confidence. I had gained a *life barometer* few people could ever imagine.

I had been out of prison for almost eighteen months, so I asked Dick for permission to travel to the West Coast, mostly because California clients were calling me. Although I was doing well on the Eastern Seaboard, there were far more opportunities for an entrepreneur in the gem business on the other side of the map. Once again, Dick granted my request, and I was permitted to travel anywhere within the continental USA. Unfortunately though, things weren't good between Tracy and me by this time. I never knew anything about it, but before we hooked up, she had developed a bad cocaine habit. While I was away, she started doing it again, admitting that she'd only been clean for a matter of weeks when we started seeing each other. She had been hanging out with people I didn't even know and staying out late most nights while I was travelling. But even when I wasn't travelling, she continued to go out after work and return home in the wee hours of the morning. Finally, I had my fill. Not about to throw my life away again, I insisted she make a decision, a choice between *coke or us.* She chose coke. Sometimes, Fate makes it easier for us to turn major corners in our lives, and it was high time for me to remain faithful to my new direction.

Within a week, I was flying to the West Coast, LA. I devised a plan where I only had to return at the end of every other month to see Dick, my parole officer. I would show up at his office on the last weekday of one month and then return to the office again on the first weekday of the following month. I'd fulfill two months obligations in just a few days' stay. The requirement was one visit per calendar month, and they didn't need to be exactly a month apart. Dick was totally cool with this arrangement.

I tried to make contact with my daughter several times, but I was always rebuffed by Rhonda who threateningly insisted that, should I even think about trying to see Debbie, she'd call the police. Although I had every right to visit my daughter, should Rhonda call them with a story, ex-convicts, historically speaking, don't fare too well in such situations. Therefore, I chose to *err on the side of caution*, at least until my parole was over.

I rented a studio apartment in Marina Del Rey. It had a view of the harbor, which was not exactly an ocean view, but close. My exercise routine and meditation and visualization practice actually increased because I was living alone without distractions. Living close to the ocean allowed me to simply breathe in the fragrant sea air while taking my daily walks around the marina. Life was good, and I was extremely grateful to everyone along the way who had helped me *regain my life*.

Before long, I found myself in a relationship with a woman thirteen years my junior. Although we never married, I developed a paternal relationship with her son from the time he was four years old. Even after we split up some years later, he and I remained close, which we continue to be to this day. In every way, he is my son and I am his father. He actually took my last name, Beckman, when he became an adult.

Working hard, I gained greater success while making a few new friends. One business contact that I'd grown close to was a Beverly Hills jeweler named Bobby Proctor. He and his partner, Tom, had a store on Rodeo Drive called *Diamonds on Rodeo*. Its first claim to fame was when their store's sign was shown prominently during several scenes of the movie, *Pretty Woman*. I had begun to consign a large number of my goods to them when I wasn't on the road, and I enjoyed hanging out with Bob. The high-roller lifestyle, late nights, and wild women constituted a big part of Bob's daily life. Although he often invited me to accompany him, I rarely accepted. I didn't know how he did what he did and continued to show up at his office first thing each and every morning. He was, and still remains, a good friend. I remember those years fondly, and Bob's still in Beverly Hills. He also has satellite offices in Geneva and Hong Kong as he continues to *dance with the stars*.

Time passed quickly for me. Once I completed my three years, I was released from the special parole at the age of thirty-four. My lawyer petitioned the Hawaii State Court to discharge me from state parole, as well. They granted the request, and I was finally free of all legal constraints resulting from my dark and sordid past. I had fought many battles to overcome great odds. Like a mountain climber, I set my sights higher. I just needed more clarification on my next goals.

One day I got a call from an English gem dealer, Jim Stubby, who lived in Tokyo. His call came on the heels of our introduction to one another through a mutual friend. Jim was a former securities trader for one of the big international firms in Tokyo. He made a killing in profits one year, quit his job with the securities firm, and invested most of his earnings in Australian black opals. At the time of his call, he was firmly established as The King of Black Opals in Japan. **Because Bob invited me to** meet clients at his store on Rodeo Drive, Jim and I arranged to meet there. By this time, I carried quite an array of loose gems and jewelry pieces, and I showed him what I had to offer. Keen to expand into selling gems other than opals, Jim asked if I might consider flying to Tokyo. When he made the invitation, I smiled and immediately asked, "When do you want me to come?"

"You make decisions quickly," Jim noted, offering a warm smile. "You'd have to come and stay for two to three weeks. Things can't be completed overnight because the Japanese take their time." I smiled back at him, thinking I had learned enough lessons in patience to last a lifetime.

"No worries," I assured him, and we arranged to meet in Tokyo three weeks later. In the meantime, I managed to convince several other dealers and private collectors to take a chance on me. One private collector had a unique collection of antique jade bowls and urns. Although, at the time, I knew little about jade, but I figured *nothing ventured, nothing gained.* One thing I wasn't short on was confidence. A truism housed in a question came to me: If you haven't confidence in yourself, why should anyone else?

CHAPTER 41

Land of the Rising Sun

Three weeks later, I was riding in a spotless taxi, with a driver wearing immaculate white gloves, and I was on my way to Tokyo City from Nikko Narita Airport. After my first night in the smallest hotel room I had ever stayed in, I took a cab to Jim's office where he had already managed to put together a list of buyers for us to visit. I immediately began making calls to the buyer's stores and offices and going out with Jim's Japanese assistant, Shirodaya San. For me, the Japanese clients were extremely difficult to deal with, not that they were anything other than the most polite, courteous, and ingratiating people I have ever met in my life, but they managed to frustrate the hell out of me. The word yes didn't necessarily mean yes, and they never just came out and said no. How can anyone do business like this? I honestly never knew if we had closed a deal or not, and most of the time, during the first few days, we didn't close any deals. I just didn't get the Japanese way of negotiating.

Before the end of the first week, I decided to let Shirodaya San do all of the business without me because my presence seemed more of a hindrance than help, a decision that left me with quite a bit of free time for exploring Tokyo. I mostly used the subway for getting around and seeing places like Shibuya, Shinjuku, Roppongi, and the Ginza. However, my days always ended up at Jim's office, where I'd get a report on the day's events, and following that, Jim and I would go out for dinner. Because Jim was a member of the Foreign Correspondents Club (FCC), we would often end up meeting others from FCC. Terry Waite, the reporter who had been held hostage by terrorists in Lebanon was a notable member. I recall a board hanging in the FCC lounge depicting the number of days he'd been held captive. (It is worth noting that after almost five years, Terry Waite was finally released in late 1991.)

When I entered the country, Japanese Customs quickly cleared all the gems I carried, but they wouldn't allow the jade urns in without more documentation because they appeared to be antiques. Jim tried his best to get them cleared, but failed. Finally, I decided to try my luck in Hong Kong. With Hong Kong being a free port, there'd be no problem importing the urns there. Conveniently, it was only a four-hour flight from Tokyo to Hong Kong. After informing Japanese Customs that I no longer wanted to bring the jade in, I picked the cases up at the airport and boarded a flight bound for Hong Kong. Upon arrival, I chose to find a hotel in Kowloon to avoid the outrageously overpriced hotels in Central Hong Kong. I managed to sell all the jade within four days. I found the Chinese easier to deal with because once we shook hands on a deal it was final.

The hustle and bustle of Hong Kong reminded me of New York City, only Chinese style. I returned to Japan and met with Jim who had sold all he could for this trip. When Shirodaya San had things wrapped up on his end, I was on my way home to LA. Over the next few years, I continued to do well in business, both home and abroad. Clearly, I had succeeded in putting my life back together while creating a successful career. But something was missing. I firmly believed that there was a special reason for me to survive my near death experience. Although I was happy with my success, this wasn't it.

Before I knew it, India was calling me. I began having dreams where I was sitting in a temple listening to prayers or songs being chanted. Perhaps I could find my answers in

India. It had been years since my last journey to her shores, and it was time to visit my spiritual home again. Mark Twain once wrote: *In religion, India is the only millionaire. The one land that all men desire to see, and having seen it once, by even a glimpse, they would not give that glimpse up for all the shows of all the rest of the globe combined.* There is no country in the world in which so many mystical saints and spiritually charged places are to be found.

CHAPTER 42
India Bound

There were no direct flights to India back then, so I flew from LA to Europe and on to wherever I could get a connecting flight, depending on timing and price of airfares. I spent the night in Amsterdam and got my connecting flight the next morning. **Previously,** I had made New Delhi my port of entry because I loved visiting Vrindavan, in Uttar Pradesh State, which was about a three to four hour drive from New Delhi. Vrindavan had inspired a deeper contemplation on the eternality of life as I walked along small lanes leading to a plethora of temples and ancient holy places. This time, however, I decided to fly into Calcutta for my first port of entry because there was a little-known astrologer there who I wanted to meet. A friend of mine had told me that this man was the most startlingly accurate astrologer he'd ever met. His exact words were, "This guy really knows who you are."

Vedic Astrology had been a passion of mine prior to the dark chapters of my life and prison. My interest in Vedic Astrology had begun in the 1970s when I had studied some books and learned how to cast a chart. But, I hadn't had the time to properly delve into finer aspects. In India, astrologers were often doctors or priests and astrology was almost unilaterally accepted as an ancient science. There, astrology was neither relegated to the realm of superstition nor was it equated to psychics, tarot cards, or fortune telling. From a young age, most great astrologers have been, and continue to be, formally trained by a guru, and academically speaking they were well educated. The science is such that it combines the intellect of a mathematician and the knowledge of an astronomer. The best astrologers were also highly elevated spiritual teachers who possess a high degree of intuition far beyond the scope of ordinary human beings.

Knowing nothing about a person, except for their time and place of birth, he or she will *know* all about the person's nature, abilities, and the hidden secrets of their destiny. The past, present, and future are laid bare before one who can truly and accurately "see." Once you hear enough accurate information about your past from an astrologer you have never met before, you begin to feel that the insightful information shared with you about your past, present, and future should be *taken to heart and seriously considered.* One great astrologer I saw many years ago told me, "Action shapes destiny, but the opportunities and events seen in the birth horoscope will manifest with certainty. Karma must be accepted as it unfolds, but we should also realize that our actions are shaping our present, as well as creating our future." **Considering** such truths, why would anyone wish to avoid hearing it? Which begs the next question: How do we *know* truth when we hear it? The answer is that when you hear the truth, you are shaken to the core of your being. Hearing the truth forces you to step back, question old patterns of thinking, and seriously inquire as to the meaning of life itself.

I was seeking a man named Rabindranath, with only an address and general directions on how to find him. My friend *Shanti* was someone who had been journeying to India most of his life and he had studied yoga and Ayurveda in India for decades. *Shanti* had met with more mystic yogis, amazing healers, and awe-inspiring astrologers than anyone I'd ever known. I knew that if he said this astrologer was a rare and gifted individual, then he was.

For a Westerner who has never alighted upon her shores, India is like stepping into a storybook. Everywhere, one sees monks in white or orange robes walking down crowded roads. There are also bearded holy men with long, matted hair carrying no more than a staff and water pot as they mingle with thousands of others. The streets and lanes are filled with women dressed in brightly colored saris as well as many who have adopted contemporary Western-style clothing. All of this blends together amid automobiles, honking horns, oxen and camel-drawn carts, elephants, horses, and cows. Cacophonies of sounds blend with smells running the gamut between exotic and putrid. India can be overwhelming for a newcomer. However, none of the Indians pay particular attention to most of it because, to them, it is all quite normal.

Moreover, in Mother India, small fruit merchants and street vendors can be seen selling tasty delicacies alongside large stores and restaurants. In the cities, the noise can be deafening and disorienting. Cars zoom by and motorized rickshaws dodge in and out of the lanes, belching out black smoke from their exhaust pipes. In between the cars and motorized rickshaws, bicycle rickshaws are often seen driven by slender young men wearing ragged clothing. Carrying multiple persons or huge piles of goods in the passenger seat, these young men struggle to pedal their overweight cargo to its destination for only a few rupees.

For many Americans, seeing so many beggars everywhere can be quite disconcerting. Immediately, upon arrival at the old Calcutta Airport, they'd accost you. (They've now been moved to outside the airport terminals.) Some of the beggars are missing arms and/or hands, while others are missing feet and/or legs as they push themselves along as best they can. Others can be seen riding carts that nearly touch the ground. This vast public display of deformity seems shocking to the Western mind, forcing many to turn away or gasp in horror and disbelief. Women carrying children hold their hands out for alms. Old men shuffle along asking for whatever anyone might be willing to give. If you were to give money to every beggar you encountered, you would be flat broke within five minutes! Discretion and selective prudence is necessary. I gave, and continue to give, to those apparently handicapped, from a fixed daily sum of money I set aside for this purpose alone. Once you meet your monetary limit, you must simply walk on, keeping your eyes straight ahead.

Westerners are often stunned by the abundance of such extreme poverty. We anguish at the deprivation or physical deformities of these, our fellow human beings, who seem forced to live their indigent lives on the streets. "Karma," the Indians say, "All comes from one's previous actions." However true this may be, compassion and charity should be shown to everyone who is suffering. Most Indians I have known consider such charity as the duty of every human being. If you have little, you can only give a little. If you have more, you should give in greater measure. *Punya* (charity) is how the Vedas say a person is guaranteed a more prosperous birth in their next lifetime.

After spending the night in a small hotel, I set out on my quest to find Rabindranath, the *pandit* (learned scholar in India's Holy Scriptures, which contain all of the arts and sciences known to man). I took a motor rickshaw to the area of the city where Rabindranath lived. Upon arrival, the driver couldn't find the street. Deciding that I was better off getting a bicycle rickshaw, I paid the driver and stepped down into the busy streets of Calcutta. Carefully making my way through carts piled high with fruits or textiles, cars with impatient drivers leaning on their horns, and cows with languid eyes, chewing their cud as they stood in the street, I crossed to the other side of the road. A bicycle rickshaw was better suited to traversing these tiny back streets, and their drivers were more willing to stop to ask directions if they were lost. I caught the eye of a young man driving a bicycle rickshaw and motioned to him. He pulled up and reached behind himself to tap the rear seat, indicating that I should climb in.

Finally, after spending half an hour asking strangers for directions and being directed to the wrong place, we came upon a man selling books from a stack on a table in the street. I approached him myself because I could see that some of the books were in English. I thought maybe he might speak

English, as many Indians do. Ever since British Colonial Rule, English has been taught in India's schools, beginning in the primary grades. He did speak English, though haltingly. When I showed him the paper with Rabindranath's name and address written on it, he smiled and eagerly bobbed his head left to right in familiar Indian fashion, exclaiming, "Yes, yes, I know him!"

Thanking him, I asked if he'd please explain to my rickshaw driver where he lived, and then we were off. After a few blocks, we turned down an alley where the rickshaw driver stopped to ask someone else. Luckily, the person knew exactly where *Pandit-ji (ji is a term of endearment)* lived, pointing toward a house across the street. Pulling over, my driver jumped down, walked up to the door, and disappeared inside. Returning shortly, he told me, "He is here. I wait you?"

"Yes," I told him, adding, "Wait for me." In India, a bicycle rickshaw driver will wait for you as long as you want, and they don't expect a fortune for doing so. He knew that I was likely to pay him more than he could earn in an entire day. Therefore, he was more than happy to sit and wait patiently for me to finish whatever business I had.

CHAPTER 43

Inspiration from a Seer

Inside the door, a young man sat at a small wooden table. He greeted me warmly and with a big smile he asked, "You are here to see Pandit-ji?"

"Yes," I answered, "I have come a long way to see him."

"Please wait a few moments. He has gone to temple and will return shortly. My name is Sanjay. I am at your service. May I get something for you to drink?" I knew better than to drink the tap water, even tea could be a bit dodgy since tap water is what they use to make it. Unless the water had been boiled for a *really* long time you could still get a bad case of the runs, or worse. Based on a few unscrupulous merchants, not all bottled water could be trusted as being safe, so in an attempt to prevent instant dysentery, I avoided it altogether. "Seven Up?" I asked, and he was off like a shot to fetch one for me.

While sitting in the front room with Sanjay, sipping my drink, I pondered on how much had transpired in my life since my last trip to India.

After about half an hour, a man entered wearing a white *dhoti* and a *chuddar* (traditional Indian dress). His eyes were bright and piercing. Upon seeing me, he said, "Ah, today is the day you were to come."

"Excuse me, Pandit-ji?" I asked.

"It is the day you were to come. I was expecting you. Please wait a moment. Sanjay will bring you," he said. His warm smile of welcome gladdened my heart.

"Thank you," I replied, not really comprehending what he meant, but figuring I would learn shortly.

Soon Sanjay returned and invited me to follow him down a corridor to an office where we found Pandit-ji seated on a cushion behind a low table. On the table there were papers and books arranged somewhat haphazardly. Behind him and on all sides were bookcases crammed with books, some of which looked like handwritten manuscripts or notebooks. Most of them looked very old based on the well-worn appearance of their bindings. To my left, hanging on the wall was a picture of Krishna and Radha (the male and female forms of the Supreme God). Several other pictures caught my eye, one of which was of Ganesha (the elephant-headed Demigod said to Remove All Obstacles) and another was of Saraswati (Demigoddess of Learning). (In the Vedas there are said to be many demigods, who are entrusted with important functions of the universe, but are not the Supreme Godhead. Nor are they eternal, but have a lifespan just as humans do, though theirs are thousands to millions of our years.) There were also a number of thin rectangular metal plates hanging high on some of the walls. These I recognized as *yantras* (powerful symbols meant to propel subtle forces from within the astral spheres or dimensions).

The *pandit* was quite youthful looking with smooth skin as though age had hardly touched him. I assumed he must be in his mid-sixties. His eyes looked unblinkingly into mine as though he could see into the depths of my soul. I knew I was in the presence of someone who knew me far better than I knew myself. I stood before him, palms pressed together and touched them to my bowed forehead in a sign of deep respect. He said, "Please, sit down, sit down." He looked through several books and some notes on a tablet, and when he was finished he sat up to look at me sitting on a cushion directly across from him. "I am Rabindranath. You have come a long way to see me. I am very pleased to receive you." Again, he smiled warmly. "Did you not believe I knew you were to arrive today?"

Staring back at him intently I asked, "How did you know, Pandit-ji? I told no one I was coming here."

He pointed to a tablet where charts were drawn and to a partially unrolled scroll of some kind, and said, "Someone from a distant land was meant to visit me today. You are *that* person." I had never believed in coincidence, but this was *one of those times* I had to accept its verity.

"My friend Shanti told me about you, Pandit-ji. He said you were a great astrologer." I told him.

"You have some questions?" Rabindranath asked, with eyebrows slightly raised.

I had already written my birth date, time, and place on a piece of hotel notepaper. "Here are my birth details," I said, passing him the paper. "I am not sure what to ask of you. I respectfully ask that you be the one to tell me what I should know." Falling silent, I lowered my gaze for a few seconds, once again bringing my palms to my forehead.

"I am but a servant of the Almighty," he said, bowing his head and folding his hands. "If I am to speak something of importance to you today, it is by His grace only. Mine is only to serve the Supreme Will of God. Whatever I am able to see is by His Grace only."

After looking in several texts, Rabindranath drew a chart and created my birth horoscope on a paper he had on the desk. After studying it for some time, he made some notes next to the chart, then he made a list of dates on another paper. When he was finished, he sat back and looked at me. The *pandit's* piercing dark eyes searched mine for what seemed like an eternity. Rabindranath began speaking slowly, occasionally glancing down at his notes and the charts.

"You have come back to *Bharata* (India) after years away from her shores. Although your guru gave you his blessings, the import of what he taught was not fully comprehended by you. It was neither fully imbibed nor completely acted upon. The woman you married almost eighteen years ago is no longer with you. She has forsaken you because she considers you her enemy." He paused momentarily to see if I was paying attention. Then he continued. Mesmerized and barely breathing, I was astonished by his poignant and accurate words.

"You had embarked on a very dangerous path and later became imprisoned. The time had come for this path to end. You were about to die and leave this world. Someone very great and powerful saved you."

My palms grew clammy as I recalled the night I overdosed on heroin. I remembered seeing the face of my guru just before I woke up and how all the other patients in the hospital ward had thought a ghost had immediately taken over my body because **I had died right before their eyes**.

Still looking into my eyes he continued, "You were imprisoned for forty-three months and seventeen days, with several short periods within this tally before you spent most of it without interruption. More than twenty-seven months were spent in a prison far from your country of birth. The remainder was spent almost entirely within your country of birth. Since that time, you have begun preparing yourself for something, but now you question what that is. You desire to find something greater." He paused to observe my reaction, but all I could do was nod affirmatively and remain silent because I had been rendered unable to speak.

"In three years, your life will again change. At this juncture you will reach a crucial time in your life. But, you still have a great deal to learn. Soon, you will once again cross the oceans to reside for some time in another foreign land. Don't worry, your destiny shall find **you**." He stopped speaking yet continued to look at me with great intensity, as though searching for a glimmer of recognition behind my eyes. After which, his gaze softened and he said, "You still have so many unfulfilled desires. Much lies ahead for you to experience in life."

I was completely dumbfounded! What could I say? What could I ask that would not sound totally insignificant in the wake of what he had just said to me? Still, I was here to find clarity, so I asked, "Will I find my mission in life?"

"All noble missions are important, both great and small," he answered. "You are not one who will be above this world. You still desire to be of it, though your desires to rise above it are sincere. Do you understand?"

I pondered the meaning of his statement before answering, "You mean to say, I think, that I will not renounce the world to become spiritually aware, but rather my mission in life will become realized while I am part of it?"

Rabindranath looked at me and smiled approvingly.

I wanted to ask him if I would marry again or if I would ever see my daughter again, but something held me back. I looked down at my lap, then I raised my head, sensing he had more to share with me.

"You have also begun to study the sacred science of *jyotish* (astrology). Your knowledge and ability will now steadily increase, as you are now picking up where you left off in your previous life. Through it, you will find the answers to the other questions that are running through your mind. Don't worry, in time all will be revealed."

Rabindranath stopped speaking. I knew he was finished, and bowing my head low, I touched it to the cushion. I also reached into my bag and retrieved some bills and left them folded on his desk. Pausing, I said, "Thank you, Pandit-ji. Thank you for your words of wisdom."

As I turned to leave he said, "Never lose faith. From both the pains and pleasures of life come experience and from experience comes wisdom. Have patience." He wrote something on a piece of paper, turned it over, and wrote something else on the back of it. "There is someone who may be willing to help you. He is a great *jyotish acharya* (master of both astronomy and astrology) who lives in the South. Take this. His address is here, and you show him this." He pointed, each in turn, to the address he'd written in English on one side and to something else he had written in Sanskrit on the other side.

I looked at him, respectfully bowing my head once again and said, "Thank you Pandit-ji. This meeting has increased my faith. I pray that someday I may have the opportunity to achieve something worthy of your words."

After thanking *Sanjay*, I quickly left. My rickshaw driver was patiently waiting for my return. Approaching me with the rickshaw, he asked, "You go to somewhere now?"

I got in and told him to take me to a hotel I had seen while he transported me. Sitting back in the seat, I went over the words Rabindrananth had spoken in an attempt to commit them to memory. I reached into my pocket to look at the paper he had given me. The address was in Trivandrum, the capital of Kerala on the southernmost tip of India. Tucking the paper into a plastic cardholder, I carefully put it back into my money belt. The money belt was always concealed underneath my long *kurta* (shirt).

I regretted not being able to record every word he had said. Certainly, I hadn't been able to remember everything, but what I did both inspired and humbled me. All that I had done, even things I'd done which had nearly ended my life, would serve to prepare me for finding my new path in life. All I could do was, as he had said: *Have faith and be patient.*

I checked into the small hotel for the night. It was a very simple room with just a bed, dresser, chair, toilet, and bath. The toilet was Indian style, but fine. After showering, I visited a temple of Laxmi-Narayan (another eternal form of the male and female aspects of the Supreme Lord) where I meditated in the sanctum. On the way back, I stopped at one of the many outdoor restaurants and had rice and *subji* (vegetable dish) served on a banana leaf plate. Falling into a deep sleep the moment my head hit the pillow, I slept soundly through the night.

In the morning, I took a taxi to the airport and booked a flight to New Delhi because, once again, I felt a strong desire to visit the hallowed land of Vrindavan. I arrived in New Delhi early enough for me to reach Vrindavan before dark. After haggling a deal with a taxi driver, I sat back for the bumpy three to four hour drive on Mathura Road, which was, at the time, a treacherous road with numerous detours.

The Mathura Road was always in terrible shape. The tarmac was full of potholes due to being built with substandard building materials and the weight of the huge overloaded Lorries. Only when President Clinton was scheduled to visit during his presidency did the government see fit to make the highway decent. Once completed, the new road, smooth and wide, went all the way to Agra, the home of the famous Taj Mahal. Today, the trip to Mathura and Vrindavan takes about an hour and a half, a great improvement to say the least.

During the ride, I thought about how my life felt so unfulfilled. Although I knew I had come a long way since the nefarious days of my past, I still found no lasting satisfaction. However, some undefined force had urged me to come to India at this juncture. As if given an urgent message, I wanted to ask the *pandit* about finding a life partner, but felt it wasn't something I should ask. At least not right then. But it was important to me. My current girlfriend and I were worlds apart. She even admitted that our relationship was simply one of convenience.

Nothing is by accident, nor are the people who come into your life. Relationships that are important to us: parents, children, partners, friends, or even the inimical relationships, somehow had their beginnings in a past life. Maybe, if I were patient, someone very special would come my way. Nothing comes either too soon or too late. Everything and everyone who are meant to be a part of our lives will arrive on schedule. The *pandit* had intimated as much when he told me: *All will be revealed in time.*

When we reached Vrindavan, I went to the guesthouse at the Krishna-Balarama Mandir and checked in. After taking a shower, I went downstairs to the temple sanctum to pay my respects and to sit and contemplate for a while. Vrindavan was always a good place for me to contemplate. Years ago, I'd thought that the spiritual path was an easy one to follow. I had mistakenly thought that my spirituality would easily become realized. How deluded and arrogant I had been. Had

I been spiritually realized, I would never have considered traversing the path of iniquity where I fumbled along.

After ten days of spiritual retreat, it was time to begin the journey home. One realization that came to me at the time was: *No matter where you go, your mind goes with you. Happiness has to come from within your heart. If your mind is disturbed, it will be disturbed wherever you are. Home is where your heart is.* I felt that whatever answers I was going to find would be found within my heart and that there was no reason to think I had to travel around the world to find them. Yet, the spiritual retreat had been a good way to put things into proper perspective and begin thinking more clearly. In the solace of the retreat, I had been able to remove myself from the everyday activities that we are all so conditioned to immerse ourselves in.

CHAPTER 44

Full Circle

After returning to LA, several thoughts came to mind: Why not move back to Hawaii? It was closer to Japan and Hong Kong, destinations I constantly traveled to. Hawaii was closer to the Far East, yet not too far from the US mainland. There was no reason not to reside in Hawaii. I had been released from parole and could live wherever I wanted. More than any other place I had ever lived, Hawaii felt most like home to me. Remembering the beautiful scenic mountains, clear turquoise-blue waters of the South Pacific, white sand beaches, and gentle ocean breezes, the islands certainly tugged at my heartstrings. Had I not fallen down the deep precipice into the heroin underworld, I probably would have never left. I was already going to Honolulu occasionally for business, and had established some good contacts there. The island lifestyle had always suited me. The lease on the house I was renting in LA was up at the end of the month, so I told the landlord I wouldn't be renewing it. A month later, I was back in Honolulu.

I rented a house in Kahala, on the far side of the extinct Diamondhead Volcano, and set up an office at the Waikiki Trade Center, where in a little over a year's time my business prospered. Materially speaking, everything was flowing in abundance. But, the gnawing feeling that something important was missing continued to disturb me. Again, I felt India calling me. I desperately wanted to deepen my knowledge of

Vedic Astrology, so I decided it was time to visit the teacher whose address Rabindranath had given me. The thought of returning to South India thrilled me. Although I had only visited once before, I remembered the awe-inspiring and intricately carved architecture of the area's many temples. Moreover, people living in South India seemed very mellow compared to people living in the North. In South India, there seemed to be a sense of natural piety. The people appeared to be less driven than their northern counterparts.

Kerala is also a place of stunning natural beauty. Its vast jungles, rivers, and waterways are phenomenal. It is like traveling through a magical lost paradise. The cascading waterfalls in the backcountry are absolutely breathtaking to behold. It is, all in all, a place that represents the best of nature's bounties. It also happened to be the Ayurveda center for all of India where the ancient medical science had been well preserved since antiquity. It is still being taught and practiced as it has been for thousands, of years. Its ancient medical and spiritual principles, irrevocably intertwined in its core philosophy, remain unchanged by the vestiges of time.

CHAPTER 45

Mystical Journey

"The knowledge of everything is there in the ether."

W ithin weeks, I was on a flight bound for India. This time, my connection was in London, followed by Bombay, my first point of entry. Bombay was closer to Trivandrum, and I wasn't planning to visit the North on this trip. I would spend the night in Bombay and fly down to Trivandrum the following afternoon. Other than his name, Ramlal, I knew nothing about the teacher Rabindranath had urged me to consult. Somehow, though, my intuition assured me that this was going to be one of the most significant and essential experiences of my life. Bombay was as maniacal and crowded as ever. What never ceased to amaze me was how the slums bordered an area that was fast becoming the most expensive real estate in the world. The wealthy elite shared a neighborhood with slum dwellers. With their hands outstretched asking for alms, beggars were everywhere, as much as they were in Delhi and Calcutta. As was my custom, I gave to eight people a day, first and foremost to the handicapped.

I tried not to think about all the stories I'd heard about children having their limbs cut off just so they could beg more successfully. Some sick adults inflicted these atrocities on children, and then became like their pimps, taking all the money the children collected. Usually, I didn't give to the street urchins, but to older people who were physically handicapped or women with children. With the latter, you still had to use discretion because too many women were obviously making a very good living by begging. Some women wore gold chains, earrings, and bracelets, yet stood on the street day and night with their children begging.

At the Indian Airlines office, I booked a ticket to Trivandrum for the following morning. Hopefully, once I got there, I would easily find the *pandit's* residence. Meanwhile, before returning to my hotel, I managed to visit a temple of Ganesha, which I had visited years before; a temple of *Siva* (the form of the Supreme in charge of the affairs of this material world); a temple of *Vishnu* (the Supreme Creator and maintainer of all creation in total, of this and other worlds); and finally, a temple of Radha Krishna. Even in the big cities there were many beautiful and inspiring temples where the atmosphere was supercharged with spirituality. Perhaps this feeling in my heart was reflecting my inner spiritual desires. Either way, I was thankful for whatever it was that gave me such a deep peaceful feeling. Certain temples seemed to touch me to the core of my being. There is a special feeling you get when in a spiritually charged environment, and afterwards, you always feel more balanced and peaceful.

I arrived at the airport early on the following morning. I carried only one duffel bag, which made travel so much easier. I boarded the flight without incident, but after sitting down in my seat, I noticed something I had never seen in the cabin of any jet aircraft before: mosquitoes! Within minutes, an airline employee entered the cabin and sprayed a noxious chemical to kill them. Only in India!

Finally, we took off for the relatively short flight to Trivandrum. Upon arrival, I went to the taxi counter and showed them the address I sought, which apparently was on the outskirts of the city. This meant I would have to take a taxi, which the person at the travel desk was only too happy to arrange for me. Soon, I was in the familiar Ambassador taxicab on my way to see the *jyotish acharya*. When we arrived in the area where he lived, the driver stopped to ask directions.

Ramlal Pandit was obviously well known because the driver immediately told tell me that he knew where Pandit-ji's house was located. Less than an hour later, we pulled up to a brightly painted house surrounded by beautiful flowers.

"Pandit-ji here," the taxi driver announced, pointing to the house. I paid him, turned, and walked up the narrow walkway, flanked on both sides by deliciously fragrant gardenia bushes. I knocked softly on the door. A middle-aged woman, wearing a sari and looking somewhat surprised, greeted me. "I'm here to see Pandit-ji," I said.

"Come in, come in," she answered, motioning toward a chair. The front room was spotless. The walls were adorned with pictures of Hindu deities, and in one corner of the marble-floored room was an altar set into an alcove. Vases of fragrant flowers lending a heavenly ambiance were strategically placed around the room. In a few minutes, a man about seventy or so years of age came to greet me. He had short grey hair with a longer knotted tuft in the back, and he wore wire-rimmed glasses, over which he peered at me. His hands were held palms together in front of him and I returned his gesture as we exchanged the greeting of *namaskar* (*I honor the same Supreme spirit that lives within us both*).

"I am Ramlal. How may I help you?" he asked warmly.

"I was given your name by Rabindranath Pandit in Calcutta who said I should give this to you when I arrived." He took the piece of paper I offered and read the Sanskrit written on it. Turning it over, he read his own name and address that was written in English.

"You wish to learn *Jyotish*?" he asked.

"I have been studying from books as best I can for about seven years, but Rabindranath said you might be willing to accept me as your student," I replied.

"*Jyotish* takes many years to master. Rabindranath has written that he recommends you for such an education. Please tell me your date, time, and place of birth."

I gave my birth details to Ramlal Pandit, writing them on the pad he'd handed to me. Then he bade me to follow him into his office at the end of a hallway. The room was spacious with windows on two walls, which allowed sunlight to enter. Like Rabindranath's office, Ramlal's was filled with bookcases. An adjoining room contained yet more bookcases, and one wall was full of books in cabinets with protective glass doors.

Ramlal immediately began drawing my horoscope while making detailed notes on a pad above it. After finishing his calculations, he sat back looking at the chart he had prepared. Finally, after consulting some books on the table next to him, he put the pages aside. "How much time would you like to spend with me?" he asked, adding, "If I am to help you learn, you must be willing to spend at least a month with me. Then, we will see from there."

I brought my palms together and slightly bowed my head, "Thank you for your kindness, Pandit-ji. I would be honored to stay a month or as long as you see fit. I will do my best to be a worthy student."

He smiled while doing the classic Indian head bob and said, "Very good, you are the first Westerner to ever come here asking to my student. And the first student Rabindranath has ever sent to me. Therefore, I am very keen about getting started. Nothing is without reason. We will begin tomorrow. Have you ever studied the *SURYA SIDDANTA* (one of the oldest treatises in Hindu astronomy)?"

"No," I answered.

"First we take our lunch, then we can talk more. Tomorrow we will begin your lessons," his words were cordially spoken.

"Thank you, Pandit-ji." I said, "It will be my honor."

He called for the middle-aged lady who had greeted me at the door and gave her instructions. Pointing to a room with a shower and sink, he invited me to wash up, which I did. Then, I accompanied him to another room, one with a low table with seat cushions around it. I recall a vase filled with flowers sitting on the table. Several young women brought in plates, cups, and bowls made of stainless steel. The bowls were filled with steaming vegetable dishes. A variety of other preparations were placed on plates at the table's center. As expected, these dishes were served with a generous helping of rice.

The meal was a divine feast. We were served a kind of south Indian *dhal* called *sambar*, which was quite spicy, and four or five different vegetable dishes including batter-fried vegetables, yogurt, and rice. I ate everything on my plate, refusing more, in spite of the women urging me on.

"You must at least take one of the sweets," Ramlal insisted, while offering a tray laden with different types and shapes of desserts that were obvious delicacies. "My wife has made them herself."

I took one of them, savoring the creamy texture and amazingly exotic sweet taste. Then another. You don't need to be hungry to eat Indian sweets, but I restrained myself from taking any more. Afterwards, Ramlal said I should rest and guided me to a room down an adjacent hallway. We were to meet together again in another hour or so.

"Excuse me, Pandit-ji, but maybe I should go now to rent a room in a hotel close by, so I will have someplace to stay while I am here? Then I can return after you have had some rest."

Ramlal raised his eyebrows, peered over his glasses at me, and with a wave of his hand said, "Nonsense, you will stay with us of course. No hotel. You will stay with me until our initial lessons have been completed." I started to say that I didn't want to inconvenience him and his family, but he waved his hand once again to prevent me from voicing any further protest. "Now go take rest. Someone will call for you in about an hour." The matter was settled.

One of the young girls took my bag and led me to my room. Then she smiled and left, closing the door behind her. It was a bright, airy room with a connecting bath. It had a dresser, a bed, and a low desk with pillows behind it to sit on, which I did. Leaning back on the pillows and stretching my legs out in front of me, I gazed out a window that overlooked the courtyard. I saw a number of children playing, laughing, and talking excitedly, and although I didn't understand Hindi, their innocent laughter instilled a wondrous and comforting feeling in me. I loved just sitting and watching them play, so carefree and filled with joy.

I wondered how much I would actually be capable of learning from Ramlal Pandit. Would he become my Jyotish guru? Would he be patient with someone like me, whose only background came from reading a few books written in English that I had managed to obtain? Regardless of whatever happened during the next month or so, I knew my progress would be significant. I felt I was at a critical juncture in my life. I surely needed additional inspiration and direction. at this point lying back against the cushions, I fell fast asleep. It seemed only moments later when a knock at the door awakened me. Looking at my watch, I realized two hours had passed instead of one. *Oh well, after all, it is India, where one hour can easily become two. People don't rush around all day and night like they do in US cities,* I told myself as I opened the door.

"Pandit-ji is waiting for you," the girl announced, motioning for me to follow her.

"One moment," I insisted, hurriedly splashing my face with cold water. She waited patiently, and in record time, I emerged and followed her back down the hallway into Ramlal's office where he was seated at his desk. He now had several books and booklets in front of him, along with several charts drawn on paper.

"Sit, *Hamsa avatar das,*" he said, using the Sanskrit name I told him my teacher had given me many years ago. "You most definitely have the horoscope of one who can imbibe this sacred science of *Jyotish.* This is not the first lifetime that you have studied it, nor have other mystic arts been unknown to you in your previous lives."

I sat before him, spellbound. No astrologer I had ever seen before in India, and I had visited many, had ever told me anything about my past lives. He continued to tell me that if the horoscope did not show an aptitude as well as previous lives' experience with astrology, it would be impossible for me to comprehend his teaching during the next month. However, he made it very plain that this was a lifetime dedication. It could *not* be a passing interest because its essence would then remain forever hidden from my eyes. If I truly wished to learn from him, I would have to tap into my experiences from my past lives.

"I also see that you suffered greatly in this life due to some mistakes you have made in both this life and in previous births. Never mind. You have come through your ordeals and emerged a different person. Do you agree?" Not waiting for an answer, he continued, "Never again will you choose such a disreputable path such as you once did. It is by God's Grace that you are still alive to learn while in your present embodiment."

Nodding my head, I answered, "Yes, Pandit-ji. There have been some terrible years."

"That time is past and this time is now," he continued. "You may rest for the remainder of this afternoon. Feel free to go outside, as you like. Ask Madhu how to get to the nearby temples, if you wish to visit any of them. We will begin tomorrow."

I thanked him, bowing my head, and returned to my room. Madhu, the girl who had been serving me, gave me directions to several of the nearby temples. First, I chose to visit one dedicated to *Laxmi-Narayana (one of these temples was inaugurated by Mahatma Gandhi)*, and I arrived there following a short rickshaw ride. After nearly an hour, I decided to walk to the other temples. I enjoyed walking; it allowed me to take in the sights, sounds, and smells of the atmosphere surrounding me. **Beholding** India's temples can be an awesome experience, but those in the South have spectacular architecture like no other in the world. Huge carved *gopurams* (entrance gates) are intricately engraved with a myriad of deities and symbols that are an intrinsic part of South Indian artistic style. Agape at the beauty of the work, I ardently examined all the intricate details of the carved stone, marveling at the phenomenal talent portrayed by such craftsmanship. The energy emanating from the artwork was intense; I felt a wave of it, like an electric current surging through me, each time I walked beneath the *gopurams*. Unaware of the time, I spent several hours exploring these unique places of pilgrimage. Finally, realizing that the sun was about to set, I began the short journey back to Ramlal's house.

On my arrival, in the evening hours, Madhu was there to offer me bread and hot milk. Indians often prepare hot milk sweetened with sugar and a bit of cardamom, which I love. Shortly afterward, I went to bed and fell into a deep and restful sleep until I awakened to the sound of a bell ringing somewhere close to my quarters. After listening for a few moments, I recognized the tinkling sound as a ceremonial *puja* bell (a small bell rung continually during worship in not only Hindu ceremonies but in other religions as well). It was just before 5AM, and I bathed quickly, dressed, and then followed the sound of the still-ringing bell to Ramlal who was just finishing his ceremonial service called *arotik* at his home shrine. Seeing me as he turned from the altar, he offered me the ghee lamp's flame, which I placed my hand over before touching my forehead. He also offered me a flower, which I brought to my nose, deeply inhaling its heavenly scent.

The shrine was beautiful. He worshipped icons of *Sita* and *Rama (another form of the Divine couple Laxmi-Narayan)*, with *Hanuman* (the monkey god) kneeling beside them. Bowing my head to the floor, I sat while Ramlal sang some *bhajans*, which I recognized immediately as devotional songs. By now, there was a heavy, near-intoxicating aroma of incense throughout the house, emanating from the shrine's marble steps. When he finished, he bowed before the altar and then walked out into his garden. I didn't want to disturb him, so I went back to my room for my *japa mala* (personal beads used for chanting) and headed out into the predawn morning for a leisurely stroll. I was profoundly at peace with myself and the world. Enthusiastically, I looked forward to a great learning experience; I knew it would be memorable and its value would be incalculable.

The sun still hadn't risen and the world was bathed in the soft light of dawn. Already, people were going about their business. Street stalls would soon open. Rickshaws and bullock drawn carts, as well as cars, careened down the road, constantly honking their horns. Suddenly, I was overcome with gratefulness for this rare opportunity to gain direct knowledge of *Jyotish* from a true master. It was an opportunity that only a few years ago, I could not have seen coming my way.

Ramlal said that I was his first Western student, and the first foreigner to ever come to his door. My heart and soul were filled with humility and exhilarating anticipation. Within my heart and mind, I earnestly wanted to be worthy of the knowledge that he would soon impart to me. Later, after a South Indian breakfast of *idlis* (small rice cakes), *sambar* (hot *dhal* taken in small quantities with the *idlis*), and *dosas* (crepes filled with potatoes and spices), Ramlal informed me that I should be at the room adjoining his office in one hour, so I could begin my first lesson.

I arrived at his office in fifty-five minutes and waited by the door for Ramlal to appear, which he did in exactly five minutes. He showed me where I should sit. "First," he said, "you must understand the structure of our universe, at least the basics, for it is within this universe that the journey from one lifetime to another takes place. Then we can begin to concentrate on the movements of the Sun, the planets orbiting around it, and their astrological significance."

Ramlal had prepared a drawing with different horizontal lines, almost like a staircase, but within it there were connecting vertical lines, which I studied with great interest. There was an arc at the top and an inverted one at the bottom of the drawing.

"There are three regions in our universe. The uppermost, the heavenly realms, are those where the planets and planes of existence of the *Devas* (Demigods) are situated, as well as the greatest of the *rishis* (yogis) of our universe. The middle portion is where our earthly existence is made manifest. The lower portion is where lower realms are situated. Human beings devoid of spiritual knowledge inhabit these lower realms.

"Karma is created throughout our lives in the middle planes of existence, directly in accordance with the quality of our work. One can earn entrance into the heavenly realms by performing many charitable and pious actions. A person can also *earn* falling into less than desirable realms of existence through impious or evil actions performed while living here on Earth. Similarly, the kind of birth we take here — man or beast, rich or poor, healthy or diseased — is due to the karma we have created for ourselves by our actions in past lives. Our incarnations are innumerable. We may live through countless lifetimes here on Earth, or move up and down through the other planetary systems. The force that determines where we reincarnate is singularly that of the Law of Karma."

I sat listening to him, focusing my complete attention on every word. As Ramlal spoke of cosmography and the cosmology taught in the *Vedas*, it was as if my mind and soul became one with the universe. Just thinking of innumerable planetary systems, linked with Ramlal's emphatic assertions that life existed on all of them, was mind-boggling. No place was devoid of intelligent life, but all had forms suitable to the planets on which they existed. He went on to explain that the Earthly Realms also had different dimensions, both within them and surrounding them. Human beings existed on the physical plane while inhabiting a human body. Although the bodies of human beings were formed of all the five physical elements: earth, water, air, fire, and ether, they were formed mostly of water and earth. Yet, there are other more subtle planes where all sorts of other beings live. Ghosts, called *bhutas*, were only one of them. *Bhutas* lived close to Earth, therefore sometimes humans saw them. However, there are many types of beings, which exist on other subtle planes as well, and all of their bodies are formed of less dense elements, meaning only air or ether. Ramlal said that on some planets the inhabitant's bodies were made mostly of fire, such as those living on fiery planets like the Sun! "On all planets there is life," he stated authoritatively. "And their bodies are suited for the particular atmosphere of the planet on which they live." Prabhupada had outlined much of this in his translation of *Srimad Bhagavatam,* but not to the depth that Ramlal explained.

Ramlal explained the transmigration of our souls, or the leaving of one's body at the time of death. At the time of death, one enters, for a period of time, a still subtler plane: The Astral World. How long we remain there is not the same for everyone. He compared it to the subtle world we enter when we dream at night. When we wake up in the morning, we realize it was all a dream. But when we *die* from this world, we also *wake up* again in the Astral World to realize that the life we have just led was also just a dream. It was no more real or permanent than the dreams we had at night while living it.

In time, we would again be given the opportunity to enter the womb of our next mother on Earth. The nature of our birth, meaning the type of family: rich or poor, healthy or sickly, endowed with physical beauty or not, and what opportunities would be offered to us in that lifetime, would be in accordance with what we deserved. Our mental natures and the qualities and attributes of our personalities were also shaped from one life to the next. Everything depended on how we had lived in our previous lives.

My studies of *Vedic* science had opened the door, but the depth of what Ramlal explained to me about the subtle planes (dimensions of existence) had never been revealed within the pages of any book I had read. In turn, I could easily write a book on just that first class. We spent the morning and afternoon singularly focused on this subject, and I tried my utmost to absorb as much as I possibly could. Pandit-ji told me that in olden-times men had such sharp memories that they would remember everything taught to them upon hearing it only once, yet in this age we are not so capable of such memorization. I did my best to take notes, and later in the evening when I was alone in my room, I wrote down everything I could remember from the lesson.

The next day was spent introducing me to the *Surya Siddhanta (Multiple treatises on Hindu astronomy edited in 1860, but written in the 12th century. They were clearly based on far older versions)*, the most important scriptural work on Indian astronomy. Its pages contain the science of planetary placements, their motions and interrelations, and an explanation of influences such as eclipses, the stars, and cosmography: the depth, breadth, and dimensions of the manifested creation of the Universe. Ramlal had given me an introduction to it the previous day, which helped me immeasurably as it served as a background for the day's lesson.

For the next few days, Ramlal taught the time cycles of the different planetary systems, the heavens and earthly realms, and how billions of years were divided into *yugas* (periods of time). Each *yuga* had many smaller divisions of time within it, an astonishing and awe-inspiring scientific explanation. The ancient *Vedic* seers, thousands of years ago, had known all of the astronomical facts and figures, which modern astronomers had discovered in only the last century. Not only this, but what has been discovered by modern science is but a drop in the ocean compared to the astronomical information that is revealed of the universe through the *Vedas*. While *modern* scientists had only been gazing at some of the worlds of our universe through telescopes first invented early in the 17th century, the *Vedic* astronomers already knew of their movements, as well as the inhabitants living on them *thousands* of years before.

There were so many mathematical calculations of planetary dimensions, orbits, and the distances between them that Trigonometry had to be used to make mathematical calculations. In awe, I knew that I would never be able to remember everything Ramlal was teaching me; however, I did my best to file away as much of it as I could. Of course, I took notes, which would help me to recall more of each lesson until I could write them down in greater depth and detail. To write too much during our lessons meant missing some of what

Ramlal was saying. Thankfully, he also allowed me to copy his diagrams, which he used as teaching aids.

As the days passed, Ramlal started teaching me about the actual structuring of the horoscope, much of the mechanics of which I already knew. Through his teaching, I gained a far greater depth of understanding of what the signs of the Zodiac, in their essence, actually represented. Astronomically, they were star systems, actual *Worlds*, but their meanings were deep and profound when it came to how a person's life on Earth was comprehended through their uniquely personal horoscope. The Houses in which the planets were situated, called Mansions, allowed a Vedic Astrologer to predict the specific events that would occur in a person's life.

Day after day, I tried my best to absorb the vast amount of knowledge he was conveying to me, much like a university student listening to a professor. I was grateful for the privilege of being the only student. Personal and intimate, Ramlal's expressions and pointed remarks were directed only to me. At other times, we went over Horoscope Charts. He would ask me what I saw, while I tried to carefully assess each chart. Ramlal commended me when I made correct observations, and corrected those that were faulty. He always provided a detailed analysis of each horoscope while forever reminding me that the chart represented a person's *Karma:* a roadmap of real interest and import *only to the person* whose chart it represented.

For days on end, I studied with Ramlal in this manner. There was *so much* to learn and assimilate. The profundity of his wisdom, insights, and realizations of the subject matter were *not available in print*, not in books written in either Sanskrit or Hindi, and certainly not those written in English. He, a master, revealed to me the essence of a vast esoteric treasure trove of knowledge. Even had there been books containing such in-depth information, reading from a book is incomparable to sitting at the feet of a learned and expert master of astrological science. For the next few weeks, he invited me to sit in with him while he counseled those who sought him out; not one of them seemed to mind the intrusion of his Western student.

A month of intense study passed so quickly that it seemed like only a few days. Knowing that I had to return to the US, I asked Ramlal's permission and blessings to go. He gave me his blessings, but said I should *please remain for only five days more* because there were still some important things he wanted to teach me. During these days, Ramlal explained what he called *advanced concepts*. He said that if I memorized them, their meaning would come with practice. "Learn to hear from within your heart," he would tell me. "You must continue to study, but know that it will then be experience and intuition that will further develop your abilities."

He took my hand in his, and in a paternal manner placed his other hand on my shoulder and continued, "Because I could see in your horoscope that you have practiced *Jyotish* in more than just one previous life, I have confidence in your ability to absorb what I have taught you since your arrival. As you practice and view thousands of horoscopes, your knowledge and ability to see another's life path will become more acute and that will enhance your ability to discern. This is what will allow you to become a true *Jyotishi* (practitioner of the science of light, Sanskrit for an astrologer).

"However, it is important that you always conduct your life in a manner that is above reproach. Perform your duties in life in a *sattvic* (pious) way. This means, first and foremost, you must live a clean personal life. Not only as a good and moral human being, but as a person engaging in higher spiritual practices. Only if you constantly walk the Path of Truth yourself, will you be able to help others do the same. Anyone can study books, and there are many students more capable than you in doing so, but what you possess within (placing his palm over his heart) is of greater importance: good intuition and a *psychic eye* (touching his index finger to the spot between my eyebrows called the *ajna chakra* [third eye]). Do you understand?"

Ramlal made his point, so I nodded yes, humbled by his confidence in me. The words he spoke were infused with love, love I could see in his eyes as though he had been speaking to his long lost son. The import of all he had said I would not fully grasp for many years. Even today, I have surely only realized a fraction of his vast range of knowledge and teachings, and yet with each passing day, I better understand that it is *the unseen* that gives us our innate abilities to perform great things in life.

One of the most important lessons Ramlal imparted was demonstrated through his humility. He took credit for nothing personally and gave all credit to God, the Supreme Source of all knowledge. The rare quality of humility in a great master was the trait that had most impressed me years before when I first met my spiritual teacher, Srila Prabhupada.

I returned to India to see Ramlal only three more times, staying for a month each time. He left this world soon after my third visit. I was astounded to discover that he had been ninety-one years old when I had first studied with him! At the time, I had thought him to be in his sixties or in his seventies, at most. At the time of his passing, he was ninety-six years old.

After my return to the US, my mind was constantly filled with questions. Trying my best to look deeply into the meaning of what life was really all about, I considered the ramifications of each and every action before I performed any of them. What was I really meant to be doing with my life? There must be something I'm missing, I thought. Or maybe the true time for seeing and achieving my destiny was still ahead. I knew my own horoscope, but it is always harder for an astrologer to be objective with himself because of an attachment to the outcome. On the other hand, with someone else's chart, I can be completely objective. Over the years, it continues to amaze me how accurate Vedic Astrology can be, if the astrologer is gifted with the proverbial *eyes to see*.

Meanwhile, back in Hawaii, the economy had begun to falter. Very dependent on the Japanese economy, which was in a tailspin in the early 1990s, business in Hawaii had slowed down to a crawl, affording me more time to devote to my studies. I was living on my savings and watched them dwindle, bit by bit. My main focus on gems changed. I began studying them for their energies, how they could heal the body and mind, and how they might impact a person's life on other, subtler levels, which was congruent with Vedic Astrology. Gems were the Astral Remedy that most Vedic Astrologers prescribed.

CHAPTER 46

Soul Mates

At this point, I had come a long way since those dark days of my past. In fact, it was hard to believe I had been there and survived. I learned some tough lessons through some very cruel experiences; experiences that included trials, tribulations, and dejection that now separated me from mainstream society. I was actually stronger now because of my misguided past. I managed to achieve successes in my life, regardless of the odds of being an ex-convict.

The visualization program I had developed for myself really worked. I was living in one of the most paradisiacal places on Earth with a lifestyle many people only dreamed of. Whatever I set my mind to while visualizing the results that I desired was coming to fruition, except one. Relationships had remained an anomaly in my life. I'd been married once, of course, and I had been in a few live-in relationships, but each one seemed doomed to failure. As a bachelor often does, I had my share of flings. In the end though, I began to grow a bit cynical about the possibility of ever finding an authentic partner let alone a *Soul Mate*. I was lonely and my life seemed incomplete even though my career was going well.

One day, I received an invitation to a private opening of a vegetarian restaurant. It was at a spiritual center nestled at the base of the Pali Mountain Range in Honolulu. Always up for a good meal in a peaceful setting, I went to the event where a *Kahuna* (Hawaiian priestess) was there to bless the opening of the *sacred space* (her exact words). The guests sat along several long tables to listen to her and sing traditional Hawaiian chants. In time, she asked the guests to stand and take the hands of those standing on either side of them. I smiled at the two women on either side of me and offered my hands, which were easily taken. The moment my hand interlocked with the woman on my left, an electric current surged through my arms. She reacted as if she felt it, too. We were both startled since we had said nothing to each other so far except a simple *hello!*

After the ceremony ended, I knew I had to speak with her. However, by this time, everyone was milling around the room or out on the estate grounds, which meant I would have to search for her. When I finally found her, I touched her shoulder so that she would turn in my direction. "Have we ever met before," I asked her, adding quickly, "This is not a pick-up line. I really feel that we must have met before." I smiled and searched her eyes for some form of recognition. There truly was a powerful feeling of familiarity, which seemed to be on a soul level; this was something I had never experienced before. Her name was Jennifer. Jennifer was tall, lithe, and had thick, curly blond hair; she was absolutely gorgeous with long legs and curves in all the right places.

She spoke with a beautiful and cultured English accent, "Yes, actually we have met! My ex-husband introduced us several years ago. You even gave me your card. Believe it or not, I still have it." Fumbling around in her handbag for a moment she produced a somewhat creased business card and said, "Here it is. I don't know why, but something made me keep it in my purse."

I hadn't words with which to answer. I'm not quite sure what I was expecting her answer to be, but I certainly wasn't prepared for her response. All I could manage was "Wow!" Shaking myself out of a momentary paralysis, I asked, "Want to take a walk out back? There's the biggest, most amazing banyan tree you'll ever see just over there. We can sit down and talk a while." Jennifer smiled, and together we walked

341

over to the bench under the banyan tree and sat down. Over the next few hours, we talked, laughed, and shared our life stories. It felt like we had known each other for years. Jennifer had lived on the Big Island in Hawaii with her ex for a year after having lived in California for several years. Her marriage had ended badly, so she had opted to return to England and live near her mother. Presently, she was staying in England with a friend, but was here to take care of financial matters that had been left up in the air for over a year since her divorce. Coming here today was a nice distraction from what she had been doing since her arrival.

Jen was leaving in a few days, and I desperately wanted to see more of her before she did, so I invited her to lunch the following day. I asked her to come to my house first. Saying she'd love to, she took my address and directions, as well as my home telephone number. By now, everyone was leaving the party, so we walked to the parking lot to retrieve our cars. Although I wanted to hug her, I restrained myself. Instead, I shook her hand, squeezing it gently before opening her door for her. "See you tomorrow," I said.

Smiling, she answered, "See you then."

I spent the next morning cleaning the house and thinking about her. This sort of sentiment was completely new to me. I felt like a love-struck schoolboy; excited, yet apprehensive. Baffled, I decided to leave it all in the hands of Fate, who always has the last word anyway.

Jennifer arrived mid-morning. After showing her around, I invited her out on the veranda where we spent hours sitting and talking and getting to know each other. I had a table reserved at one of my favorite restaurants, the *Hau Tree Lanai* on Kaimana Beach in Waikiki. Its name is due to the exceptionally large and very old Hau tree that forms a natural canopy over most of the restaurant. The scenery was picture-perfect, as always, and from our table we watched surfers riding flawless waves on a turquoise-blue ocean under a broad expanse of blue sky. You couldn't ask for a more romantic setting.

After sharing a long and luxurious lunch together we drove back to my house, where Jen stepped outside to the veranda while I went into my office to check for phone messages. In a few moments, I joined her and asked, "Can I get you anything to drink, tea or juice, maybe?" We looked into each other's eyes for an *extended moment*. Then, we were locked together in an embrace. In the following hours, we came together as if after a long and lonely separation, so passionate were the feelings between us. Relaxed and comfortable, I mused on whether I had finally found the perpetually elusive Woman of My Dreams. I sensed that our liaison had the potential to last a lifetime. Neither of us wanted the day to end, but when evening arrived, we had our last embrace before saying a tearful goodbye.

I wondered if I would ever see her again. After all, I lived in Hawaii and she lived in England. How would we manage to spend any quality time together let alone develop a relationship with such a huge distance between us? Could we manage this, ten thousand miles across two oceans and the breadth of the North American continent? With a deep sigh, I left it all in Fate's sometimes merciful hands.

Jen and I spoke on the phone regularly after that. Over the next year or so we got to be close and intimate friends. We wrote to each other constantly, sharing things that neither of us had ever shared with anyone else before. We only saw each other once during that time when we both went to the East Coast. Even though so much time had passed since we were last together, it was as if no time had elapsed at all. We spent a magical few days together, each of us wishing it wouldn't end.

After returning to Hawaii, I deeply contemplated the feelings I had for Jennifer. And, as had become my custom, every morning I'd go for a long walk and allow my eyes and senses to soak up the heavenly beauty of this island paradise. I felt an overwhelming gratitude for the blessings in my life, but Jennifer had changed everything. No matter where I was or what I was doing, she was forever on my mind.

Each day, while meditating, I prayed to find something meaningful to do with my life. I had learned and experienced so much, but I yearned for greater spiritual depth. Meanwhile, I did a lot of thinking, contemplating, and visualizing on what I'd like to manifest here and now and carry into the future. I felt in my heart that something new and wonderful was just on the horizon.

CHAPTER 47

Merry Old England

Jennifer and I were on the phone, as well as the fax, with each other all the time. No one had e-mail in those days. Back then, we used faxes to send letters and documents *quickly*. One day, Jennifer asked, "Why don't you come over here for a visit? I could contact yoga centers, healing centers, and other places that might be interested in Vedic Astrology and Gem Therapy. Who knows? They may be interested in inviting you to speak at their centers. Maybe you could also teach the meditation and visualization techniques that you told me about. It would be fun, don't you think?"

Jennifer was on the board of a New Age healing center in Sussex, so she knew they would be interested. She also felt certain that others would be, too. Why not, I thought? Besides, it would be a great excuse for spending time with her, whatever the outcome. *Nothing ventured, nothing gained*, one of my catchphrases for years, prompted me to affirm, "Sure, that would be great!"

We decided on a two-month visit, which would give us enough time to build upon whatever she had managed to arrange before my arrival. Hopefully, initial talks would be met with requests for workshops as well as referrals to other centers. Jennifer would begin contacting prospects and sending out my photo and press kit. Because she had previously worked for a publishing house, she had tons of promotional experience. She used articles I had written, newspaper clippings, and booklets I'd created to promote the talks I was giving in Hawaii. She distributed my press kits to places all over the United Kingdom (UK).

Six weeks later, I was on a plane bound for London, anticipating a good time, but without any specific expectations, whatsoever. Not only would it be nice to have a change of scenery, I was also very excited about being able to spend quality time with Jennifer. We felt like we knew each other really well at this point, but there's a big difference between a long distance relationship and one where you are constantly together for two months on a 24/7 basis.

I arrived at Heathrow Airport, and after clearing Immigration and Customs, I looked around for her. There she was, waiting with a big smile and a garland of flowers! Her deep blue eyes shined with excitement as we hugged and, once again, our electrical circuitry coursed through and around us. Walking through the airport together, it seemed as if we both had that same anticipation of something wonderful being on the horizon.

We walked with the luggage cart to the parking garage to fetch her car, a little Nissan Micra, which was to be the vehicle in which we would travel all over the UK during the next two months. It felt so strange, whizzing along the M-25 motorway, sitting shotgun in what was normally the driver's side at home. Then on the two-lane "A" Road toward the coast, I felt like I was on a theme park ride.

Jennifer's flat was the entire top floor of an old Victorian house. She lived on White Rock Gardens in Hastings, East Sussex, where she had a fantastic, expansive view overlooking the English Channel. Hastings has a rich and meaningful history dating back to the eighth century, but it is best known for the Battle of Hastings in 1066, which marked the beginning of the Norman Conquest.

There were seagulls everywhere, reminding me of the New Jersey beach towns where I once vacationed with my family as a young boy. Seagulls sat on the rooftops all along the houses at White Rock Gardens, crying out to those within earshot.

Jen had a tiny office in the back where a flat roof extended the entire length of the attached homes on the block-long road. Each family claimed their own section of the collective rooftop. The seagulls congregated along the roof each morning and evening. Jennifer and I got in the habit of putting stale bread and leftovers out on the roof for the gulls, and they quickly grew accustomed to this daily smorgasbord. Their favorite dish was Greek *moussaka*, made meatless of course since we were both vegetarians. It got to the point where the gulls would be waiting for handouts morning *and* evening. Should we be slow with our delivery, they began to peck relentlessly at the window until we gave them something. We found the gulls behavior hilarious, but that was not the case with our next door neighbor. When we weren't home, the gulls pecked relentlessly at *her* window to see if the magic worked there as well. In exasperation, she would often give in and throw something out, sometimes an entire loaf of bread.

Jennifer had sent out almost 300 letters to educational institutions, temples, healing centers, western astrology groups, New-Age centers, yoga studios, ashrams, and any other groups she thought might be even remotely interested in hearing talks on Vedic Astrology, meditation, or yoga philosophy. I was amazed that there were so many places to send letters to in such a small country. Her efforts quickly generated a slightly higher than three percent return; we thought that was pretty good. She ended up with nine places that booked my speaking engagements.

Jen also had a job doing massage at a health club in Brighton. While I was there, she only took appointments three days a week, Tuesday through Thursday, which gave us long weekends to do the venues, and to simply be together. The locations stretched the entire length of the country, from the south of London to northern Scotland.

During our two months together, we visited many cities, towns, and villages, and we met interesting and heartfelt audiences everywhere we went. It was the most wonderful and intimate time I had ever spent with anyone before in my life. Jennifer and I laughed often, and we talked about so many things. We could also sit and be quiet. It was comfortable just being together, whether talking or in silence, laughing or stone cold serious. We completely connected in mind, body, and spirit, becoming like two halves of a whole. And then it happened. We really and truly fell in love. Sadly and too soon, the day came for my departure. After a bittersweet parting at Heathrow Airport, I boarded my flight back to the US. Jen was crying, and although I did my best to control myself, I failed. My eyes brimmed over with tears as I waved goodbye one last time, then turned to board the plane.

I couldn't just up and move to England, I thought. I was also probably a bit afraid of such new and deep feelings. I had never felt so emotionally vulnerable before. I needed to think about it all and sort out my emotions. It was the craziest thing, but going to England had felt like returning home. On the flight back to Hawaii, I could think of nothing else. Not just the joy we felt in each other's company, but something else very special had happened while I was in the UK. I had developed a strong bond with many of the people who came to hear me speak. They had all seemed like old friends for whom I felt an overpowering affection.

Once back at home, I returned to doing all the things I loved about my island lifestyle: going to the beach, body surfing, and hiking. I would hike up to my favorite mountain ridges to sit and contemplate on the past few months, while simultaneously appreciating the awesome views of the Pacific Ocean. There were an inordinate number of vantage points for me to watch from. After three days of such activities, plus eating out at my favorite restaurants, as well as visiting with friends, I grew glum. *Something* was missing, and that something had, all along, been *someone* – Jennifer. I decided to call her first thing in the morning and explain how I felt.

I awoke early to a glorious Hawaiian day. The sun was shining, only a few clouds were in the sky, and a warm breeze was softly blowing. But, before doing anything else, I called Jen. As soon as I heard her voice, I became all choked-up, yet somehow I managed to speak. We made small talk for a while, and then I opened up my heart. Here goes, I thought, I can't stop now. Clearing my throat, I said, "I love you. I miss you, and I miss England. I want to come back just to be with you. That is, if you want me to."

For a few brief seconds there was a pause, and then I heard her choked-up voice. "Of course. I love you, I miss you, and I want you to come back as soon as possible." Long story short: I sold my car, all my furniture, and even my piano!

CHAPTER 48

The First Day of the Rest of My Life

Four weeks later, I again arrived at Heathrow Airport. This time I had three large suitcases, a large duffel bag, some electronics, and my two Guild acoustic guitars. By the time I cleared Immigration and Customs, I had to use the bathroom so badly I could hardly walk. I looked around for Jennifer, but she was nowhere to be seen. Announcements over the PA system reminded everyone not to leave their bags unattended while in the airport. Although this was prior to 9/11, the Irish Republican Army (IRA) continued to create a great deal of havoc in England. At the time, it made US security appear lax compared to the UK. I didn't know what to do. People kept rushing by me. Somehow, I managed to hold myself together. Just as I was about to take my chances and abandon my luggage and precious possessions to run for the bathroom, Jennifer showed up. Out of breath from having to run all the way from the parking garage, she started to explain, but I dismissed her explanation saying, "Bathroom! Quick!" and I ran off to relieve myself.

"Whew," I exclaimed when I returned. "Where were you?" She explained that there had been a traffic jam on the M-25. I took her in my arms and hugged her tightly, and whispered, "Never mind, you're here now. Let's go."

How we got all my belongings into her car I'll never know. The trunk was completely packed and the back seat was stuffed to the roof. I even had a bag under my feet. I managed to place the guitars between us for the long ride to Hastings. Neither one of us was at all bothered, however. We were ecstatic to finally be together. Although unsure what the future held for us, at this moment, we didn't have a care in the world. The world was beautiful! Life was wonderful!

The next few days were spent talking, laughing, and giving ourselves completely over to one another without any pretenses or worries. We were in complete and total abandonment to love. When Jennifer was away, I would take long walks by myself to explore the town. Hastings is quite hilly, so I got plenty of exercise. The people were great. It seemed like nobody was too busy to stop and chat with me whenever I asked for directions to a particular place. Sometimes I ended up standing and talking for half an hour with a stranger. I developed relationships with people who worked in the post office, the bank, the local shops, and even with a guy that used the *Green Machine* (a pressurized air machine used to clean sidewalks, under benches, and other public places).

I was barely there six months when we started getting some great press. Several local magazines published articles I had written, and I was invited to do a few interviews on the radio; one was with the British Broadcasting Corporation (BBC). There were even a few blurbs written about our workshops in the *Daily Mail* newspaper. My entire life had completely changed in only a matter of months. I began receiving calls and letters from people who had attended my workshops and classes. They graciously thanked me. The simple methods of meditation I taught them had changed their lives for the better. Life was a joy, plain and simple.

One day, however, I received a telephone call from my ex-girlfriend. She had called me, not knowing who else to turn to for help. Her son, Adam was depressed, and he missed me terribly. He and I spoke on the phone regularly, but he missed having me, his Dad, around. Even after his mother and I split up, our father/son bond had continued. After hanging up the phone, I confided in Jennifer that I felt torn. What could I possibly do to help him from such a long distance? Without reservation, she immediately said, "Have her send him here to live with us."

Looking at her incredulously I answered, "You know he's not my biological son, and you have never even met him. How do you know what you might be letting yourself in for?"

Gazing back at me lovingly, she answered, "Sometimes you have to do things in life that are above and beyond the call of duty. You love him, so I'll surely love him, also. Hopefully, he'll also like me."

Drawing her close, I said, "I've never met anyone like you before, and that makes you special, very special."

A few weeks later, eleven year old Adam stepped off the plane alone at Heathrow Airport where we awaited him. That was over two decades ago. Jennifer was a phenomenal mother to him. She helped him with his homework, listened to his tales, and shared his youthful disappointments. As well, they both enjoyed sharing her brilliant sense of humor. This was another testament to just how remarkable she is.

In over five years in the UK, we lost count of how many people, organizations, healing centers, yoga centers, as well as many other groups we interacted with. But, because we kept all of the press clippings, we could see we had made a sizable impact. I was able to bring my own realizations and life experiences to the teaching of meditation, thus adding a new dimension to what some had already learned.

I spoke before audiences from St. James of Piccadilly, in London, to the Theosophical Societies of Scotland, to universities and yoga centers in Wales and England, and to Spiritualist groups and astrological associations on the Channel Islands. The joy of being permitted to share what I had learned at the *School of Hard Knocks* brought a sense of purpose and satisfaction to my life, which I had never known before. During my years in the UK, I wrote several books on Vedic Astrology, mantra, yoga philosophy, and the use of gems for Ayurveda healing. My articles on these subjects also found their way into quite a few magazines and other publications, many of which still remain in some form, and are accessible on the Web.

CHAPTER 49

My Four Legged Teachers

At the end of 1998, Jennifer and I had been married for four years when we decided to move to the US. We wanted to find a place to develop a spiritual retreat and healing center. We were drawn to Santa Fe, New Mexico, where we built a yoga and Ayurveda center nestled in a valley on the Pecos River, about half an hour or so from Santa Fe. There, I developed relationships with animals, something I had never really had the opportunity to do before. The animals opened my heart, allowing me to experience and share *reciprocal and unconditional love* with them. We rescued quite a few dogs, mostly because they either showed up at our property on their own or were dropped off there. We were forced to find homes for the majority of them, but four remained permanently with us.

The first dog to enter our lives, we rescued from the shelter in Santa Fe shortly after we arrived there. His *time* had expired, and had we not adopted him, he would have been put down within twenty-four hours. Half German shepherd and half Rottweiler, he had been found near a freeway exit when he was about six months old. We named him Ram Das (after Lord Ram of the famous epic *Ramayana* of India), and he became one of my best friends. He was a wonderful, gentle, and loving soul. He was a people dog, loving everyone who came to *New Rishikesh*, our center. But he didn't seem to like other dogs; so at first, we thought he would be the only one to stay with us. That is, until something happened one day, in the dead of winter.

We were out in the snow at the back of the property when we heard Ram Das crying near our fence. He kept looking out through the fence and then back at us. We'd had to build the fence because early on because numerous coyotes, mountain lions, and bears seemed to like to use our place like a thoroughfare. Although we loved the wildlife, it was decidedly safer for all concerned if the wild animals went *around* us. We looked on the other side of the fence and saw a puppy. He looked like a Labrador mix, about six months old.

Ram Das was crying for him, and we couldn't just leave the pup out there in the snow. So, I went down to the river and around to the adjoining field to get him. He was wonderful and *so* grateful. He also knew just what to do to appease Ram Das. He would lick his new friend's face and wash his ears each day. Ram even let him share his doghouse! We named him Laxman Das (after Lord Ram's brother).

That same year, we rescued our first horses. My first rescue was a Tennessee Walker — all black, seventeen hands high, and gorgeous. But this beauty had been abused and was scared to death of everything and everyone. He'd been beaten, tied down, had his ears twisted, had been severely kicked (there were scars from broken ribs), and altogether defiled. When I found him, a gelding not a stallion, he was used to being kept isolated in a paddock. I was told that he had never been allowed to be with the other horses. His only friend had been a bird, which had recently died. Now, he was alone. Still, as they say, he didn't have a mean bone in his body.

His former owner had stated, "You have to corner him to catch him; otherwise you can never get him. You have to keep jumping back and forth and yelling at him. Eventually you'll corner him." I looked at Shadow, quickly renamed Shyam (meaning *black* in Sanskrit, referring to the blackish complexion of Lord Krishna), and back at the owner, then back at the horse whose eyes were laden with fear. That afternoon, he was moved to our place on the Pecos. "You'll have nothing to be afraid of here Shyam. I promise," I told him.

I knew nothing about horses at the time. I had only ridden about a half dozen times in my life. Jennifer had been around horses most of her life, having grown up in England where she was introduced to them as a toddler. To learn about horses, I purchased Monty Roberts' (who is famous for his training programs on natural horsemanship) books and videos. Every day for hours and weeks on end, I coaxed Shyam, talking to him, and communicating mentally and with gestures. I did my best to reassure him and let him know that I was his friend. One day, when I had my back turned to him (as I occasionally tracked him over my shoulder), I experienced one of the most emotional moments of my life. I was just waiting for him to acknowledge me, hoping to achieve *join-up* (when the horse comes to you of his own volition).

Suddenly, his face came into view and he began edging closer to me, an indication that his fear was dissipating. I looked away for a moment, and when I turned toward him, his nose was almost touching my shoulder. For me, this was a miracle. When he did not shy away, tears began running down my face; they continued to flow for several minutes. The feeling of having gained his trust was indescribable.

People began telling me how remarkable it was that I had managed to heal *Shyam*. Soon, I was riding him along mountain trails with my wife who rode her *ex-working* quarter horse. We rode to places we otherwise could never have reached. Furthermore, Shyam had a healing effect on me. He had a way of teaching me unconditional love beyond what I had learned from the dogs. I used to think I was a spiritual person and that my yoga and path of nonviolence were the primary means of achieving my life goals. They were important principles, no question of that, for without them, my life would have seemed like a road to nowhere. But, once I began my relationship with horses, everything I had contemplated, even everything I taught others, really and truly came together and touched my soul. My relationship with horses was another catalyst for bringing everything together in my life.

Horses not only communicate with each other, they can also communicate with us. We just need to be good listeners. Without a doubt, horses are sensitive beings, so spending quality time with them can change a person's life. I believe that a human being can develop a truly special relationship with a horse, like no other animal on Earth.

CHAPTER 50

The Story Never Ends

One of the things that can never be stopped is the passage of time; so, just as they should, the years moved on. But just when you think you've seen it all, there's always another lesson waiting to be learned. That is, if you take the time. The greatest of them all is to appreciate being alive, to be here now, in the present, today, and every day. *Be Here Now.* The future comes in its own time and it certainly doesn't need us to worry about it.

I am grateful for being able to experience the world around me, for the love I have shared with my near and dear ones and with the many friends I have met along the way. This is what makes life all it can be. Never mind the challenges, the pains, or the heartbreaks. The hopes, joys, and pleasures will balance it all out. Since that day many years ago when I decided to have faith, I also vowed to never let it go.

Sure, we all have our good and bad days. Just as there are occasions for laughter, there are times when we must experience sorrow. There are times in life when we need to grieve, when we have to release our pain-laden emotions. And, it's simply not true that *big boys don't cry.*

Many people have told me they could never have lived through what I did, undergoing the physical and mental torture I experienced in prison. I believe, regardless of what life throws at us, that we *can* and *will* somehow find a way to survive, especially when we embrace our faith. Most of us do, no matter how intolerable our circumstances may appear. The will to live is very strong in human beings. The same is true for animals. Life always comes around, no matter how hard it may seem to believe at the time. You can be sure that: *This too shall pass.* Soon enough, we'll smile again.

It has been just over thirty years since the day I walked out of that Thai prison. For all these years, I have kept the dark secret of my sordid past from nearly everyone. I had no inclination to reveal my heroin addiction, the drug smuggling, or the torturous years of imprisonment where hope for the future seemed lost. It seemed to me that it would be counter-productive to tell anyone about my past. Would it have affected people's opinions of me? Curtailed opportunities? Without question, the answer I heard in my head was always *yes.*

Somehow, through all the hardships, hair-raising experiences, and the long journey home, I finally found myself. Nobody can possibly accuse me of not knowing what it is like to suffer or not being able to understand what it is like to *hit rock bottom.* I am not proud of my past, yet overcoming it laid the foundation for who I am today. I am thankful for having lived through it all, and I am sincerely remorseful for the suffering I caused others.

Sure, if I could do it all over differently, I would. But, life doesn't work that way. At some point, we all end up saying *if I knew then what I know now.* Well, we didn't know then what we know now, and at the end of the day we just have to live with it. Suck it up, as they say. What matters is today: *What you do today and who you are today is what really matters.* It is undeniably true that we receive in return what we give in life.

Many of us have experienced failures, and want and need to start again. We want to take a different turn in the road, but feel lost and don't know where to begin. It is only fear that stops us from forging ahead with positive change. Therefore, as soon as we stop being afraid, the road to a successful and satisfying future will appear before us. Renewal begins with taking that first baby step. And no one can take it for us. Anyone can change direction in life. Anyone can turn a life of sadness into a life of joy. You have to believe in yourself and in the possibilities of your own destiny. As Mahatma Gandhi once said, "Be the change you want to see in the world."

I'm grateful beyond words that I am still here to share my story. The story won't end because it never ends. As long as we live, anything is possible.

CONCLUSION:

When Knowledge Becomes Wisdom

*Om ajnana-timirandhasya jnananjana-salakaya
cakshur unmilitam yena tasmai sri-gurave namah.*

*Translation: I offer my respectful obeisance
unto my spiritual master,*

*who has opened my eyes, which were blinded
by the darkness of ignorance,*

with the torchlight of knowledge.

Through the light of knowledge imparted to me by my eternal teacher, then through the pain resulting from my mistakes in life, came a dawning of wisdom, which caused a profound change in my heart. With this change came the determination and confidence that I needed so I would never again be covered by the darkness that had once enveloped me. Whenever a man needs an antidote for healing his fears and the wounds on his soul, the only panacea is to attain knowledge. Whenever we seek knowledge and actually acquire it, it becomes our responsibility to put what we learn into action. This simple yet profound life-altering formula has become the foundation for the way I drive all my missions in life.

Knowing what to do is part of the curing process. I have not learned all the remedies, but I have learned enough of them to make a difference, to myself, and when given the chance, to others. Knowledge gained of things in this world is an ongoing process, not just during this life, but also through our many births and subsequent rebirths where we will again find ourselves walking upon, and adapting to, the world around us.

In furtherance of my conviction and dedication to helping others heal, I would like to address the illness of drug addiction. My own experiences that led to a deep and intense change of heart has given me a very poignant understanding of this problem. Initially, most people begin as recreational drug users, social pressure usually being the prime factor. The drug either produces a pleasant feeling or reduces an unpleasant feeling, like anxiety. Before a person knows it, he/she has gone through a subtle change whereby recreation grows into dependency and therein lies the hidden danger.

Countering a dependency requires a spiritual and psychological paradigm shift. Becoming aware is the first step for any healing to begin. Having been an addict myself allows me insights that are based on experience, not simply learned through reading and hearing about the experiences of others. I can immediately recognize that same germ in others that once caused a disease that almost killed me.

Notice how I said, "having been an addict", not "I am an addict"? I am no longer a drug addict, and I continue to live life to its fullest without being dependent on attending addiction meetings or accepting that I am forever helpless. The 12-Step Program that has been the Bible of almost all addiction recovery programs is a beginning (it is also *not* the only method for a successful recovery), but you have to take charge of your own life from there. This is a proven fact … if you really want to be successful and actually satisfied with life, you have to take control.

It's up to each one of us whether we want to label ourselves as forever weak and helpless or give ourselves the chance to soar to the greatest heights possible. Sure, in the beginning, once you cry out for help, and are serious about it, you first have to detox. Then you need a support group of some kind that can relate to exactly what you've been through, and are still going through. Intense rehabilitation with the right people is a must. But then there has to be a plan for change and that plan must include a new you and a new life. It requires an inner spiritual *realization*. To become free of substance abuse forever, one must address what was missing that caused such dissatisfaction with life in the first place. Circumstances in life can at times lead to depression, but becoming chemically dependent will only exacerbate it. Nobody is happy all the time. Take life as it comes and always remember that *this too shall pass*.

Keep searching. Have faith in yourself ... and in God. If your experiences in life have made this an uncomfortable thought, then at least you can acknowledge there's a higher, Divine power that is behind the workings of everything animate and inanimate. Through your own heart, you can tap into this power, finding what I call your *higher self.*

All human beings are capable of spirituality. That is because this is our inherent nature. We are units of consciousness, not these bags of bones that we usually look to as us. *"Aham brahmasmi,"* the ancient Vedas sing to mankind. "I am spirit." A well-defined spiritual path is paramount to a successful recovery, but that takes more effort than just giving your power over to a higher source. Following a spiritual path means following a process to get there, a means to an end. Belief or faith alone will not do it. Such convictions may change, but when realization opens the lotus of our hearts, all doubt is instantly cleared from the mind. Doubt is like a cloudy lens obscuring our vision and it must be cleansed and removed. We must see the world for what it is, and more importantly, we have to see ourselves as we truly are.

That I managed to crawl out of the dark abyss of addiction is proof that it is possible. I have been clean for almost 33 years, and after the first year I never came even close to a relapse. The endeavor takes a great deal of courage and commitment, so you must give it your full measure of effort. Prison or an untimely death are not options any of us would want to choose. There are no other ends to this game, unless you escape from your addiction and clean up your act. This is the stark reality of drug addiction.

You have to become a philosopher in life. You can never go back to just living the life you used to live. Something wasn't right about your life when you became an addict or you wouldn't have gotten yourself into that situation. You don't need to pretend you're someone other than who you are, or to declare your allegiance to one religion or another. But you do have to become the best possible version of yourself and that includes asking important questions about God, the universe, and your own existence. What you need is knowledge of who you are, why you think the way you do, and why your mind is such that it got you into such a bad state. Once you begin to understand by answering these questions, it will be time for action.

There are many spiritual paths out there, but none of them will work without faith, perseverance, and actual knowledge of the philosophy. My own spiritual path allowed me access to the Vedas and its thousands of years of tried and tested theories and methods.

Within the pages of this book, I have only been able to scrape the surface of the spiritual techniques and remedies that are openly available to those who truly desire to become the best version of themselves possible.

When it comes to religion verses spirituality, although they can be, they are not necessarily always one and the same. But these concepts are not competitive with each other. What they do is complement each other. For example, Mahatma Gandhi was a spiritual leader, as well as an activist who advocated non-violent protests against discrimination, especially when it came to the poor. He displayed a great deal of humility and his legacy will live forever. But he wasn't necessarily a "religious" leader, at least not as we think of them. But he possessed personal ideals and traits that showed him to be spiritually inspired.

When it comes to religious leaders, I include Catholic popes and other Christian, Jewish, Hindu, and Muslim advocates in this list. They also advocate for the poor and often display a great deal of humility. Moreover, neither popes nor others at the religious helm get a free pass because of their position. We have all seen those who profess a life of divinity, but are later seen living a life very much in opposition to their stated beliefs.

If a Catholic pope, bishop, or priest is sincere in his heart, he must go to confession or engage in other remedial measures to address sins and transgressions just as anyone else would. Popes go to confession every day because they are human and have a free will like all of us; that's what makes us vulnerable to evil and wrongdoing. Thus, we must be careful when it comes to the choices we make. Whatever your choices have been so far, confronting the reality of an addiction is never easy. But do it you must.

One of the keys to succeeding in life is our ability to face our fears. Our spiritual paths, and our faith in them, become magnificent tools for meeting the challenges we will face. But we have to be fully engaged, not mindlessly leaving everything for God to sort out for us. Remember, once we give up, we are dead to this life, so failure should not be an option. In the words of Napoleon Bonaparte, "*Impossible* is the word found only in a fool's dictionary. Wise people create opportunities for themselves and make everything possible."

Throughout this book, I have shared my story and you can see how many times I came close to giving up. My path, my faith in it, and the experience gained from its practice is what worked for me. What is of primary importance is to first and foremost seek knowledge. You have to know what to do before you can begin actually doing anything.

Eventually you will find the path that speaks to your heart, and through your dedication and patience, you will eventually gain some degree of wisdom. The result is finally finding peace with this thing we call LIFE. Though transmitted in every language, the song remains the same. Learning to sing without thought, and dance without effort ... well, that's when knowledge becomes wisdom.

But before we can really begin to tread the higher path, we have to take control of our own health. There are many modalities for healing what ails us that we can take advantage of to bring our bodies and minds into a healthy state of equilibrium. Only then can we properly commit ourselves to finding the ultimate goals of life.

Gem therapy illustrates one of these ways for improving health and wellbeing. Since I am a certified gemologist, it should not come as any surprise that I investigated the healing capacity of gems. Because of time constraints, I feel compelled to dwell only lightly on this subject. For readers further interested in this topic, my books *Mantras, Yantras & Fabulous Gems* and *Vibrational Healing with Gems* will give you an excellent introduction to this healing modality. Within the parameters of my experience and expertise, I would like to share some prudent generalities.

I discovered a paradigm at work here. You see, we humans are integral parts of our vast universe, and as such, we not only have the attribute of free will, we also have the ability to reason and draw conclusions. For instance, we know from experience that matter is a form of energy. We possess the capability to harness this energy and use it to treat illness and even discontent. Thus, gems, used properly by skilled practitioners, can be used to enhance our health. Not surprisingly, Gem Therapy has quickly risen above the realms of intuition, hunches, and folklore. Thus, my application of Gem Therapy has been both useful and rewarding on a multitude of levels.

Another topic that is dear to my heart is our relationship with animals. Animals inherently occupy every environment on our planet that we humans do, as well as some that we do not. We are all children of Providence and all are born with a right to pursue life, liberty, and happiness. Since we coexist, why shouldn't we live in harmony together? Our God, or our understanding of God, has put us all here together to share our environment, not to exploit it and all others living in it with us. So it is incumbent on us to respect the animal kingdom. Taking this thought one step further, we are the custodians of this planet, endowed with the responsibility of protecting it and all others living on it. Sadly, human society has lost its way when it comes to protecting and honoring all the other inhabitants of this Earth.

My experiences with animals have taught me a lot about life and the way we treat others, including animals. There is no secret that human beings are capable of willfully inflicting harm and pain, even without provocation. Some people seem to relish the infliction of pain on animals, and that is not only shameful, but such actions are unconscionable. Such terrible travesties inflicted upon innocent animals, unable to defend themselves, are surely the epitome of evil intent in this world. Animals generally will only attack humans out of self-preservation and even instinct, but never do they attack for the thrill or fun of it. Domestic or farm animals almost never attack or behave aggressively toward human beings. Yet the industrialized world sees domestic animals as nothing more than objects to be used for clothing, food, and entertainment.

Have you ever seen the look in the eye of a frightened cow, horse, pig, or sheep? It is no different than the look of terror you may have seen in the eyes of your pets, or in the eyes of other human beings. If all human beings simply realized that animals really and truly are *people*, that they are capable of the same feelings and emotions as we are, they would have to rethink the whole way they live their lives. Because our intellect is more advanced than theirs, does it mean we should abuse, torture, and kill them, as though their life meant no more than that of a potato or a ball of cotton?

Imagine a race of beings that conquered us and used the human race for the same purposes that we use animals today.

Is that not the same as our species conquering all other species on Earth, deciding who lives and who dies? So why do we not speak of it in terms of mechanized wholesale slaughter of millions worldwide every day?

I have personally witnessed the results of human cruelty to animals. Such persons usually come to abuse their own family members, as well, until finally they may be barely discernable as even being human at all. We humans have a distinct advantage when it comes to the animal kingdom. We have the means to either make a positive contribution to their welfare or to harm them without any worthy reason. After all, we share our environment with those who are at a disadvantage. Violence without a reason, such as self-defense or protecting the innocent, is evil.

I have rescued a multitude of animals, both wild and domestic. When it comes to caring for an abused animal or a fellow human in need, there are either two winners or none at all. Rescuing an abused or neglected animal will undoubtedly build on my positive karma, instead of making a mess of it. Evil acts today will bring suffering to the performer in the future, while acts of kindness and charity return to the performer in kind. This realization has no end, especially when it comes to our desire to become the best version of ourselves possible.

One of the missions here at the Vedic Cultural Fellowship is our Equine Rescue Program. Horses are unique among animals. Domestically, they work hard for their owners and have a long history of proving their value. They also have an amazing capacity for demonstrating their feelings for, and their devotion to, their owners. By comparison, people also can form strong bonds with their horses. However and sadly, this is not always the case.

Abuse and neglect have always been around. However, in recent years, it seems that they have been on the rise. Our hearts should always go out to any creature that has been abused or neglected. The emphasis of government agencies is more aligned with legality, and almost never to long-term care; thus, they are somewhat inadequate when it comes to rehabilitating and caring for rescued animals.

Our program focuses on horses, although we also have rescued dogs, geese, and ducks, and they remain here on the farm with us. Horses are large animals with huge appetites. Their medical needs can also be expensive. There are 13 ways a horse can founder, and the outcome is rarely good. Many are emotionally damaged when we rescue them and it takes patience, experience, and a great deal of love to treat them successfully. Horses, especially the number we have on hand, require land, and that is also expensive. The bottom line here is that rescuing and caring for abused horses is a costly endeavor.

Our program does not generate any money, only expenses. We are extremely grateful for the donors who contribute to our cause. Whatever proceeds are gained from telling my story in this book will go exclusively to our Equine Rescue Program. It is imperative that we keep this program afloat. We will be forever thankful to anyone wishing to donate to this worthy cause. Additionally, our welcome mat is always out for anyone wishing to visit and witness first-hand the loving work we are doing here.

We are a not for profit 501 C 3 charity.

Our contact information is as follows:

e-mail: howard@vedicworld.org or

howard@ocalaequinerescue.org

Web: http://www.howardbeckman.com

http://wwwvedicworld.org/

http://www.ocalaequinerescue.org

EPILOGUE

It's funny how life eventually comes around. Everything changes. People and our environment change just like our attitudes and views on life, and sometimes we end up right back where we started. Just when you're sure something is going to happen, it doesn't. And by the same token, when you think something can never happen, it does. I've learned over the years to *never ever say never*. Just when you think you've seen it all, well, you know what I mean.

In the summer of 2008, my wife and I decided to attend the annual Festival of India held in Los Angeles, CA. Jen wanted to browse around an India import store there, so I accompanied her. As I stood next to a wall at one end of the large shop, I saw someone I recognized. He was the now ex-swami, *Ramesh*, who had caused me so much grief back in the seventies when my first wife became one of his fanatic followers. He had been very unkind to me, personally, which I chose not to elaborate on in this book. Upon recognizing him, an old animosity re-awakened within me. I have always done my best not to hold any animosity for anyone, but suddenly an intense and powerful revulsion for this man welled up inside of me. As I walked over to him, we locked eyes.

"Don't I know you?" he asked.

"Yes, don't you remember me?" My answer was somewhat curt. I reminded him of how he had once treated me, how he had voiced his approval for my wife to leave me to better serve him, thinking little to nothing about what my daughter's life would be like without her father's presence.

As I related my side of the story to him, he began to remember, and his eyes filled with tears, which streamed uncontrollably down his face. He bowed his head and said, "I'm so sorry. I hurt so many people. How can you ever forgive me? You can't. I know that." And then he sank down to his knees and grasped my ankles, saying repeatedly, "I'm so sorry. I'm so sorry."

I had not expected such a passionate apology; it melted my heart. And suddenly, my animosity was gone. Tears filled my eyes, and I too bent down. Grasping him under his arms, I lifted him up to his feet and put my arms around him.

"I forgive you. I forgive you," I said. "It's over."

I experienced a profound sense of release. My heart grew lighter. I had been carrying anger toward this person around for all these years and never realized it. Ultimately, Fate has her way with us, yet it is never too late to right a wrong, never too late to forgive. For me, a deep emotional wound began healing at that very moment.

On a snowy winter morning in New Mexico during January of 2009, I entered my home office to check my e-mail. One e-mail stood out to me; it was from *Debbie*. I hadn't had contact with her in years. In fact, it had been twenty-eight years since we had last held one another tightly in a loving embrace. Following my arrest, *Debbie* was only four years old when I left Hawaii. Over the course of all these years, she had somehow worked her way through school, earned a doctorate degree in Psychology, and found work in a university as an Assistant Professor. She had been married for about three years and had recently given birth to her own daughter. Having a child of her own caused her to think about the father she never knew, the one she had learned to fear and hate. For *Debbie*, questions arose as to the validity of her fears and negative feelings toward me, questions she needed to address with me. We have found our way back into each other's lives. And as Fate would have it, my wife and I now have two beautiful granddaughters, the apples of granddad's eye.

As for *Adam*, he and I talk to each other all the time, and see each other regularly. *Shyam*, the Tennessee Walker we rescued in New Mexico, is still with us, as is *Chandra*, Jen's quarter horse, along with a dozen other horses my wife and I have rescued. *Ram Das* and *Laxman Das* both died over the years, yet two of our rescue dogs remain with us, along with a menagerie of rescued geese and ducks.

Writing these memoirs was the hardest thing I've ever done. Sounds funny after all I've been through, I know. I had to relive all of those memories, and more. My effort to recall all the pain, the hopelessness, the fear, and the sadness has been difficult. But I also gladly and joyfully relived my awakenings, the healing, and the regaining of my confidence. Thankfully, I embrace the love that I have been so fortunate to share with so many wonderful beings on this Earth. I feel blessed to be able to share my love with so many near and dear ones, which includes fourteen horses, two dogs, five geese, and four ducks. And through it all came the realization that I can share this love with everyone, no matter who they are or where they are from. True and pure love does not discriminate, even when it comes to divergent species.

In the aftermath, I had to cry because I realized that this love was always deep inside of me. Had I not found my capacity to love, I would not have found myself. I had survived all the lessons that Fate had thrown my way, both heavy-handed and merciful. What a gratifying achievement I had earned.

I now feel overwhelmingly grateful. I am grateful to all those who have helped me along my journey, and even all those who had caused me so much pain and suffering. Had I not experienced all of it, I would not be the man I am today. Fate does not play favorites. Whatever happens to us is a result of actions we have performed in the past, so it is incumbent on us to connect the dots and understand the *why* of it.

Ultimately, life is what one makes of it. What comes to us may be a product of Fate's uncanny ways, but what we do with what comes to us is ours to work through. As for me, I know that I have released what needed releasing. Through the process, I have truly learned to earnestly live each and every moment of my life. And, I am grateful to be able to be here to share my memories with you.